A New Paradigm of
LEADERSHIP

**Visions of Excellence for
21st Century Organizations**

Ken Shelton, Editor

Executive
Excellence
Publishing

The publisher offers discounts on this book when ordered in bulk quantities.
For more information, write, call, or fax

Executive Excellence Publishing
1344 East 1120 South
Provo, Utah 84606
phone: (801) 375-4060
fax: (801) 377-5960
web: www.eep.com

Printed in the United States of America

10 9 8 7 6 5 4 3 2 1

ISBN 1-890009-18-0

Situational Leadership is a registered trademark. Copyright 1991 by Authors Media Syndicate

CONTENTS

INTRODUCTION

Leaders at Every Level

 by Ken Shelton, Chairman and Editor-in-Chief of Executive Excellence Publishing and author of *Beyond Counterfeit Leadership*

WHY IS THE IDEAL of leaders at every level so elusive? It stems from misconceptions of leadership, from the idea that leadership is something you possess or acquire—or is synonymous with a person, position, or title.

To think of leadership as a possession or position is meaningless and misleading, notes Gregory A. Gull, founder of Practicum Unlimited. This perception fits the elitist orientation, erects barriers, protects the "right" of a special few to direct or control the fate of the many, preserves as primal the position of those in power, and perpetuates dependency and envy.

Viewing leadership as a possession also fosters idol or hero worship and forms a dependent or codependent relationship between the leader and the led, where each, being dependent upon the other, becomes powerless toward realizing his or her potential.

When you relinquish powers to another, you also give up your ability to act in a self-directed way. This dependency inhibits you from real learning and progress, and from the life-enriching experiences that promote productivity, synergy, and creativity.

Erich Fromm has written: "Only to the extent that we decrease the mode of *having*, that is of nonbeing—stop finding security and identity by clinging to what we have, by sitting on it, by holding onto our ego and our possessions—can the mode of *being* emerge."

Authentic leadership experience springs from a genuine concern for the growth, well-being, and empowerment of people.

DRIVING FORCES

The hullabaloo over empowerment is no longer confined to the "elephants" learning to dance—everyone is getting into the act. And for good reason: empowerment, the dispersion of power and responsibility, is high on the list of needs to survive and succeed.

Why are so many leaders at least paying lip service to empowerment? Is it the crazed quest for quality? The fashionable harangue against hierarchy? The open admission that organizations of every size and type must now reinvent themselves and more fully tap the potential of people? It's all of that and more. But the driving factors appear to be the following three:

1. Competition. As foreign and domestic competitors become flatter, faster, and more flexible, many *Fortune* 500 corporations are shedding management layers and adopting empowerment as a creed. In flat organizations, people and teams must be empowered to engage in self-improvement, make decisions, improve quality, boost productivity, enhance service, and take pride in their work.

2. Changing nature of work. More work is knowledge-based, requiring people to acquire and use information and knowledge to create products or to help customers improve their business performance. As the working world becomes more idea and information-intensive, the people who will rise to the top will be those who are intellectually aware and excited by ideas and information.

3. Shifting employee expectations. Leaders are needed at every level to manage change effectively and sustain competitive advantage. These leaders must be aligned with the direction, vision, policies, procedures, strategy, and systems of the organization if they are to have a sense of ownership—a stake in the success of the business—that motivates them to take initiative, risks, and responsibilities.

To be empowered, people need information, support, and resources, notes Rosabeth Moss Kanter, former editor of the *Harvard Business Review*. Companies that excel in empowerment, she says, "make more information available to more people at more levels through more devices; permit collaboration so that people can build supportive problem-solving coalitions; and decentralize resources to make them more available for local problem solving."

Even though this is elementary, Empowerment 101, it is still counterintuitive for many control-centered or power-based managers. That's why anyone who hopes to empower people must be principle-centered, notes author Stephen R. Covey. The taproot of empowerment is trust, he says. If you have no or low trust in the culture, if you lack character or competence, you have to control people and measure their performance. But if you have high trust and clear performance agreements, people will supervise themselves and evaluate their own performance.

You create a sense of ownership by providing clear expectations, local control of resources, and personal responsibility for results. You coach and offer help without removing responsibility. It's guided discovery. People retain ownership of a problem or idea while they work out a solution together.

THREE CHARACTERISTICS

Empowering leaders share three characteristics:

1. *They create a compelling vision*. Great leaders create a compelling vision and manage the dream by communicating, recruiting, rewarding, retraining, and reorganizing. People are more threatened than excited about a new vision unless there are empowered change agents who champion the vision at every level, bringing it down to the gut level of each person by showing them how the vision will help them solve the biggest job-related problem confronting them.

To CEO Fred Smith, empowerment means that employees don't just work for Federal Express—they *are* Federal Express: "Daily, they go above and beyond to serve our customers. They are the ones who trek through all kinds of weather; deliver every package, each one critical; they persist in solving every customer's problem; they ferret out the root cause of every problem to prevent it from ever happening again. Their talent, ingenuity, and commitment drive our quality standards closer to our goal of 100 percent customer satisfaction." In a service company, says Smith, "each interaction with a customer can be priceless or disastrous. Customer satisfaction begins with employee satisfaction. If we put our employees first, they will deliver impeccable service, and profit will be the natural outcome."

Everybody feels that they are a legitimate part of what is going on. The magic, the zest that produces ideas and then converts them into quality products and services, comes from being a legitimate part of what is going on. All members pull their own oars because they know that if they don't, the boat won't move. People exhibit immense creativity and motivated behavior without being prodded if they are getting growth-enhancing feedback and soul satisfaction from what they do.

Jan Carlzon built Scandinavian Airline Systems (SAS) on the belief that the leader who expects results must first give people free access to information. A person without the information can't take responsibility. With information, he or she cannot avoid taking it.

2. *They break down barriers.* The artificial barriers between people and departments must come down, along with all else in the system that creates adversarial relationships among people who need to cooperate, said Edwards Deming. Florida Power and Light went through an amazing transformation—from a beleaguered utility to the surprise winner of the Deming Prize—when team leaders began to see each employee with new eyes, to assume that every worker was an intelligent individual who genuinely wanted to give his or her best to the company. While some people resented the new emphasis and the extra demands and left the company, those who stayed volunteered for extra duty to prove something to themselves.

3. They bust the bureaucracy. They learn and teach the art of self-leadership, and replace fear with feedback, order giving with decision making. Successful companies fight bureaucracy aggressively on every front—preventing it when they can, attacking it when they find that it has crept in. Winning performers are obsessively dedicated to keeping their systems and structures simple. They find that doing so is far easier and more fruitful than trying to cope with cumbersome reporting arrangements and layers of delegation. Empowerment efforts often fail, and people fall far short of the dreams and goals they set because of shortcomings in self-leadership. To enhance self-leadership, build more naturally rewarding features into your activities and focus your thoughts on the naturally rewarding aspects of your work.

WHAT ARE THE BENEFITS?

Among the many benefits (fruits) that grow from the "roots" of empowerment are the following six.

1. Commitment. The primary challenge of leaders, say John Naisbitt and Patricia Aburdene, coauthors of *Megatrends 2000*, "is to encourage people to work effectively in teams and to be more entrepreneurial, self-managing, autonomous. The dominant principle has shifted from management in order to control, to leadership in order to bring out the best in people and to respond quickly to change. While capital and technology are important resources, people make or break a company. To harness their power, leaders inspire commitment by sharing authority, thus enabling their firms to attract, reward, and motivate the best people."

2. Quality products and services. The Malcolm Baldrige National Quality Award won't be won without empowering both employees and customers, says its former director, Curt Reimann. "The leaders of the past delegated or relegated quality and its internal standards to a department within the company. The new manager must have a different focus: quality driven externally by customer requirements." Every employee must be empowered to deal effectively with internal and external customers. When John Grettenberger, General Manager of Cadillac, winner of the Baldrige Award, was asked, "How do you prepare 10,000 people for a Baldrige examination?" he replied, "You can't. People either accept ownership for the process or they don't."

3. Speed and responsiveness. Many companies are working on the symptoms instead of the root causes of non-competitiveness, says

Philip R. Thomas, CEO of The Thomas Group and an expert in speed and responsiveness. "They are trying to improve forecasts instead of reducing cycle time so they won't have to forecast so far in the future. They are trying to control customer changes instead of reducing cycle time so that they are responding to the changes on a real-time basis. They are trying to manipulate work-in-process to meet a given need instead of removing barriers that reduce cycle time and improve process predictability." When these efforts fail, executives apply excess resources in the form of people, inventories, equipment, and risk in a vain attempt to improve cost, quality, and customer service. Excess resources only compound problems, says Thomas: "To solve quality and competitiveness problems, you must create a short-cycle-time, rapid-feedback culture."

4. Synergy. Synergy results from valuing differences, from bringing different perspectives together in a spirit of mutual respect. Mature people view differences as potential strengths. They not only respect those with different views, they actively seek them out. They also seek objective feedback from both internal and external sources on their performance, products, and services and look for ways to build complementary teams where the strength of one compensates for the weakness of another. At 3M, for example, managers act like "sponsors" who express a strategic vision and then let people with different ideas and styles find creative ways to contribute.

5. Human development. What W. Edwards Deming first taught the Japanese 45 years ago were people empowerment principles, not product quality practices. His 14 points constitute basic human development, and his "deadly diseases" are descriptions of anti-empowerment crimes committed by well-intentioned management. "The wealth of a nation [or company]," says Deming, "depends on its people, management, and leadership more than on its natural resources. All must adopt a new [empowering] style of management and acknowledge that the aim of leadership is to help people and machines do a better job."

6. Management leverage. Amateur managers try to direct the efforts of subordinates by attempting to think out everything for them, says Bill Oncken III of the William Oncken Corporation. The result? "One-to-one leverage and a back-breaking assortment of monkeys. The amateur never gets over the feeling that to stay away is to move in the opposite direction from where he or she should be moving. Knowing when to stay away is the mark of a pro, whose leverage is much greater than the number of subordinates because of the number of self-assignments each empowered individual takes on and completes without the manager even knowing about it."

Today, we are replacing the manager as order giver with the manager as teacher, facilitator, and coach. Facilitators draw out answers from those who know them best—the people who do the job.

Facilitators ask questions, guide a group to consensus, and use information to motivate action.

Effective empowerment efforts result in more "co"-mission, "co"-ordination, "co"-operation. As the interests and activities of individuals are more closely aligned with those of organizations, people act more as responsible agents who are empowered at their level to make decisions. We all need the power to do and to be, because when we lose our agency, we abdicate our power to act and become things to be acted upon. We may actually disempower people who are competent, if all the systems say, "We really don't trust you that much." Until we give people the keys and say, "You alone decide," we won't get empowerment.

Empowerment grows from the roots of trust, character, and competence—and without the roots, we simply won't get the fruits, season after season.

SECTION I

Changing Times

LEADERS CAN SURVIVE in the 21st century when they evolve with the changing times. A new century demands a new paradigm of leadership, one that rides the crest of change, rather than wallows in the wake.

Warren Bennis tells us that "the key to making the right choices" in the face of change and transition lies in "embodying the leadership qualities of a new generation of leaders." These new leaders, he says, innovate, originate, develop, inspire, envision, question, and challenge—they "do the right thing."

Lynne Joy McFarland and **Larry E. Senn** see change as being driven by globalization, increased competition, and the decrease of hierarchies. They see leaders not only at the top, but at the bottom of organizations. Every person needs to contribute his or her creativity. Every person needs to be a leader. "Leadership is the currency of the 21st century."

Especially in the 21st century, leaders need to be authentic, not counterfeit. **Ken Shelton** warns that "not all models of leadership are worth following as they contain elements of counterfeit in conception or implementation. . . . When leaders think of their roles narrowly in terms of discrete compartments, followers tend to get only bit parts and sound bites. Where context and perspective end, fanaticism begins." Through all the haze and maze, drama and death, reflection and synchronization of changing times, leaders need to be genuine models.

Leadership needs to take on a new dimension. It must be broad and deep, spread across every function and department at all levels. **John W. Humphrey** says that "organizations are finding they must rely on the personal leadership of individuals at every level if they are to manage change effectively and sustain competitive advantage." Also, as **James A. Belasco** informs us, a leader must change from being a Head Buffalo to forming a flock of geese, whose "V" formation allows leadership to change frequently.

Leaders have certain characteristics. **Ronald R. Fogleman** believes that since leaders work with the same basic resources, what distinguishes the good from the bad are their courage and firmness, their framework for making decisions, and their loyalty to their followers. **Charles C. Manz** adds that SuperLeaders are not the "commanding, charismatic, one-of-a-kind magnetic" types. Rather, they are leaders who help their followers become leaders themselves.

For **Horst Shultze** and **Kevin Dimond**, the essence of leadership is a constant focus on vision. During tough reengineering processes, leaders who center themselves on vision can endure the darker days. **Francis N. Bonsignore** notes that the focus on vision must include people and their contributions: "The perplexing challenges of change argue for a renaissance of people responsibilities—a clarified set of responsibilities that are broader than profit and loss, and focused on outcomes further away than the next quarter." Leaders must "acquire, retain, and mobilize people resources."

Leaders in changing times forge ahead. For example, **Gerald L. McManis** writes that leaders must be willing to transcend traditional ruts and comfort zones. They must "continually question and challenge to help keep the organization vital and alive." **David Neidert** maintains that "leaders must strive to acquire not just skills alone but a set of virtues that move all stakeholders toward excellence. . . . The leader is essential as people seek purpose for rising each day to engage in work."

John F. Welch, Jr., of General Electric Company shows how it's possible to keep an organization moving ahead in changing times. He says, "We're focused on getting bigger, not smaller." General Electric's vision is "to shape a global enterprise with the reach and resources of a big company—the body of a big company—but the thirst to learn, the compulsion to share, and the bias for action—the soul—of a small company."

CHAPTER 1

Leadership in the 21st Century

 by Warren Bennis, Distinguished Professor of Business Administration and Founding Chairman of The Leadership Institute at the University of Southern California

CONSTANT CHANGE disturbs some managers—it always has, and it always will. Machiavelli said, "Change has no constituency." Well, it better have one—and soon.

On the eve of the 21st century, we must look now at what it will take simply to remain a player in the game. We can do that because the 21st century is with us now. Cultures don't turn sharply with the pages of the calendar—they evolve. By knowing what is changing today, we know what we must do better tomorrow.

Can we compete successfully in the new, spirited global economy? If there is reason to despair and join the handwringing and head shaking of doomsayers, it's because most American managers were brought up in a different time, when all they had to do was build the greatest mousetraps and the world beat a path to their doors. The competition was fierce but knowable. If you played your cards right, you could win. But the game has changed: Strange new rules have appeared; the deck has been shuffled; and jokers have been added. Never before have leaders faced so many challenges, and never before have there been so many choices about how to face those challenges. Uncertainties and complexities abound. The only thing truly predictable is unpredictability. The new chic is chaos chic. As Yogi Berra put it, "The future ain't what it used to be."

Given the nature and constancy of change and the transitional challenges facing business leaders, the key to making the right choices will come from embodying the leadership qualities necessary to succeed in a global economy. To survive in the 21st century, we'll need a new generation of leaders, not managers.

The distinction is an important one. Leaders conquer the context—the volatile, turbulent, ambiguous surroundings that sometimes seem to conspire against us and will surely suffocate us if we let them—while managers surrender to it. There are other differences as well, and they are crucial:

- The manager administers; the leader innovates.
- The manager is a copy; the leader is an original.
- The manager maintains; the leader develops.
- The manager relies on control; the leader inspires trust.
- The manager has a short-range view; the leader has a long-range perspective.
- The manager asks how and when; the leader asks what and why.
- The manager has his or her eye on the bottom line; the leader has his or her eye on the horizon.
- The manager accepts the status quo; the leader challenges it.
- The manager is the classic good soldier; the leader is his or her own person.
- The manager does things right; the leader does the right thing.

Field Marshal Sir William Slim, who led the 14th British Army in one of the epic campaigns of World War II, said: "Managers are necessary; leaders are essential. Leadership is of the spirit, compounded of personality and vision. Management is of the mind, more a matter of accurate calculation, statistics, methods, timetables, and routine."

I've spent 20 years talking with leaders, close to 1,000 men and women, some famous and some not. In the process, I've learned something about the current crop of leaders and something about the leadership that will be necessary to forge the future. While leaders come in every size, shape, and disposition—short, tall, neat, sloppy, young, old, male, and female—every leader I talked with shared at least one characteristic: a concern with a guiding purpose, an overarching vision. They were more than goal-directed. As Karl Wallenda said, "Walking the tightwire is living; everything else is waiting." Leaders have a clear idea of what they want to do and the strength to persist in the face of setbacks, even failures. They know where they are going and why.

MANAGING THE DREAM

Many leaders find a metaphor that embodies and implements their vision. For Charles Darwin, the fecund metaphor was a branching tree of evolution on which he could trace the rise and fate of various species. William James viewed mental processes as a stream or river.

John Locke focused on the falconer, whose release of a bird symbolized his "own emerging view of the creative process"—that is, the quest for human knowledge.

Leaders manage the dream. All leaders create a compelling vision—one that takes people to a new place—and have the ability to translate that vision into reality. Managing the dream has five parts: *communicating the vision*; *recruiting meticulously*; *rewarding*; *retraining*; and *reorganizing*. As Jung said: "A dream that is not understood remains a mere occurrence. Understood, it becomes a living experience."

Jim Burke spends 40 percent of his time communicating the Johnson & Johnson credo. More than 800 managers have attended J&J challenge meetings, where they go through the credo line by line to see what changes need to be made. Over the years some of those changes have been fundamental. But like the U.S. Constitution, the credo itself endures.

General Electric CEO Jack Welch said: "Yesterday's idea of the boss, who became the boss because he or she knew one more fact than the person working for them, is yesterday's manager. Tomorrow's person leads through a vision, shared values, shared objectives."

The single defining quality of leaders is the capacity to create and realize a vision. Yeats said, "In dreams begins responsibility." Vision is a waking dream. For leaders, the responsibility is to transform the vision into reality. By doing so, they transform their dominion, whether an airline, a motion picture, the computer industry.

Thoreau put it this way: "If one advances confidently in the direction of his dreams, and endeavors to live the life he has imagined, he will meet with a success in common hours. If you have built castles in the air, your work need not be lost. It is where they should be. Now put the foundation under them."

All leaders' guiding visions provide clearly marked road maps; every member can see which direction the corporation is going. The communication of the vision generates excitement about the trip. The plans for the journey create order out of chaos, instill confidence and trust, and offer criteria for success. The group knows when it has arrived.

If you're not sure of your company's vision, how can you tell what the advantages of an alliance would be? You must be certain you have the right map before embarking on the journey.

If you think your company's vision lacks definition, here are some questions that may help give it color and dimension: What is unique about us? What values are true priorities for the next year? What would make me professionally commit my mind and heart to this vision over the next five to ten years? What does the world really need that our company can and should provide? What do I want our company to accomplish so that I will be committed, aligned, and proud of my association with the institution?

Ask yourself those questions today. Your answers will be the fire that heats the forge of your company's future.

WHERE HAVE ALL THE LEADERS GONE?

We are witnessing a high turnover, an appalling mortality—both occupational and actuarial—among leaders. The shelf life of presidents and CEOs has been markedly reduced. Their days at the top are numbered from the moment they take office.

Corporate heads are either organization men who have risen to the level of their incompetence, celebrities, or one-man bands, who devote at least as much time and energy to blowing their own horns as to business. It is no accident that the most celebrated businesspeople now are those who spend their days demolishing rather than creating companies.

Things are no different in politics or public service. More distinguished people announce that they will not seek the presidency than announce that they will.

Never before have individuals wanted and been able to seize so much power unto themselves, and never before have they had so many tools to ensure their autonomy. The automobile, the TV, the VCR, the microwave oven, the computer all serve not only to separate us from our fellow humans but to render us independent of them. But it is the anarchic instinct that has blossomed in so many of us, not the tools, that are at the heart of the problem.

Bereft of leaders and bereaved, we turned on the managers and bureaucrats, the organization men who had reduced great private corporations to money mills and great public institutions to red tape. They had not made life easy for us, and now we were going to make life difficult for them.

As individual autonomy waxed, institutional autonomy waned. External forces impinged and imposed more and more on the perimeter of our institutions; the incessant concatenation of often contrary demands grew. The government had for decades assumed more and more power over corporations and institutions. Now the people were challenging not only the government, but the corporations and institutions, too. An incessant, dissonant clamor grew.

This fragmentation marked the end not only of community, a sense of shared values and symbols, but of consensus. Everyone went his or her own way.

NEW ALLIANCES

Decades of organization men have spawned, perhaps inevitably, anti-organization men. Junior executives rank their fealty to their own ambitions above any loyalty to the company. And why not? Traditionally, corporations have seen employees as adversaries, not allies. Business is the concentrated epitome of our culture, and is inseparable from it. Environmental encroachments and turbulence, the steady beat of litigation, the fragmentation of constituencies, along with their newfound eloquence and power, multiple advocacy, conflicts between internal and external forces, and an everyone-for-himself climate in the executive suites, have turned corporate chiefs into broken field runners—dodging, ducking, moving fast, and demanding "golden parachutes" to soften the inevitable fall.

More and more chiefs, aware of the rancorous mood of the Indians, play it safe and, living up to the inverted proverb, "Don't just do something, simply sit there." Such people avoid trouble, but they also stop progress. The sense of individual responsibility that animated the Constitution has vanished, as both chiefs and Indians now trumpet the new credos: "It's not my job" or "It's not my fault."

Nothing counts except profits, and profits count because they are the sole measure of the CEO. Conscience and competence take a backseat to ambition, as the wheel that turns the fastest gets the bonus. There was a time when CEOs were civic leaders and corporate statesmen. Today, they have no interest in anything but their own bottom lines. The visionaries, too, are gone. Only surefire products and systems win the attention of the CEO, who has neither the time nor the inclination to commit his or her company to a potentially innovative or even useful product. If it isn't likely to be an instant bestseller, it isn't likely to get an okay.

Business leaders never had many moral imperatives, but they did feel some obligation to their employees, the towns they operated in, and the national economy. That's no longer true. In the same way, as Prokesch says: "Many chief executives preach the virtues of employee involvement, teamwork, and participative management, but for a calculated reason. Personnel cutbacks have taken a heavy toll on employee loyalty, which, in turn, threatens to take a toll on company efforts to bolster productivity and product quality. As a consequence, executives face the difficult paradox of having to convince employees that they really care about them—until the axe falls in the next wave of cutbacks." As corporate employers increasingly require their employees to sign "fire-at-will" clauses, the last ray of the covenant is dissolving.

Where have all the leaders gone? They're out there pleading, trotting, temporizing, putting out fires, trying to avoid too much heat. They're peering at a landscape of bottom lines. They're money changers lost in a narrow orbit. They resign. They burn out. They decide not to run or serve. They're organizational Houdinis, surrounded by sharks or shackled in a water cage, always managing to escape, miraculously, to make more money via their escape clauses than they made in several years of work. They motivate people through fear, by following trends or by posing as advocates of "reality," which they cynically make up as they go along. They are leading characters in the dreamless society, given now almost exclusively to solo turns.

Thus, precisely at the time when the trust and credibility of our alleged leaders are at an all-time low and when potential leaders feel most inhibited in exercising their gifts, America most needs leaders—because, of course, as the quality of leaders declines, the quantity of problems escalates.

MICROWAVE OR MCLEADERS

As countless deposed kings and hapless heirs to great fortunes can attest, true leaders are not born, but made, and usually self-made. Leaders invent themselves.

What is true for leaders is true for each of us: We are our own raw material. Only when we know what we're made of and what we want to make of it can we begin our lives—and we must do it despite an unwitting conspiracy of people and events against us.

As television producer Norman Lear put it, "On the one hand, we're a society that seems to be proud of individuality. On the other hand, we don't tolerate real individuality. We want to homogenize it."

A couple of studies underscore the benefits of self-invention. First, middle-aged men tend to change careers after having heart attacks. Faced with their own mortality, these men realize that what they've been doing, what they've invested their lives in, is not an accurate reflection of their real needs and desires.

Another study indicates that what determines the level of satisfaction in post-middle-aged men is the degree to which they acted upon their youthful dreams. It's not so much whether they were successful in achieving their dreams as the honest pursuit of them that counts. The spiritual dimension in creative effort comes from that honest pursuit.

There is evidence that women, too, are happier when they've invented themselves instead of accepting without question the roles they were brought up to play. Fortunately, the changing times have meant changes in relationships, too. Many women leaders have managed to invent themselves, even though married.

I can't stress too much the need for self-invention. To be authentic is literally to be your own author (the words derive from the same Greek root), to discover your own native energies and desires, and then to find your own way of acting on them. When you do that, you do not exist simply to live up to an image posited by the culture or by some other authority or by a family tradition. When you write your own life, no matter what happens, you play the game that is natural for you to play.

LEADERSHIP FOR TOMORROW

One of my favorite quotes is by E. B. White, who once said, "I wake up every morning determined both to change the world and have one hell of a good time. Sometimes this makes planning the day a little difficult."

Every leader today shares a similar wake-up call and charge: both to change the world and have a good time doing it. But I would add an important footnote: The noble mission of the leader can't be used to justify the means.

In the leadership arena, character counts. In fact, I think leadership is character. Character is a word that comes from the Greek "engraved." It's from the French "inscribed." It isn't just a superficial style. It has to do with who we are as human beings, and what shaped us. I also believe that character is a continuously evolving thing, as we continue to acquire and to grow and to develop. The process of becoming a leader is much the same process of becoming an integrated human being. So I see a real connection between what it takes to be a leader and the process.

Integrity, the basis of trust, is not as much an ingredient of leadership as it is a product. It is one quality that can't be acquired, but must be earned. It is given by co-workers and followers, and without it, leaders can't function.

There are three essential parts of integrity: self-knowledge, candor, and maturity.

• Self-knowledge. "Know thyself," said the inscription over the oracle at Delphi. And it is still the most difficult task any of us faces. But until you truly know yourself, strengths and weaknesses, know what you want to do and why you want to do it, you cannot succeed in any but the most superficial sense of the word. Leaders never lie to themselves, especially about themselves, know their flaws as well as their assets, and deal with them directly. You are your own raw material. When you know what you consist of and what you want to make of it, then you can invent yourself.

• Candor. The key to self-knowledge is based in honesty of thought and action, a steadfast devotion to principle, and a fundamental soundness and wholeness. Any person who trims his principles—or even his ideas—to please, lacks professional integrity. The leader cannot cut his or her conscience to fit this year's fashions.

• Maturity. I've never seen a person derailed because of a lack of technical competence. But I've seen lots of people derailed from positions because of a lack of maturity, judgment, and character.

To keep their organizations competitive, leaders must create a social architecture capable of generating intellectual capital, or brainpower. The frustrating thing is that it's hard to measure. When I talk to executives from big and small companies, they say, "My biggest challenge is: How do I release the brainpower?" Certain leaders are more capable of generating intellectual capital than others. We've got to think carefully about the qualities that make leaders effective as we move into the next century.

CHAPTER 2

21st Century Leadership

by Lynne Joy McFarland, President
and CEO of LINC and Larry E. Senn,
Chairman of Senn-Delaney
Leadership Consulting Group

WE LIVE IN an unprecedented period, on the eve of a new century. Profound changes are taking place. We are reinventing not only our organizations, but also ourselves as leaders.

Major shifts have put great pressures on leaders in every sector. These enormous changes have been brought about by increased global competition, economic, political, and social upheaval, and demand leadership that is so completely revolutionary, it challenges all our old models for thinking and acting. We are all witnessing a fundamental transformation in what leadership is and what the elements of effective leadership need to be for the 21st century.

Most effective leaders are refocusing energy on tools and processes that received only scant attention a decade ago. For example, we now make a clear distinction between management and leadership, and place a far greater premium on leadership than ever before. In fact, a whole new definition of leadership has emerged.

A BLUEPRINT FOR SUCCESS

When we interviewed about 100 top leaders representing a cross-section from business, education, government, healthcare, and the service sector, we discovered certain themes—themes as old as civilization, and yet imbued with new meaning, new hope, and new application.

This rich tapestry of leadership concepts provides both an understanding of the times we're facing and a blueprint for building successful organizations in the 21st century.

Three major driving forces of change must be understood—globalization and its consequence of increased competition, the acceleration and complexity of change, and the decrease of hierarchies and "position power."

How do we best address the challenges of this changing game? The overwhelming response is that we can't provide all the answers at the top. We need the contribution and creativity of every person—we need *empowerment.*

The movement toward empowerment is threatening for some and challenging for all. With less hierarchy and more participation, it is difficult to keep people aligned, pulling together in the same direction. At the same time, in an empowered organization guided by vision, there are fewer rules, regulations, and unquestioned policies. How will order be kept and what will govern behavior? The answer seems to be that a healthy culture and shared vision will be the critical leadership tools for moving organizations forward in the future.

We are moving toward a redefinition of leadership. As empowerment, vision, values, and healthy cultures become essential for success in organizations, we must examine what this will mean for leaders. How do they now reinvent themselves?

Diversity will be at the heart of many of these questions, with special focus on the role of women in leadership. Competing in the new global economy calls for the full use of all human resources in organizations. Increasingly, women and people of diverse backgrounds will impact the workforce and direction of leadership. Of primary importance is ensuring a world-class education system. A well-educated work force is essential if we are to compete in the global community. Leaders must also recognize their responsibility to educate and mentor the next generation of leaders.

We must focus on the expanded application of leadership beyond the organization and into society. Our success—as a person, corporation, or nation—requires our concerted leadership efforts toward addressing and solving social and economic problems. Leaders must define the most critical economic and social issues of our time, along with their visions of solutions and models for effective action. Tomorrow's leaders need to be concerned not only with the health of their organizations, but also with the health of their people, communities, countries, and the world.

LEADERSHIP—OUR FUTURE CURRENCY

Leadership will be the currency of the 21st century. We must invest wisely for our current and future generations. Leaders must be willing to share their passion and expertise, to empower others to be leaders, and to effectively lead their organizations. Leaders must inspire people to tap their enormous human potential, to challenge conventional ideas, to take risks in pursuit of their goals and dreams, to create enthusiasm for excellence, and to focus on visions that guide both our organizations and nations, and embrace all humanity.

Highly innovative leadership is emerging in every sector of society. The leadership style is shifting—from autocratic to participative, from a leadership elite clustered at the top of organizations and nations to a leadership distributed at the grass roots; from leadership run by quantitative, short-term, bottom-line measurements to qualitative, long-term, people-oriented, and value-rich indices. This is, in effect, the redefinition of leadership; we are exploring what it will take not only to survive, but to thrive in the 21st century. We are entering a whole new era for the advancement of civilization, a period best characterized by the Chinese symbol that stands for both crisis and opportunity.

Our institutions, our cities, our nations, and the world are in many ways at a crossroads. Tremendous crises need to be faced. There is, however, a window of opportunity for enormous breakthroughs. And these breakthroughs will come to the degree that more of us from every segment of society see ourselves as leaders, stretch beyond our current comfort zones, and commit to making a greater contribution.

The key to enhancing our leadership effectiveness is the courage to live by a powerful vision. One of the most frequent themes for vision is making a difference. We all would like to be known and remembered for having left our "footprint in the sand." Another powerful personal vision is being the best we can be. This is what fuels Olympic athletes and other high achievers in our society.

Equally important is a set of personal values—values based on the highest possible standards of excellence. Some of the most self-empowering values include integrity, honesty, trust, "can-do" attitude, personal accountability, respect for all people, and openness to change. These values make a profound impact on our health, well-being, and success in life.

The difference between those who gain mastery and those who simply dream is commitment to action. We invite you to create an action plan around your new vision and personal values.

SELF-EXAMINATION

In light of this new model for 21st century leadership, you may wish to re-examine yourself as a leader using these and other questions:

1. What is my highest vision for my personal and professional life?
2. What values guide my life and how can I use them to enhance my leadership?
3. How can I empower the people and teams I am in a position to influence? How can I bring out the best in myself and others?
4. What can I learn and apply from the leaders I personally admire most?

5. Do we have a compelling and motivating vision that effectively aligns everyone?
6. Do we have a healthy culture, with positive habits that foster leadership and enhance performance?
7. Do we value diversity and develop everyone's potential?
8. Are we socially responsible? Do we give back to the community, education system, environment, and society?

LAUNCHING A NEW ERA OF LEADERSHIP

As we near the end of this decade, century, and millennium, we approach the beginning of a new era of leadership. Never before has there been a greater need for outstanding leadership. We each have the unprecedented opportunity to play a crucial role in human history and make a profound contribution as we launch a new era of leadership for the 21st century.

"We all stand on common ground," says Peter C. Goldmark, Jr., president of the Rockefeller Foundation. "We are all in danger. We must change. We all share the same planet. If the weak do not get stronger, the strong will not survive. If we do not use our knowledge, our wealth, and our comparative advantages toward common objectives, as partners, then we will consume nature's capital and make development impossible throughout the world."

Leadership is the currency for the 21st century: How do we want to invest it? It's time to invest in building a new 21st century society. We need to launch a worldwide leadership campaign to empower people to make a difference.

We call for compassion and caring—the highest quality leadership—among current leaders and emerging leaders, and that includes everyone.

• *To our youth*—the next generation of leaders—we encourage you to get a good education and to step forward and lead in whatever you do: We need your fresh spirit of optimism. We need your rich talents and boundless energy. We need your conviction and commitment.

• *To the current generation of leaders*, who have to be stronger perhaps than any other generation before to lead us through the next century: Be impeccable about your values because you are setting an example and are the role models for our future generations. You have many hard decisions to make to prepare us for the next century. These choices must be made wisely for the long-term benefit of our organizations as well as for our countries. The key to making the right choices will come from understanding and embodying 21st century leadership qualities.

Take action and take heart. Today's leaders invite each of us to participate as leaders in our own right.

CHAPTER 3

From Counterfeit to Authentic Leadership

 by Ken Shelton, Chairman and Editor-in-Chief of Executive Excellence Publishing

NOT ALL MODELS of leadership are worth following as they contain elements of counterfeit in conception or implementation.

Whenever something is highly prized, whether it be gold coin or genuine leadership, we can expect to see masterful counterfeits.

Real leadership is often hard to detect—even harder to reward once recognized—because of rules and biases built into social, academic, and professional systems. Hence, we are short on leadership, long on counterfeit. Our coffers are filled with fool's gold (pyrite), and our offices filled with gold fools (pirates).

Professional counterfeit is an art, and the artful imitation has the look and feel of the original. To the eye, even the educated eye, it may even appear to be identical. And to the child or the uninitiated, the cheap imitation not only has the same look, but the same worth and value as the genuine article. In fact, to the child, the cheap imitation may be even more valuable than the real thing because it is affordable, available, and accessible.

But alas, children soon learn what is and what is not legal tender—what trades over the counter or on the exchange.

And yet as adults, in the business world of buy and sell, we still mistake coins and currency, credentials and character; we fail to detect and reward the legitimate and then learn to live with sham, fraud, forgery, and deceit; with fakes, impostors, impressionists, impersonators, and third-generation copies of genuine and original folks and works.

One reason is that we see counterfeit by degree—a continuum of counterfeit. And when one area or aspect of our personal lives or of our organizations is more or less legitimate, all other areas then borrow credibility from the Bank of Strength.

Indeed, even as educated and experienced professionals, we may be hard pressed to tell the difference between counterfeit and genuine articles, especially when the cultures we live in (and help create) have a high degree of counterfeit built into them.

CAUSES AND SOURCES OF COUNTERFEIT

Why do we see so many feigned, false, forged, fabricated, and other counterfeit forms of leadership? What are their origins or causes? What are the seeds and the sources?

Counterfeit leadership often begins with counterfeit followership— with the notion that passive resistance or assistance, ignorance, activism, apathy, ambition, and aggression are traits of true followers— with the idea that the tallest, toughest, biggest, loudest, most articulate, best dressed, most popular, or the most physically or financially endowed ought to be leader. Counterfeit election, selection, and promotion processes compound the problem.

While counterfeit leadership often defrauds, defames, misguides, maligns, or simply mismanages people, it rarely starts with sinister intent; in fact, *much of it is manufactured with good intentions and with noble missions and motives in the most reputable of academic, business, and social institutions.*

Counterfeit leadership is made in many fine factories. Some cynics might say it begins in the womb with genetic, intergenerational imprinting. Although that may be argued, it's certain that by the time children are five years old, many indelible impressions are made upon them in homes and neighborhoods, preschools, and day care centers. And the stamping, engraving, foiling, embossing, and die casting continue through the teenage years. Our skin, our souls become tattooed with inks and ideas.

Genetic imprinting, parental modeling, and cultural conditioning greatly influence us—no question. But our "adult" choices of leadership models also contribute greatly to the degree of genuine or counterfeit leadership we build into our personal and corporate characters. In fact, it is in and through these choices that we move along the continuum, in one direction or another, toward the legitimate or the counterfeit.

MODELS OF LEADERSHIP

Many attractive "models" of leadership pass before our eyes each day. We typically assess these; accept and adopt some; and begin to integrate or implement them.

- *Schools of management* market various academic or conceptual models of leadership that celebrate intellectual, cerebral, compartmental, statistical, financial, analytical, theoretical, functional, and measurable elements with an explicit trust in credentials and accreditation.
- *Corporations* have culture models that spotlight lore, legend, myth, tales, and larger-than-life wizards and folk heroes.
- *Governments* push political models that reward the compromiser; the facilitator; the diplomat; the speech, law, and policy maker.
- *Societies* make mirror models that encourage observations, comparisons, criticisms, and competitions based on style, skills, and appearance—all coming with different distortions.
- *Management consultants* make wonderfully creative models that feature jargon and jerry-rigged constructs.
- *Performing arts and athletics* elevate talent models that stress performance, charisma, personality, creativity, style, points.
- *Media* sell their celebrity models—the mogul, master, mentor, actor, anchor, commentator—that venerate visual and verbal images.

But before we buy any models of leadership, we would be wise to try them and to put them to one or more reliable tests.

THE MISSION, MOTIVES AND MEANS TEST

A basic cause of counterfeit is misalignment of mission, motives, and means. When the leadership is so misaligned, many odd problems develop, and these spread like cancer into other healthy parts of the organization. Soon the mission begins to justify the means; the means gain momentum and override the mission; the motives become polluted; good intentions masquerade for real reasons. We then begin to substitute expediency for priority, imitation for innovation, cosmetics for character, style for substance, pretense for competence, rationalization for research, and public relations for ongoing development of people and improvement of products.

Counterfeit leaders often profess to have noble motives, missions and purposes—even clean hands and pure hearts—which is why so many heinous crimes are committed in the name of religion, patriotism, and nationalism. It's a distortion of a good that creates a false god, an unhealthy adoration that creates an aberration, a selfish or possessive love that creates a hate.

- ***Mission.*** The mission of leadership may be to create market, margin, money; to provide for basic needs; to supply incentives and reward hard work, resourcefulness, efficiency, and effectiveness; to benefit in win-win ways all the stakeholders; to enrich and refine the soul; to supply light, leaven, and salt.

Inevitably, even in the most mundane, militaristic, or malevolent of organizations, the mission is articulated in such artistic, if not altruistic, words. People want to believe that what they do makes a difference; that the company or the cause they work for is constructive; that the products and services they provide are needed and valued in society. Hence, looking at the mission statement alone won't reveal much.

Moreover, mission-centered, cause-driven organizations are rather easily counterfeited by con artists who learn the right buzzwords and passwords, gain entry and corrupt the systems. Self-deception and ego-centricity set in, often accompanied by feelings of euphoria or invincibility. There's honor among thieves and philosophers alike. In fact, one of the worst corporate cultures I have worked in was a "Camelot culture," complete with warring and ever-sparring knights of the round table.

Time may be the best test of the validity of a professed mission. But who can afford to wait for 20-20 hindsight to determine if the mission is, in fact, self-serving or selfless? This leads us to an examination of motives.

• *Motives.* Trust is the tender of trade, and if the motives are pure, there is sanctity and trust in relationships, an openness in style, a simplicity in systems, a candor in communications. The motives of genuine leaders engender trust and encourage the growth and development of people. They are tempered by a long-term view, disciplined by systems with memory, and checked and filtered by counselors.

Counterfeit leaders profess purity of motive but are tainted by pride, ambition, desires, and passions for power, wealth, fame, publicity, or sensuality. Their motives often shift during the course of events; secrecy and privacy become mandatory to counterfeiting. Such leaders begin wearing two or more faces and many hats. Few followers dare question or challenge their motives. Even with foul motives, their behavior may be very believable and commendable, which is why so many loved ones are "shocked" and "stunned" to learn of the sordid deeds of esteemed leaders who are found out.

• *Means.* To counterfeit leaders, the means are ever justified—even such messy means as murder, spying, stealing, cheating, lying, fighting, deceiving, etc. Notable leaders have, throughout history, done such things to achieve a worthy mission. While there must be exceptions that allow such extremes, these certainly must be rare. Rape, pillage, and plunder are not the everyday means of genuine leaders. Experienced leaders need not see results overnight; they understand natural growth cycles and seasons.

THE CHARACTER TRAITS TEST

Certain traits characterize counterfeit leaders. They tend to be proud, vain, and self-promotional. They bring about uniformity and sameness as opposed to unity and oneness. They often judge on appearances. Their style is to use, abuse, exploit, deceive, consume, create dependency. Their voices are full of vanity, vulgarity, dogma, jargon, and sentimentality. They relish politics, theatrics, dramatics, short-term flashes, shortcut finishes, as well as artificial highs through alcohol, drugs, and pornography. They are masters of symbolism.

Counterfeit leaders enjoy the expansive and the expensive; they waste and exploit resources. Their view of the public is that the masses are asses. Their appetites and passions are either socially and systematically checked or out of control. They both want and need much money, and to get it, they will do whatever is necessary, including start their own press. They try to fool people, even mother nature. They profess to stimulate creativity but in reality control speech and expression, and manipulate media. They imitate originals, copy and plagiarize materials.

Genuine leaders, on the other hand, have something original to them. They reflect a home-grown character, a respect for roots. They prize light and knowledge, virtue and industry, without believing they have a corner on the market. Their charisma is quieter, but evident in their wisdom, perspective, and life balance. Their style is to build, empower, and create self-reliance.

From a wellspring of love and trust, great leaders perform anonymous acts of service, even sacrifice. They are responsible stewards over time. They continue to discipline appetites and passions, budget time and money, even after acquiring an abundance. They also continue to do real work and maintain close ties to nature or to natural processes. Their speech is unaffected and unpretentious—natural, efficient, and effective. They would often rather make a clear difference on a small scale than endlessly seek advancement. They are appropriately meek, humble, contrite, submissive, and obedient to proper authority.

THE RELATIONSHIP TEST

We can also apply certain behavior and relationship tests to detect counterfeits. Genuine and counterfeit leaders tend to manage relationships differently, especially in times requiring originality and creativity; in times of disaster, chaos, confusion, conflict, opposition, competition; in times of contests, games, sports, recreation. By examining intimate family relationships, close professional relationships and other stakeholder relationships, we begin to see true colors.

Genuine and counterfeit leaders differ also in how they treat children, minorities, and people who others might consider to be "poor, dumb, ugly, and plain."

COUNTERFEIT VERSUS GENUINE CORPORATE CULTURE

The signals are all important: who gets hired, rewarded, promoted, recognized; who gets resources; what gets celebrated; what gets punished; who and what gets attention; who and what gets forgotten or ignored.

People attend to such signals, and when they point to counterfeit, there is a lot of gameplaying, posturing, positioning, politicking, parading, patronizing, pleasing, appeasing, pandering, palavering, and pushing palliatives.

The genuine corporate cultures recognize good work, team effort, origins, originals, significant contributions. They are based on the agricultural principles—faith, seed, plant, cultivate, weed, water, harvest—and on natural processes, correct principles, constitutional and participative forms of government.

CURES: FEW MIRACLES BUT MUCH MEDICINE

Transformations or reformations are possible, but it's hard to cure counterfeits. They are usually addicted to one of several "drugs" and "quick fixes"—everything from caffeine to cocaine, from power to politics.

The cure for such malignant growth and tumor is to get mission, motives, and means back in alignment—and that may require surgery or the equivalent of chemotherapy to keep counterfeits from spreading and ulcerating.

Although we must allow for repentance, change, and reformation, old habits are hard to break. Once one masters the martial art of hardball negotiation, once one has the habit of taking candy from children, of getting one's own way, of controlling lives and situations, one is a compulsive counterfeit.

Cures involve the following process:
- Return to roots, the soil, the seed;
- Get close to nature, agriculture, land, garden;
- Experience anew natural processes, cycles, seasons;
- Identify and discipline toward best self;
- Associate with genuine articles/models;
- Work for or with companies with quality products/services;
- Oppose and boycott garbage, dirt, waste, pornography;
- Strive for balance; work with both mind and hands;
- Keep fit; consume right foods and drinks;
- Get in touch with real self, talents, capabilities;
- Submit to divine/inspiring influences.

History shows us that even the wisest men and women are occasionally deceived by counterfeits. Hindsight is always 20-20; foresight is flawed; and present vision often prejudiced. Hence, when the dust settles after a storm, we can expect to see some paradoxes, ironies, and dramatic reversals: The first may be last, the greatest the least, the master the servant. Genuine leadership stands the test of time.

CHAPTER 4

A Time of 10,000 Leaders

by John W. Humphrey, Chairman of the Board and Chief Executive Officer of The Forum Corporation

THE MAJOR FEATURE of today's business landscape is dramatic, sudden, and often unexpected increases in both the amount and speed of change. In such a turbulent setting, organizations are finding they must rely on the personal leadership of individuals at every level of the corporate structure if they are to manage change effectively and sustain competitive advantage.

ALIGNMENT AND EMPOWERMENT

A key requirement for creating broad and deep leadership within an organization is a high degree of workforce alignment and empowerment in direct support of the corporate strategy. I use *alignment* to mean communication of a clear direction, shared vision, and well-defined policies, procedures, systems, and methods throughout the organization. *Empowerment* in this context denotes a strong feeling of authority, power, and ownership that motivates all employees to take initiative, responsibilities, and risks. Prevailing thought once put alignment and empowerment at opposite ends of the same scale, but we now know they are entirely different dimensions that, according to the degree to which each of them is present, create distinctly different organizational climates.

1. Abdication. This climate is created when an organization is low in both alignment and empowerment. It is characterized by managers who do not take much initiative, and large numbers of unmotivated, unenergetic employees with seemingly no sense of common purpose.

2. Autocracy. This is a climate of high alignment and low empowerment, a "do it my way or hit the highway" style of management that fails to tap into the discretionary efforts of employees. It does a good job of making sure everyone understands the corporate direction, and an even better job of telling everyone exactly how things should get done.

3. Heroism. With a high degree of empowerment but low alignment, there is a potential for everyone to run around like an entrepreneur and do his or her own thing. The frequent result is lots of redundancy and people often working against each other. And because heroic actions are situational, they are not predictable, and heroic producers get burned out.

4. Leadership. This climate is created when high levels of both alignment and empowerment are built and sustained. Throughout the organization, people have a clear picture of the company's strategic direction and feel they have an ownership stake in assuring the outcome is successful. This climate takes a long time to achieve, even when enormous resources are committed to the effort, because it requires mobilizing and inspiring large numbers of people.

DRIVING PRINCIPLES OF LEADERSHIP

People have been thinking about and defining leadership since antiquity, and everyone has his or her own ideas. In our most recent leadership research, we wanted to identify specific practices that distinguish high-performing leaders in today's environment of change. This research has produced a number of important conclusions. Many of the findings are fresh and exciting; others confirm what we have known for years. All of them have important meaning for modern corporations.

• *Leadership is not exclusive to the executive suite.* The business environment is simply too complex to have one, two, three, or even a layer of executives at the top assuming the role of leadership. Progress depends on the personal initiative and skills of every person at every level. This contrasts well with the concept of the critical few, a handful of strong leaders who perch at the top but are relatively isolated. Leadership must be evident from the boardroom to the shop floor.

• *Organizations will crumble without leadership.* Change makes people feel tentative, vulnerable, and reluctant to act. A paramount value of leadership in turbulent times is that it helps people see clearly and act decisively. Strong leaders are able to build and maintain the confidence and trust of their people in order to overcome organizational paralysis.

• *The right to lead must be earned.* Businesspeople tend to think in terms of ascribed leadership: the leader as CEO, military commander, or captain of the team. Forum's research found that people today are extremely skeptical of this idea. In fact, there is an inverse relationship between having a title or position of authority and the degree to which people feel they can easily earn the right to lead.

• *Leadership focuses on relationships.* Most definitions of leadership reflect the theory of "the great man," the daring but isolated achiever who goes off into the sunset to find the next challenge. However, most of the practices we identified that differentiate high-performing leaders focus on relationships with other people, not acts of individual heroism.

• *Leadership is contextual.* The qualities of high-performing leaders are grounded in extensive knowledge of the general business environment; intimate understanding of their industry, company, and work group; and a strong sense of their organization's strategy, culture, and values. People need to understand how the leadership practices they learn relate to, and are best applied, in their own situation.

• *Leaders inspire others to lead.* Leadership is not about winning followers. It is about showing others how to lead by empowering them to do so and supporting their efforts. The challenge is that most people do not see themselves as leaders. They may feel confident in their abilities, but have a hard time taking on the sense of ownership that leadership demands. Conversely, managers may fear that sharing power will create "too many chiefs" and stymie the group's progress. I have found, however, that it allows leaders to be more creative and moves innovative work forward more successfully.

• *Management skills are an essential component of leadership.* Most leadership studies argue that organizations need leaders in times of change and managers in times of stability. But in today's business environment, the pendulum of change moves too fast to parcel out leadership work and management work. To ensure progress, companies must foster leadership and management capabilities within each individual.

• *Leadership can be learned.* The ability to lead is not native talent. Some skill development is necessary, but the key is to help people understand what it means to lead and why it is important for them to be leaders if their organization is to remain competitive. In our own practical experience, we have found statistically significant improvements in the leadership abilities of participants after training, both in their own eyes and in those of their associates.

PRACTICES OF HIGH-PERFORMING LEADERS

The roots of effective leadership are really quite practical and based upon a set of observable behaviors. We have grouped these into four clusters.

1. Interpreting. There is a strong correlation between leadership performance and a passion for information. Leaders are extremely good at making sense of the world and doing things that are linked to real situations. They are able to track a wide variety of factors and analyze their impact on the business environment, the organization, the work unit, and themselves. It is interesting to note that the level of confidence people have in someone as a leader is directly related to how skilled they believe that person is at interpreting conditions.

2. Shaping. Leaders are highly effective at shaping a vision and strategy that give meaning to the work people are doing. In the face of dramatic change or even crisis, an effective vision acts as a catalyst that drives the group forward.

3. Mobilizing. This means moving people from vision to reality; rallying the group, getting people aligned, giving people a sense of ownership, and helping them understand where they are going. Of all the leadership practices the Forum study identified, managers are least proficient of those that mobilize other people. One reason is that traditional business education focuses on critical thinking and crunching numbers, not on appealing to people's hearts and minds or demonstrating confidence in their abilities.

4. Inspiring. Inspiration can move nations. Think of Martin Luther King, Jr., or Joan of Arc and their ability to change history. In business, however, helping people develop their own talents matters more than stage presence, and showing one cares for people counts more than charisma. In the long run, inspiring others, recognizing their contributions, and building their enthusiasm pays enormous benefits.

DEVELOPING LEADERS

Many organizations persist in pursuing selective recruitment strategies as the means of replenishing their leader rosters. This is not the answer. Middle- to senior-level leaders are hard to find and even harder to hire away. Developing leadership from within is invariably faster and more reliable. Still, it isn't easy. It demands executive persistence, courage, careful planning, constant communication, and a highly focused, contextual leadership development effort.

Leadership development must be linked to the corporate strategy. To achieve this, people must be challenged to explore their intellectual and emotional limits. Beyond tactical leadership skills, they must know where the group is headed, realize they have control over its direction, and feel that the direction is consistent with their own beliefs.

The pressure today for an applied view of leadership is the result of heightened competition, intense technological change, globalization, and an increasingly diverse work force. As we approach the 21st century, the winds of change will howl more fiercely. In this climate, an organization's ability to cultivate broad and deep leadership is not a short-term solution, but an imperative for the future.

CHAPTER 5

Leading the New Organization

by James A. Belasco, Chairman of Management Development Associates and Professor of Management at San Diego State University

THE NEW LEADER must change from being Head Buffalo to forming a flock of geese. The mandate is, "Be different or be gone."

Some time ago, I met with the president of a major corporation. As we talked, he shifted nervously in his chair. Worry creased his face. With his Ivy League training, he was a leading spokesperson for American business. Although greatly admired and frequently cited, his eloquence now deserted him.

He got up, strode to the window, and peered out at the bucolic setting. "Not on my watch," he said to the huge oak tree outside his window. "This can't happen on my watch." After a silent shuffling of feet and clasping and unclasping of hands, he whirled and faced me, steel flashing in his eyes. "I've got five years before I retire. What can I do to make these five years count?"

The challenge was daunting. The company, despite its favorable press, was losing market share in every phase of its business and was very late in launching several new products. Despite its cash hoard and dominant market position, the company was in serious trouble as its cash cow was under attack by the Japanese. The CEO saw with crystal clarity the dire consequences if the business did not change radically now. The unthinkable could happen on his watch, and he did not know what to do. Nothing in his experience or training had prepared him to deal with this. He felt powerless to make the changes he knew had to be made. He saw clearly what had to be done. He knew well the management mantra of teamwork, quality, service, and speed. He preached them to anyone who would listen. Yet, he was unable to produce any of these outcomes in his organization.

It was not for lack of trying. In the last six years, he'd instituted programs designed to improve quality, service, and teamwork. He'd trimmed the organization, reorganized functional groups into customer-focused units, and reduced the management layers. Yet, he continued to lose market share, competitors continued to beat him to the market, and he'd lost 50 percent of his market value. He just couldn't move his people to do what he knew had to be done.

In the end, this president failed. Despite his good intentions and herculean efforts, he took early retirement after drowning in the flood tide of red ink he was unable to stem with his traditional leadership approaches.

I know how that president felt. I've sat in the same chair, felt my gut crawl, and felt like throwing chairs through windows in frustration. I know it is easy to talk about being different. It is a lot harder to *be* different.

OLD PARADIGM: HEAD BUFFALO AND HERD

The old leadership models and paradigms no longer work. How leaders develop and live a new model is and will be the critical success factor for most organizations.

For a long time, I believed the old leadership paradigm that told me my job was to plan, organize, command, coordinate, and control. And I saw my organization functioning like a herd of buffalo. Buffalo are absolutely loyal followers of one leader. They do whatever the leader wants them to do. In my company, I was Head Buffalo.

Originally, I liked that arrangement. After all, my brilliance built the organization. I wanted people to do exactly what I told them, to be loyal and committed. I loved being the center of power, and I believed that was the leader's job.

But I realized, eventually, that my organization didn't work as well as I'd like. Because buffalo are loyal to one leader, they stand around and wait for the leader to show them what to do. When the leader isn't around, they wait for him to show up. The early settlers could decimate the buffalo herds easily by killing the lead buffalo. The rest of the herd could be slaughtered while standing around awaiting instructions from their leader.

I found a lot of "waiting around" in my buffalo-like organization. Worse, people did only what I told them to do and nothing more, which meant that I got zero creativity from my buffalo.

I also found it was hard work being the lead buffalo. Giving all the orders and doing all the "important" work took twelve to fourteen hours a day. Meanwhile my company was getting slaughtered out there in the marketplace because I couldn't respond quickly enough to changes. All this frustrating work as the leader of the buffalo herd was growing old—and making me old before my time.

NEW PARADIGM: A FLOCK OF GEESE

Then one day I got it. What I really wanted in the organization was a group of responsible, interdependent workers, similar to a flock of geese. I could see the geese flying in their "V" formation, the leadership changing frequently. I saw every goose being responsible for getting itself to wherever the gaggle was going, changing roles whenever necessary, alternating as a leader, a follower, or a scout. When the task changed, the geese would be responsible for changing the structure of the group to accommodate, similar to geese that fly in a "V" but land in waves.

I saw clearly that the biggest obstacle to my success was my role as the head buffalo. I had to become a different kind of leader, so everyone else could become a leader in his or her own right.

So I decided it was time for "out with the old, in with the new." The old command-and-control paradigm of leadership was given us over 100 years ago by Henri Fayol, Max Weber, and Frederick Taylor. I practiced and believed in it. And it worked when physical assets were the critical tools of production. Today, the precious tool of production is the intellectual capital held by programmers and machinists. The people who perform the work hold the real power.

The ground rules for the leader's new role in this era of intellectual capitalism are as follows.

1. Change your own leadership behavior first. My desire to be the head buffalo, my wanting to rescue people, and my previous success all got in the way of successfully handling the current situation. Nothing constructive happened until I recognized myself as the obstacle and changed my behavior. My leadership effectiveness grew when I learned to ask, "What did I do or not do that caused the unsatisfactory performance to occur?"

2. Make your customer the boss. Far too often, it's the person in the corner office who gets served first with the deference and swift response to requests. My organization didn't thrive until I established systems that provided each person with monthly personalized feedback from customers and fellow employees. Then I linked these monthly customer and employee data with profit contributions and tied it all into compensation. When I gave the customers control over the paychecks, my people started treating them with the deference accorded the real boss.

3. Think strategically. I used to begin with what we could be and managed forward. We struggled to make inches of progress and usually finished out of the money. It wasn't until I began with what we must be for customers and managed backwards from there that we won gold medals.

4. *Transfer ownership.* Create conditions where the intellectual capital holders, the performers, assume responsibility for delighting their customers. In the new organization, everyone becomes a leader when the systems provide real-time real-data on: profit contributions, customer evaluations, and peer/colleague upward feedback. People assume ownership when they see the consequences of their own behavior.

5. *Learn continuously.* To keep ahead of the rapid changes, everyone, including the leader, must learn faster. We set pay and performance appraisal systems that evaluated and rewarded learning. Then, we prospered.

In the new organization, the employees who hold the intellectual capital do the managerial work of planning, organizing, commanding, coordinating, and controlling. Leaders perform the leadership tasks listed above. In this upside-down world, leaders lead, and employees manage. Leaders who recognize this phenomenon and change their behavior will survive. Leaders who don't change will pass from the scene.

CHANGE BEGINS WITH ME

If leaders in the new organization hope to change some things in the company, they might start by changing their own ways and means.

Vaughn Beals, former Chairman of Harley-Davidson, looks straight into the camera and says: "We tried all the usual solutions—the culture routine, the robot routine, the low wage routine—and none of them worked. We couldn't avoid the unescapable conclusion. We, the management, were the problem."

In the early 1980s, Harley was flat on its back, leveled by Honda. Honda was selling motorcycles that had better styling and didn't leak oil. It looked as if Harley had a one-way ticket to the corporate graveyard.

Then, Vaughn Beals woke up. He realized that his fundamental problem was not Honda, or the unions, or whoever was the excuse this week. Rather, his biggest problem stared back at him in the mirror every morning. As Michael Jackson sang, change begins with the "Man in the Mirror."

Beals began to empower his people. He organized his people into teams and gave them responsibility for scheduling, quality, and production line design. He slimmed the hierarchy and got supervisors out of the way of the people so they could do the job they needed to do. He put in a *Just-In-Time* inventory system. With the help of his people, he even made it work. Today, Beals says, "The power from those teams is damn near infinite." What a turnaround—in the way he thinks.

WE-NEED-TO-FIX-THEM MENTALITY

So many leaders feel, "We need to fix them (the employees). They aren't doing it right. Let's straighten them out quickly, so we can get back to business."

With that mentality, is it any wonder that "they" don't take responsibility? It's not a surprise that most often "they" wait for instructions, and then do only what "they" are told. This "I'll think and you do" mentality is the biggest obstacle to empowerment.

Mr. Matsushitu, president of the most successful consumer electronics company in the world, put it best when he said, "We are going to win, and the Industrial West is going to lose out; there's nothing you can do about it, because the reasons for your failure are within yourselves. Your bosses do the thinking while the workers wield the screwdrivers—and you're convinced deep down that this is the right way to run a business. For you, the essence of management is getting the ideas out of the heads of the bosses into the hands of labor."

What many leaders fail to understand is that "they" (the people) are the business and that the primary purpose of any leader is to empower "them" to use the vision to execute the strategy.

This may require managers to change their mentality. For example, I recall my attendance at a crisis meeting of the executive committee for a major software company. They were ten months late on a major new product announcement. And, the best guess from the R&D head was at least six more months. The day went with the usual finger pointing and recriminations.

After eight hours the weary CEO asked, "What can we do to get the product out sooner?" The shoulder shrugs and upturned palms all said, "Nothing." When I suggested that they put together a tiger team of employees, the president turned to me and said, "What do they know?"

FIRST CHANGE YOURSELF

Empower people by looking squarely in the mirror and asking, "What am I doing that either empowers people to change, or prevents them from changing?" Make a list, and don't be surprised if your empowering actions list is a whole lot shorter than the disempowering list. Then, do more of the empowering behaviors and fewer of the disempowering ones.

It won't be easy. You've got many years of programming and education to overcome. I know. We at the universities turn out thousands of people a year with the misguided philosophy that their job is to "fix them." Virtually all of your previous successes have come from "fixing them." But what got you here, unfortunately, will not get you further. Previous success prevents us from trying new behaviors.

Seek help. I did. So did Ralph Stayers from Johnsonville Sausage: "I asked my people to give me a sign when I was overpowering them, which I did frequently. It took me a while to accept that feedback without getting angry. It's still difficult. I also tape recorded my interactions and held frequent replays. I was astounded by my domineering actions. I was the smartest, best person in the company—and I made certain everyone knew it. I cut people off. I argued strongly for my point of view. I didn't listen very well to anybody else. I found it hard to believe that it was really me on the tape. The evidence was overwhelming, though. I couldn't avoid the conclusion that I was the biggest obstacle to the successful empowerment of my people."

Try it yourself. Listen to yourself and ask, "Did my behavior really help to empower others? What else could I do to help my people take responsibility? What else could I do to get out of the way?" But, be ready. It'll take time to change, and lots of courage. My experience tells me that the current rash of writings on empowering leadership misses the important point: Empowerment only works when the leaders throughout the organization—at every level—change.

CHAPTER 6

Leadership for Changing Times

by Robert R. Fogleman, Joint Chief of Staff for the United States Air Force

GENERAL GOERGE S. PATTON, JR., defined leadership as "The art of getting subordinates to do the impossible."

I can say from my military experience that the difference between a good unit and a bad unit is leadership. Where you find poor units, you find poor commanders. In the military, and I suspect also in the corporate world, leadership is the key, because the personnel system in the aggregate deals everyone an even hand. Every unit will get some superstars, some middle-ground folks, and some who are not up to standards.

So how does a leader best use the resources he or she has been given? In his book *Managing for the Future*, Peter Drucker says that there is no substitute for leadership, and he defines leadership simply as "getting things accomplished by acting through others." And in the book, *In Search of Excellence*, Tom Peters says, "All excellent companies have strong leaders at every level."

When you are put into a leadership position, you need to take stock of your people and get to know them not just as names, but as people. You must treat them with the dignity with which you would like to be treated. That won't always be easy, because you will have people who don't live up to your expectations. But successful leaders determine how to make the best use of each talent assigned to them.

COURAGE AND CONSIDERATION

It takes courage to accept leadership responsibility, especially knowing that not everybody is going to like you and your decisions.

You will need to make hard decisions that affect people's lives. To be an effective leader, you must make those difficult decisions, but guard against becoming insensitive to the fact that you are leading people. The decisions you make impact people who have children, who have lives, expectations, and goals outside of work.

I am the court-martial authority for many men and women, and frequently, cases are referred to me by the Staff Judge Advocate. By the stroke of a pen, I decide whether a person goes to prison at Fort Leavenworth or gets rehabilitated; whether a person gets released with an honorable or dishonorable discharge. In the Military Justice System, there has to be justice, but there also has to be fairness, because your decisions impact people's lives.

General George Marshall, chief of staff of the Army during the Second World War, and later the secretary of defense and secretary of state, was once asked what he sought in future and potential leaders. He answered, "Courage, because all else depends on that." General Marshall was talking about people who have the courage of their convictions, the ability to make decisions based on the best available information, and then get on with life.

FRAMEWORK FOR MAKING DECISIONS

It helps if you have a framework or frame of reference for making your decisions. That framework starts to build the very first day you enter the organization. You look around to see how things are done, and you make mental notes, such as, "I never want to be like that person," or, "Faced with this situation, I will make this decision."

People often say to me, "You seem to make decisions very fast." I say, "Yes." And they ask how I do that. I explain that I have built, over time, a set of references, and I stay within those references. When I am presented with an issue, I compare it to my set of values. If it is compatible, I support it; if not, I ask for more information or I reject it.

This idea of building a set of references has to do with how we go about educating ourselves. If left to our own devices, we tend to stay engaged in the things we know best. We do not like to venture into the unknown or the unpleasant. But to be an effective leader, you have to do some things that you do not like to do. Executives may not like to visit the workstations of employees, but they have to visit them, because the troops are looking to them to get the resources to improve them, to improve their quality of life.

As you go up through the ranks, you get a few stripes or a couple of promotions and start to think, "I want a nice, cushy office, where I can put up my 'I love me' wall, and have people come to me," rather than stay on the flightline, engaged, where the primary mission is.

You need to understand the whole organization. You need to know about a lot of things, and you have to do things you do not necessarily like to do.

A leader must ask, "How can I make good things happen?" You are supposed to provide the vision for the organization. There were years when we actually encouraged people to kill good ideas. When a good idea came up, we would check every regulation, if not to kill the idea intentionally, to at least ensure that we were not violating anything. We have turned that around. Now, rather than ask, "What do the rules say?," we give all inputs a fair shot. Rather than look first to what the rules allow us to do, we first seek to make every good idea work, even changing the rules to give us greater latitude, if necessary.

You ought to treat your machines as if they were people, but never treat your people like machines. You need to care for your resources, but you have to treat people like people. You have to lead by example and be where the action is.

I teach four basic principles:

1. *Absolutely no rule through fear.* You will get much more out of people if you lead them in a positive fashion.
2. *Don't display raw emotion in public.* If a person can't control himself or herself, how can I trust him or her to control a large organization?
3. *Tolerate no outright breaches of integrity.* In the reporting of mission activities, security responsibilities, and financial data, we can't afford altered reports.
4. *Don't use your office to abuse anyone.* Every individual is vital. We will get the very best out of people if we create a climate that allows them to function at their best.

LENIENCY IS NOT LEADERSHIP

Some people in the military confuse leniency with leadership. Everybody wants to be popular, but you can't always be popular and still be a good leader. Real professionals are turned off by leniency. Remember: When you identify a problem, you should deal with it. I tell people not to use a shotgun to fix a problem when they ought to use a scalpel. Avoid the tendency to call everybody together to give them a lecture, when only one person in the outfit is generating the problem. Go take care of the individual. Troops don't like being harangued when they know they are not the real problem.

Firm, fair, and consistent discipline is essential to good human relations. We must understand the difference between a crime and a mistake; and an honest mistake is not a crime.

Loyalty is a big part of leadership. And we need to understand that loyalty is a two-way street: loyalty to your bosses, and loyalty to your people. In the military, we say that our first loyalty is to our country, our mission, and our people. Loyalty to people, especially superiors, can be very difficult. At times, I must simply exercise faith in my superiors. They will not always be right, but generally, the basis for their decisions is sound. They have more sources of information than I do, and they are exposed to a larger picture.

You must have goals for yourself and for your unit. Your people must have goals, because goals give direction to life and to work. Periodically, we set new goals. Hopefully, as we set those goals, we "aim high." We ought to set goals that are quantifiable and achievable." Good leaders have a passion to succeed. Leadership is a tough task. Shifting from talking about leadership to actually being a leader is not easy. To become successful leaders, we must first learn that, no matter how good the technology, people-to-people relations get things done. People determine our success or failure.

CHAPTER 7

SuperLeadership

by Charles C. Manz, Professor of Management at
Arizona State University

WHAT COMES TO MIND when you hear the word "leader"? You probably think of a commanding, charismatic, masterful figure who powerfully influences others to do what the leader thinks should be done. These images stem from historical themes that have been acted out through centuries.

In the early decades, leadership was a male-dominated process, and the image of an effective leader was frequently a "strong man" (or someone who appeared to be) who led through commands and the threat of punishment. An image of John Wayne commanding troops on the battlefield through barked-out orders backed by hard fists comes to mind. This same style of leadership was replicated in many organizations. The wisdom and direction for action came solely from the leader, and followers complied with orders through a sense of fear. Followers could be counted on to do what the leader wanted done and no more. They exemplified the classic term "yes men."

Knowledge of new influence methods such as behavior modification led to a different approach. Many leaders became "transactors" who exchanged incentives and rewards for follower compliance. The wisdom and direction for action were still primarily tied up in the leader. Followers complied with what the leader wanted done, and again usually no more, as long as the rewards kept coming. Followers became "calculators" who asked, "What's in it for me?"

More recently, the popular view of effective leaders paints a picture of a "visionary hero" who is charismatic and inspires followers to commit to the leader's vision. The source of wisdom and direction is still primarily the leader. Followers are expected to commit to the leader's vision and cause and to go above and beyond the call of duty to see that they are achieved. Although this approach holds some advantages over the previous views, if taken too far, followers can become "enthusiastic sheep" that rely on the leader as a source of vision and inspiration. As with the other leadership types, followers can become overly dependent, and the system, like a house of cards, may collapse if the leader leaves.

To address this potential danger and many recent world trends— such as intense international competition, a more educated and demanding work force, rapid change that requires greater organizational adaptability, and the many other pressures that require a fuller use of organizational human resources—we developed a new leadership approach called SuperLeadership.

WHAT IS SUPERLEADERSHIP?

What comes to mind when you hear the word "SuperLeader"? My suspicion is that for many, a similar image comes to mind as for the word leader, only more so. Is a SuperLeader an even more commanding, charismatic, one-of-a-kind magnetic individual who attracts the spotlight because of superior abilities that set him or her apart from everyone else? Even if there are individuals that fit this description, would it necessarily be good for the organization? The answers to these questions are "no" and "probably not."

As stand-out leaders supposedly become stronger and receive more of the spotlight and attention, followers will often become weaker and feel less significant. And leaders with weak followers who feel insignificant are really weak leaders, and their entire organizations are vulnerable to failure.

This perspective is based on my research and writing on leadership over the past 15 years, with my colleague and coauthor Henry P. Sims, Jr., that culminated in our book *SuperLeadership: Leading Others to Lead Themselves*. Our study of leadership has led us to a distinctly timely and effective approach that focuses on followers who become self-leaders.

The strength of the leader is multiplied many times because it is founded on the multiple abilities of those who surround him or her. Followers are encouraged and led to be dynamic, creative, and capable self-leaders who provide much of the wisdom and direction for their own actions. These self-leading followers commit to performance out of a sense of ownership rather than passively complying with the limited view of one sole human being who happens to be designated as a leader. They become strong pillars upon which the organization can stand, even if the leader must leave the system.

Strength and power reinforce the entire organization from top to bottom, enabling it to withstand much greater shocks than a system that concentrates its strength and power in a handful of central leaders who steal the spotlight and the opportunity for growth and development. The SuperLeadership approach promotes the organization's adaptability through well-informed, self-directing employees capable of meeting environmental pressures in their specific work areas.

SEVEN STEPS TO SUPERLEADERSHIP

Becoming a SuperLeader is a challenging journey that must be taken one step at a time. In fact Henry Sims, Jr., and I have identified seven specific steps:

1. If you want to become a SuperLeader, you must master the art of self-leadership. Self-leadership consists of a set of behavioral and cognitive strategies designed to provide personal direction and self-motivation. Some of the behavioral-focused strategies include self-set goals, self-observation, self-reward, constructive self-criticism, and practice or rehearsal. The cognitive-focused strategies include self-job redesign to meet responsibilities in ways that are more personally motivating. There are many ways to get a job done, and some of those ways are going to be more personally energizing and effective, and will fit each unique human being better than others. Other cognitive strategies include managing personal beliefs and assumptions, mental images, and self-talk to establish constructive thinking patterns or habits.

2. Modeling self-leadership for others is one of the most powerful ways to practice SuperLeadership. People in leadership roles occupy highly visible positions that are watched by subordinates. Consequently, it is important to demonstrate through action the behavior desired from followers. The credibility and vividness with which this is done is important. Leaders who have established their own trustworthiness, sincerity, and ability to perform—and who then openly and clearly demonstrate enthusiastic, innovative, self-directing behavior— are likely to have subordinates with the same qualities. After all, actions do speak louder than words. Self-directed and self-motivated leaders who can effectively apply self-discipline strategies, who adapt their jobs to their own unique interests and strengths, and who constructively manage their own thinking patterns, can and should be powerful self-leadership models to learn from.

3. SuperLeaders also encourage followers to use self-set goals. Peter Drucker pointed out long ago that doing things right (efficiency) is not enough. Doing the right things is crucial for being effective. Part of SuperLeadership is helping followers to set their own goals for higher performance and improved self-leadership capability. SuperLeaders promote goal-oriented followers who have desirable targets for their efforts. These targets include both immediate short-term goals and longer-term work and career goals. Generally, self-set goals will be more helpful if they are challenging but achievable.

4. SuperLeaders promote positive thought patterns in followers. Two positive thought patterns concern the way problems are viewed and self-image. SuperLeaders help followers to obtain the habit of being opportunity-focused—to develop the ability to see the opportunities nested in challenges rather than being paralyzed by the fear of potential failure. They also promote followers' confidence and positive self-image, particularly during the transition to becoming independent self-leaders who can stand on their own two feet.

5. SuperLeaders reinforce follower self-leadership and facilitate a constructive critical feedback process. They do not view independent initiative and creativity as threats. Instead, they see such follower behavior as valuable energy for progress and as the basic raw material for building a self-leadership system. As a consequence, employee self-leadership becomes a primary focus of rewards, even more so than high performance. And plenty of room is left for honest mistakes and failures in the pursuit of progress and improvement.

Critical feedback is offered, but it is feedback, not punishment, that is focused on, thus promoting development and improvement. Gradually, the critical feedback process is transferred to the individual followers themselves, as they become the experts in their own work areas and develop the self-confidence to constructively critique themselves and one another.

6. The SuperLeadership approach is not designed to create an anarchy where hundreds of independent self-leaders run off in totally different directions. The SuperLeader helps to coordinate the many creative independent efforts, and part of this coordination is accomplished through promoting teamwork. Followers (self-leaders) are encouraged to work together and help one another, both in getting the job done and in maximizing individual growth and development. The SuperLeader encourages followers to feel good about themselves as individuals, but as part of an overall team. Through encouragement, rewards, and guidance, the SuperLeader helps the many developing self-leaders to become sources of encouragement, strength, and inspiration for one another.

7. Finally, through SuperLeadership actions, a self-leadership culture should naturally unfold. This serves as the ultimate integrating mechanism for SuperLeadership. Over time, values, norms, principles, and a sense of overall purpose tend to bubble up—and these emphasize the value of every individual as a unique source of ideas and talent. People learn to look to themselves and one another as important sources of motivation and wisdom for solving problems. A system that is capable of continuous improvement in terms of quality, overall performance and individual talent is the usual result.

HOW CAN YOU BECOME A SUPERLEADER?

So what is the answer to becoming a SuperLeader? Simply, develop a philosophy that strong leadership is not the domination of others to do what you want them to do. Rather, it's a process of unleashing the vast talents of followers who become self-leaders.

Become a capable self-leader yourself. Then, help your followers become dynamic self-leaders by setting a positive example and encouraging, guiding, and rewarding them for initiative and effective self-leadership practice. And coordinate this vast self-leadership energy with the aid of teamwork and an integrating culture. Most importantly, becoming a SuperLeader means having SuperFollowers and often, just getting out of their way to help them do their stuff.

NATURAL SELF-REWARD

One of the most powerful methods to lead ourselves to new achievements is self-reward. We can positively influence our actions by rewarding ourselves at both a physical and mental level. To achieve self-motivation through self-reward:

- *Identify what objects, thoughts, and images motivate you.*
- *Identify desirable behaviors and activities.*
- *Reward yourself when you successfully complete an activity or engage in a desirable behavior.*

Potential rewards might include: desired physical objects such as an expensive dinner, a night out on the town, or simply a cup of coffee or a snack; enjoyable or praising thoughts such as thinking to yourself that you performed well and reminding yourself of future benefits you might receive from continued high performance; pleasant images such as imagination of your favorite vacation spot.

- *Develop the habit of being self-praising and self-rewarding for your accomplishments.*

Naturally rewarding activities make us feel more competent and help us feel self-controlling or self-determining. To discover your naturally rewarding tasks, examine activities that you naturally enjoy—where the rewards for doing them are built into, rather than are separate from, the tasks themselves. Look for activities that help make you feel competent and provide you with a sense of self-control and purpose.

Enhance your self-leadership by building more naturally enjoyable features into your life's activities, and by focusing your thoughts on the naturally rewarding aspects of your work.

Both natural and self-imposed approaches represent ways to achieve more effective self-leadership. Actually, the two strategies can complement each other. The intention is to maintain the self-leadership necessary to work through the "undesirable desirables" on the way to activities and future job positions that we can naturally enjoy.

In the meantime, make an effort to build in and focus on the natural rewards that are available. To the extent you do this, you will experience greater enjoyment of your present moments. Norman Vincent Peale once said: "Do your job naturally, because you like it, and success will take care of itself."

If we practice a self-leadership style that allows us natural enjoyment of our activities, we can indeed derive the motivation we need to be successful—especially at enjoying life.

CHAPTER 8

The Essence of Leadership

by Horst Schulze, President of Ritz-Carlton Hotel Company, and Kevin Dimond, Director of Quality for the Ritz-Carlton Hotel Company

A CONSTANT FOCUS on vision is the essence of leadership, especially during reengineering processes.

Today's approach to reengineering requires leaders to pack their own parachutes and be the first ones to make the jump. The troops are standing behind, waiting for the word.

Before you jump, your heart begins to race as you ask: "Did I check to be sure my parachute is packed properly?" The consequence is clear once you're out of the plane. Every person who has skydived has encountered that moment of truth.

We encountered such a moment when we added three positions in each hotel—a quality manager, a repeat guest coordinator, and a training manager. Several investors asked why we needed those positions; in fact, some insisted that we do away with them because at first we had no results to show, only agony and cost.

During the dark days, what pulled us through was vision, and the constant focus on that vision. That's the essence of leadership. Leadership doesn't go away. In fact, only leadership can pull you through the tough times. You can have a vision, be committed to the vision, and do things to get there. That's easy. But to keep focused on it, to keep people motivated behind it, and to not be sidetracked by excuses and by superficial effects is hard.

It would have been very easy to say, "We have 30 hotels, each having three optional employees. We can dismiss 90 people tomorrow. That will save a few million dollars and show everybody our ability to reengineer." It was very tempting to do that during a recession. But when you have a clear vision, you resist the temptation to sell out.

At the top, we kept focused on our vision and the values we teach because we came here for a dream. We came here because this challenge was the only one left. And we're not only colleagues in this quest, we are dear friends.

LEADERSHIP FIRST

Leaders encounter moments of truth as they commit to reengineer business processes. Leaders must build a relationship based on trust with the reengineering team to fully understand the process being reengineered. Lack of involvement by leaders hurts the entire process. Companies spend more time trying to manage their approach to reengineering than actually managing the process to be reengineered.

Leaders build trust through active involvement. Teams must see and feel the presence of leadership daily. And leaders must work with the team to attack deep cultural issues. The failure to confront cultural issues kills any chance to achieve revolutionary results. Companies facing less than revolutionary results end up scrapping the entire process at a great loss. At best, the company uses the reengineering process as a tool to streamline the business or simply to reduce jobs. This builds resistance and limits improvement.

The reengineering process demands full active involvement of leadership. Leaders must not only set standards and goals for the team, but also participate as active members on the team, thereby placing themselves at risk. Involvement on this level ultimately places them accountable for the team's success.

In the past, leaders would stand at the doorway of the plane encouraging the troops to jump. This approach was easy for leaders because they never put themselves at risk. However, the team was expected to take a "leap of faith" for the benefit of everyone. The plan was clear: After the jump, leaders would rendezvous with the team and consultants at the targeted landing site. Consultants, gurus, and team members were held responsible for results in reengineering the process. This "jump and rendezvous" method marginally improved our ability to hit the target. Using this method, we spent more time packing the parachute than jumping.

FLIGHT PLAN CHECKLIST

Before you make the "jump" to reengineering, complete the following checklist.

1. Align yourself with your mission. Is your personal and company mission statement strong enough to guide you on your 10,000-foot plunge? Will it guide you back on target if you become disoriented in the fall? Missions based on fundamental principles and values will increase the team's ability to be successful. Of course, because real reengineering must address the accepted cultural norms, the value of the mission statement will be questioned. As a result of reengineering efforts, the very mission of the company may have to be revisited.

2. Commit to being a "prophet in your own land." As a leader, you need to lead the charge daily for change and put your reputation on the line. At Ritz-Carlton, we learned this lesson early. Processes that were being reengineered needed the personal commitment of the president. He could not abdicate ownership of the process to the quality director.

3. Focus on rallying points that everyone can own. If you want the team to jump with you, make it for a noble cause. Companies all too often make such statements as, "We will reengineer the company to reduce manpower by 10 percent." Efforts with these objectives are doomed from the beginning. Obviously, no one jumps under these conditions. These shallow efforts take place constantly and are misnamed as reengineering; these "cut and burn" methods only weaken the entire environment within the company.

4. Make customer needs, wants, and wishes the Alpha and the Omega of the reengineering model. Make the model simple to learn and easy to repeat. Your models and methodology should also allow the team to relate to your mission. When your mission is aligned with your reengineering model, it serves to build an increased level of trust in the reengineering process as well as strengthen the culture.

5. See consultants as necessary evils. Their natural tendency will be to continually sell you on their methodology used to reengineer your process. Although this is an important part of the learning process, leaders within the company should make clear what results are expected from the process being reengineered. When this expectation is not set by leadership, consultants quickly act as the surrogate leaders of the process. But consultants can't eliminate cultural barriers without the deep involvement of leadership.

6. Make sure the payoffs are worth the expense. Radical change is required when reengineering any process. Look for processes that cut across the entire structure. Customers should benefit both tangibly and intangibly by improvements. Measurements must show results for any benefits.

7. Prepare yourself to coach and mentor teams. Leadership involvement builds trust when the team is allowed to eliminate, simplify, and combine steps in the work process. Leadership should stand back when the team is working on these issues. Leadership must move quickly to remove barriers that stand in the team's way. Cultural issues will be seen automatically as barriers. Ultimately the success of the process falls in the hands of the workers.

CHAPTER 9

People Leadership

by Francis N. Bonsignore, Senior Vice President of Human Resources and Administration at Marsh & McLennan Companies

MANAGEMENT'S RESPONSIBILITIES to shareholders, workers, customers, and boards of directors are coming into clearer view. Top management is being "reintroduced" to its constituencies—and its obligations for the people resources.

With this reawakening comes a challenge: to face up to the fact that the leaders of business have not distinguished themselves on the people management dimension. Responsible stewards of people resources remain in short supply.

The reformation of management thought and practices argues for a reexamination of such principles as, *Who is responsible for people?* and *How can we best fulfill that responsibility?*

DEFICIENCIES AT THE TOP

Though notable exceptions exist, CEOs continue to be characterized and popularized as manifestations of the American rugged individualist style. Closer examination of these free-wheeling, tough guy CEOs reveals a pattern of disturbing attributes:

• A streak of anti-intellectualism with frighteningly superficial mastery of the world and its different social systems.

• Insufficient attention to identifying and understanding the external factors affecting the enterprise's performance and perpetuation.

• Detachment from day-to-day operating requirements and associated problems.

• A disposition to manage more in the style of the intimidating boss than the knowledgeable leader who delivers empowerment and provides a framework for responsive adaptation and change.

• Outdated, often myopic views of people as expendable and replaceable commodities, in contrast to competitive resources to be marshaled for distinctiveness.

True people-leadership qualities have been diluted and, in their place, a fixation on the "right stuff" has emerged, a lazy vernacular for what we think should be the distinguishing (but often superficial) qualities of leadership.

Packaging of high profile, expensive CEOs as folk heroes has overtaken substance. Questions of what they contribute and the permanence of their influence to justify their rewards are increasingly posed by shareholders at large, prominent institutional investors and a few others confident enough to challenge. Not surprisingly in this context, management resources and the cultivation of talent have not been shepherded as they deserve.

INTO THE BREACH

Are we familiar with those CEOs whose behavior has truly enriched the enterprise? Bolstered the success of senior executives? Influenced for the better the company's people resources and long-term capabilities? Can we identify what is notable among CEOs whose reigns have been both memorable and beneficial for their customers? Sadly, too few examples emerge against these standards. More likely, we recall the tough, the rich, and the controversial.

Historically, the framework for people leadership has been defined by a philosophy, rules, a code of what is right and wrong, and commonly held values—amorphous stuff for CEOs to concern themselves with and certainly quicksand for boards of directors to tread on. Indeed, motives, values, and competencies are concepts we seem to eschew as levers for change.

Executives face the challenge to move to a new plateau, one that transcends trivial solutions or lip service to leadership and people management and embraces more broadly defined and accepted obligations for all people resources. The perplexing challenges of demographic change, a reshaped world political and economic order, social responsibility, as well as environmental and "global village" problems, argue for a renaissance of people responsibilities—a clarified set of responsibilities that are broader than profit and loss, and focused on outcomes further away than the next quarter.

ELEMENTS OF A PRESCRIPTION

The precarious state of American competitiveness has sounded the alarm. We must heed the warning. Facile prescriptions are not remedies. A successful solution has several elements worthy of consideration:

• *Introducing performance measures* for the CEO that balance financial results with people results (competencies, behaviors, productivity, and innovation) and the tone that the CEO sets for how people behave.

• *Reshaping management education* to make ongoing awareness building, personal growth, and development an integral part of preserving the enterprise.

• *Infusing the organization* with more managers who have liberal arts educations to provide the perspective and sensitivities (balancing techno-managerial skills) for dealing with the complexities of managing in a world shrunk by technology and market interdependencies.

• *Reexamining roles* of boards of directors to provide for more active and constructive governance of the corporation's people dimension and its array of skills, competencies, creativity, and leadership depth.

• *Nurturing work force skills*, competencies, and management concern for shared success. Balance, respect, and honesty are not "new age" management principles to pursue. They are enduring characteristics that can make for a clear self-image and consistent behavior over time.

THE CEO'S PEOPLE ROLE

Distinctive companies design and implement distinctive plans to acquire, retain, and mobilize people resources. Among the people leadership tasks that fall to the CEO and his senior colleagues are:

• *Creating* a sense of urgency that contributes to responsiveness to market and competitive circumstances.

• *Communicating* unequivocally and consistently on what aspects of people performance contribute to competitive advantage—and make for individual rewards and recognition.

• *Balancing* an understanding of the external competitive environment with intimate insights about company operations and people practices.

• *Reengineering* people processes that link strategy and operating responsibilities.

• *Coaching* top-level people relationships and management processes to avoid blockages and promote the vertical and horizontal communications that contribute to teambuilding.

The ultimate people measure for CEOs will be how management resources are deployed and motivated to achieve business goals and change. Scrutiny of senior resources and their alignment to the most critical operating tasks can help maximize the talent and the impact of the CEO on adaptation, change, and competitive outcomes. Moving people resources from the requisite skills needed to compete toward distinctive competencies that can help achieve competitive advantage should be a driving influence on how CEOs conducts themselves on people resource management subjects.

The best and most deserving CEOs are paid to make things happen, not to control, preside, or be caretakers. Not the least of their obligations is to shape the character and chemistry of the enterprise. Such a "soft" objective can be met by the CEO taking the lead to examine such questions as: *Who are we? Where are we headed? What needs to get done? Who's responsible? or How will results and contributions be measured?*

Successful CEOs engage in active scrutiny of these questions and share their insights with senior managers for application in their day-to-day roles. Questioning what people competencies will respond best to markets and contribute to achieving strategic goals is a central and continuing leadership task.

The CEO should be measured for ability to manage people selection risks, making executives responsible for people (as well as financial) resources, and, of course, results. Challenging and intervening in key people processes is an integral part of the CEO's job—to ensure that the application of talent to goals and needs is occurring.

The CEO has to judge how well equipped his or her executives are to manage the talent within their spheres. Honest and demanding evaluations of how executives carry out this role are essential for the CEO to create and maximize the "people franchise" of the organization.

Improved clarity regarding the CEO's role for people resources and the board's responsibilities in this dimension of senior management's performance can help American enterprise win back its competitive standing and, maybe, its position as the standard setter for people management expertise and practice.

CHAPTER 10

Leadership: Charisma or Competence?

 by Gerald L. McManis, President of McManis Associates, Inc., management and research consultants

THE ROLE OF senior management is changing and becoming more challenging. No longer is it enough to be a good manager. What is needed to make U.S. companies succeed in a competitive, global economy is leadership.

Our productivity is lagging behind that of other countries; our quality is not what it should be; our ability to compete is declining. As Ross Perot said, "Lack of leadership is the biggest problem we have in making this country competitive."

What is leadership? Can we develop it in ourselves and in others? There have been numerous "studies" attempting to define leadership and hundreds of experts with hundreds of different opinions about it. I will not even try to come up with yet another definition of leadership, but I would like to dispel a couple of myths.

TWO MYTHS

The first myth is that leaders and leadership qualities are only found at the very top of an organization and that the top is the only place we need it. If that is how our CEOs and managers in this country think, no wonder we are having problems being competitive.

CEOs are not the only leaders nor the only persons in an organization that we should be able to look to for leadership. All our business executives and managers can and must provide leadership. As Warren Bennis and Burt Nanus stated in their book, *Leadership*, "The problem with many organizations, and especially the ones that are failing, is that they tend to be overmanaged and underled."

Another myth is that leaders must have "charisma." A critical evaluation of effective leaders against the charisma standard can lead only to one inevitable conclusion—leaders don't have to be charismatic. The successful CEOs of many *Fortune* 500 companies are filled with top executives that managers below describe as bland, if not downright boring. In fact, many of our nation's most highly effective leaders have been described in like terms when it comes to personality.

Over the past quarter of a century, I have had the privilege of working with a number of CEOs of major corporations. I have met many executives who were far from charismatic, but they were successful and respected leaders. Moreover, I have yet to find the "perfect" leader, at least not in the conventional sense. But I have found leaders who were perhaps "perfect" for an organization at a particular time.

Leaders also seem to simply be in the right place at the right time. That is, recognizing what an organization needs to succeed at a particular point in time. It will differ depending upon the situation and environment, both external and internal. For example, when John Sculley joined Apple Computer, the company needed a more disciplined approach to management and a stronger thrust in marketing. Apple needed to transition from the loose, entrepreneurial style of Steven Jobs in order to grow and prosper, and Sculley was right for the times.

INSTILLING THE VISION

Leadership is also having a vision—a clear vision that can be articulated and instilled in others. But it must be a vision of what is right for an organization at that time and in that situation. And, once that vision is created and developed it has to be articulated and shared with those who will help to achieve it.

Years ago, John Reed had a vision of what Citicorp should become: the number one national "consumer" bank in the country. Reed faced opposition from both insiders and outsiders who thought that Citicorp should concentrate on traditional banking services and maximize near-term profits. But he held to that vision and instilled it in others. It took almost ten years, but today Citicorp is first in nationwide consumer banking, and exceptionally well-positioned in the financial services industry. John Reed was not the CEO then, but he is now.

IMPLEMENTING THE VISION

It is one thing to have a vision, but another to implement it. There are traits and styles of leadership that each of us can learn. Here are some examples and some of the leaders who have possessed them.

1. Demonstrate strong commitment. Irving Shapiro, former Chairman of the Board of DuPont, commented: "How will a person behave under adverse circumstances? That is the real test. Any fool can do it when things are going well. But how do you stay with it and keep things right when you're really in trouble? I've seen fellows who look like the greatest guys in the world and yet, when the crunch comes, they fold."

Donald Peterson showed commitment in troubled times and engineered changes in Ford's culture, structure, and technology to improve quality and productivity—precisely what was needed to revitalize Ford. Ford is an entirely different company now, but Peterson remains committed to his cost-cutting and quality improvement campaigns. Once you have determined what is needed, commit yourself and your management team to achieving it.

2. Encourage followers to take calculated risks and forgive mistakes. Years ago, IBM was at a crossroads in the development of a particular technology. In order to syndicate the risk, several different approaches were taken. One young executive was involved in a high-risk venture for the firm and lost over $10 million in the gamble. Tom Watson, Sr.'s response to this risk-taker's offered resignation was, "You can't be serious. We've just spent $10 million educating you." As more and more companies attempt to reposition, executives and managers will need to take prudent risks. Encourage an environment of action and calculated risk taking, and let followers know it is better to ask for forgiveness than permission.

3. Be open-minded and inquisitive. Listen to and foster ideas and suggestions from followers. William Hewlett of Hewlett-Packard recognized that, to be successful in a highly competitive and rapidly evolving technology industry, people must be able to cut through the "bureaucracy" and reach their maximum potential. Hewlett promoted the "HP Way" of management, believing that "Men and women want to do a good job, a creative job, and if they are provided the proper environment, they will do so." Today, Hewlett-Packard is not only successful, but is consistently cited as one of the best companies to work for in the U.S.

Be open, curious and inquisitive and recognize that people on the front line have valuable input and ideas. Show recognition and appreciation for those ideas.

4. Foster leaders throughout the organization. During the 1970s, General Foods became over-centralized, with executives and managers spending too much time analyzing and too little acting. Philip Smith, Chairman of the Board, believed that developing leaders in the organization was vital and would be "the foundation for all growth at General Foods." Smith spent time personally with his executives and managers in retreats to help develop that leadership deep down through the company.

The source of success of any organization is the individuals in it. True leaders know their power comes from people, and that is where they must make an investment. Also, they realize that in order to gain power you must give up power, and that the performance of everyone who works for you is a reflection on your performance.

5. Inspire enthusiasm and a winning attitude. Sam Walton of Wal-Mart knew that building a really successful business in discount retailing would depend largely on the sales clerks who meet customers every day. Walton shows respect for his "sales associates" and consistently and publicly states, "I wouldn't have gotten here without them." His corporate culture is strong and imbued with hard work, dedication, and enthusiasm—as well as a sense of humor. One year, Walton challenged his employees to reach new heights in pretax profits, pledging that he would dance a hula on Wall Street if they succeeded. Walton danced that hula, on Wall Street, grass skirt and all—much to the delight of his employees and himself. Today Walton is described as a man with "unique human skills and energy"—not to mention a $10 billion company.

Believe in what you do, be enthusiastic about it, and create an environment in which employees have a sense that work is rewarding and fun.

6. Do not fear change, but instead embrace and create it. Under John Welch, Jr., General Electric is undergoing drastic and controversial changes, but Welch says they are necessary to survive in a "faster-changing, less predictable, and far tougher global environment."

To be a leader you must be willing to clear away what may appear to be sacred and continually challenge to help keep the organization alive. Never rest on your laurels or be content with the status quo, for change, good or bad, is inevitable, and complacency can be a killer.

There are leadership qualities in each of us that can be developed. Don't worry about charisma—the magic and novelty usually fade anyway. Be more concerned with integrity and consistency and your followers will stay with you for the long haul. Do not let a fear of not being the "perfect" leader hold you back. Recognize and have confidence in your own abilities and acknowledge your shortcomings as well. Then surround yourself with people who have the skills to complement yours.

Each of these executives was successful, yet none of them can be called the perfect leader. Their styles and strengths are different and their primary areas of focus are different. But what they have in common are many of the skills and traits mentioned here and insights and ability to focus their leadership skills and energies in the areas their companies and situations need most.

CHAPTER 11

The Best Leadership

by David L. Neidert, Director of Auxiliary Services at
Anderson University

FOR CENTURIES, people have tried to understand the character elements of effective leadership. But just when it seems the golden fleece is found, a new set of questions emerges.

And yet, we should still seek answers about the nature of leadership because in doing so we reflect not only on work, but also on purpose.

The philosopher Aristotle reasoned that living with a purpose brings us ultimately to happiness. This purposeful living was more than achieving the creature comforts and collecting assets. To live with purpose rests upon the examination of one's life, so that in the end a person may live as fully as possible.

Great leadership is about moral character and living to the most excellent qualities valued in the human experience. Leaders are expected to guide those around them in examining their lives, in finding fulfillment, in answering the question, "Am I fulfilling my meaning in life through my work?" The leader is essential as people seek to make sense of their lives and the purpose for engaging in work.

FIVE EXPECTATIONS

Although Aristotle constructed a framework of what people should expect from others, his reasoning may also be applied to leaders. These expectations may be few, but they are powerful if lived.

1. Set vision and mission. A leader's purposeful reflection and action in setting the vision are critical for the climate and direction. Beyond this task, leaders seek ways to challenge people to construct their own personal mission—one that reflects not only their relationship to the company, but their connection with families and communities.

2. Think. A leader asks "why?" and also gives quality thinking to clarify the issues. Leaders must be reflective in their thinking, seeking wisdom as they consider what is best for the enterprise. Learning and careful reflection must be modeled by leaders, so that the urgencies of the moment do not sidetrack the principles of long-term health.

3. Keep promises and tell the truth. We have a duty to keep our promises and tell the truth. Keeping our promises means people can rely on us to do what we say. Trust is built on commitment to goals and consistent behavior in carrying them out. Truthfulness and credibility do not come from words, but spring from consistent action and reliability of behavior. Effective leaders do as they intend.

4. Be mutually accountable. Mutual accountability is a two-way street between follower and leader. Leaders share their personal performance goals with the entire entity, and they acknowledge where they are not meeting their goals. Trust emerges from this display of humanness and action rooted in commitment to personal performance.

5. Expect financial health and solvency from each other. Leaders know that debt restricts people, saps productivity and energy, and may force institutions to compromise standards of excellence in serving their constituents. Staying financially solvent is among the priorities that leaders have on the agenda, as they seek to balance money and assets with people and relationships.

The bottom line of leadership is to create an empowering climate where people find energy, adequate resources, and a control of their own destiny. Aristotle's ultimate reasoning about virtuous living is that our personal lives influence the good of all society.

CHAPTER 12

Big Is Beautiful

 by John F. Welch, Jr., Chairman and CEO of General Electric Company

THE HOTTEST TREND in business, and the one that hits closest to home, was the rush toward breaking up multi-business companies and "spinning off" their components, under the theory that their size and diversity inhibited their competitiveness. The obvious question to General Electric, as the world's largest multi-business company, was, "When are you going to do it?" The short answer is that we're not. We've spent more than a decade getting bigger, faster, and more competitive, and we intend to continue.

BODY OF BIG, SOUL OF SMALL

Breaking up is the right answer for some big companies. For us it is the wrong answer. Our dream and plan is to shape a global enterprise with the reach and resources of a big company—the body of a big company—but the thirst to learn, the compulsion to share, and the bias for action—the soul—of a small company.

Here's how we did it.

1. Changing the hardware. The foundation for our future was to be involved in only those businesses that were, or could become, either number one or number two in their global markets. The rest were to be fixed, sold, or closed. We made this decision based on our observation that when a number-one market-share business entered a down cycle and "sneezed," number four or five often caught galloping pneumonia. Consistent with this view, we divested $10 billion worth of marginal businesses, and made $19 billion of acquisitions, to strengthen the world-leading businesses we wanted to take with us into the nineties.

While we were restructuring the businesses, we also changed the management hardware. We delayered. We removed "Sectors," "Groups," "Strategic Business Units," and much of the extensive command structure and staff apparatus we used to run the company.

We cleared out stifling bureaucracy, along with the strategic planning apparatus, corporate staff empires, rituals, endless studies and briefings, and all the classic machinery that makes big-company operations smooth and predictable—but often glacially slow. As the underbrush of bureaucracy was cleared away, we began to see and talk to each other more clearly and more directly.

As the company moved through the eighties, the businesses grew increasingly powerful. Freed from bureaucratic tentacles and charged to act independently, they did so with great success. Corporate managers got off their backs, and instead lined up behind them with resources and support.

2. Changing the software. As the big-company body was developing, we turned toward creating the spirit and soul of a small company. Most successful small companies possess three defining cultural traits: self-confidence, simplicity, and speed. We wanted them. We went after them.

• *Self-confidence.* We valued self-confidence as the absolutely indispensable ingredient in a high-performance business culture. Self-confident people are open to good ideas regardless of their source and are willing to share them. Their egos don't require that they originate every idea they use, or "get credit" for every idea they originate. We began to cultivate self-confidence among our leaders by turning them loose, giving them independence and resources, and encouraging them to take big swings.

• *Simplicity.* The inevitable surge of self-confidence that grows in people who win leads to simplicity. Self-confident people don't need to wrap themselves in complexity, "business" speech, and all the clutter that passes for sophistication in business—especially big business. Self-confident leaders produce simple plans, speak simply, and propose big, clear targets.

• *Speed.* The boldness that comes from self-confidence and the clarity that comes from simplicity lead to one of the greatest competitive advantages: speed. Simple messages travel faster, simpler designs reach the market faster, and the elimination of clutter allows faster decision making in the upper echelons. At GE, we saw the leadership come alive with energy, excitement, and the crackle of small-company urgency.

3. Involving everyone. The challenge then became to involve everyone—to spread our new openness into every corner of our company; to give our 222,000 employees what the best small companies give people: voice. We were running out of models at this point, and moving into uncharted territory—at least for big companies—and so our next move, and the centerpiece of culture change, was one we had to invent ourselves. We call it *Work-Out.*

Work-Out was based on the simple belief that people closest to the work know, more than anyone, how it can be done better. It was this enormous reservoir of untapped knowledge and insight that we wanted to draw upon. Across GE today, holding a *Work-Out* session is as natural an act as coming to work. People of disparate ranks and functions search for a better way, every day, gathering in a room for an hour, or eight or three days, grappling with a problem or an opportunity and dealing with it, usually on the spot—producing real change instead of memos and promises of further study. Everyone today has an opportunity to have a voice at GE, and everyone who uses that voice to help improve things is rewarded.

At *Work-Out* sessions, it became clear that some of the rhetoric heard at the corporate level—about involvement and excitement and turning people loose—did not match the reality of life in the businesses. The problem was that some of our leaders were unwilling, or unable, to abandon big-company, big-shot autocracy and embrace the values we were trying to grow. So we defined our management styles and how they furthered or blocked our values. And then we acted.

We rewarded managers who not only delivered on performance commitments, but also believed in and advanced our small-company values. We encouraged managers who believed in the values but sometimes missed commitments. We removed managers who did not meet commitments or share our values. And we even began to remove managers who delivered short-term results, but who did so without regard to our values—in fact, they often diminished them by grinding people down, squeezing them, stifling them. The decision to remove these managers was a watershed—the ultimate test of our ability to "walk the talk," but it had to be done if we wanted GE people to be open, to speak up, to share, and to act boldly outside traditional "lines of authority" and "functional boxes" in this new learning, sharing environment.

Throughout this change process, our Management Institute has served as a forum for sharing experiences, aspirations, and frustrations. Our Management Institute has become a vehicle for learning and sharing the best practices that can be found anywhere around the globe. Leaders return from these intense courses to their businesses prepared to put new ideas quickly into action. Entire classes are regularly sent to Europe or Asia to wrestle with specific opportunities. After data gathering and intense *Work-Out* style discussion, each class returns and presents recommendations directly to the top 35 officers of GE, who act on them—often on the spot. The Institute combines the thirst for learning with an action environment usually seen only in small, hungry companies.

4. Promoting boundaryless behavior. These changes in culture—the profound and pervasive effect of *Work-Out* and the steady reduction of managers who did not share our values—developed a fresh, open, anti-parochial environment, friendly toward the seeking and sharing of new ideas, regardless of their source. It also encouraged looking outside boundaries that shackle thinking and restrict vision. Ideas began to stand or fall on their merits—rather than on the altitude of their originators.

An endless search began for the best practices—for ways of getting better, faster. Meetings that used to consist of self-serving "reports" and windy speeches became interactive forums for disseminating new ideas and the sharing of experiences. A whole new behavior has invigorated and freshened this century-old company. We've seen the emergence of true small-company phenomena: dreaming, which is at the heart of stretch goals; and constant celebration of the milestones toward those goals—even if we occasionally don't quite get there.

We describe our emerging culture as "boundaryless." It is the soul of our integrated diversity and at the heart of everything we do well. It is the small-company culture we've been seeking.

The sweetest fruit of boundaryless behavior has been the demise of "Not Invented Here." We quickly began to learn from each other. And we embarked on an endless search for ideas from the great companies of the world.

"Stretch" simply means moving beyond being as good as you have to be—"making a budget"—to being as good as you possibly can be: setting "impossible" goals and going after them. Crucial to stretch is the trust that grows in a boundaryless organization, as self-confident people come to know it is the quality of their effort toward achieving the "impossible" that is the ultimate measure.

To reinforce the boundaryless and stretch behavior, we adapted our compensation system. Today, 22,000 individuals, at all levels, have stock options, and thereby have a clear financial incentive for driving total company performance by doing everything they can to help their colleagues.

Today, stock option compensation, based on total GE performance, is far more significant than the salary or bonus growth associated with the performance of any individual unit or business. This aligns the interests of the individual, the company, and the share owner behind powerful one-company results.

A NEW KIND OF COMPANY

We have created a new kind of company—one that has, and uses, all the strengths of a big company while moving with the speed, hunger and urgency of a small company. During the past five years, as boundaryless behavior has taken hold and the best practices have taken effect, we've returned to share owners about $2.3 billion a year in dividends and repurchased an additional $5.3 billion of our stock.

The pace continued to accelerate in 1995 when $5.9 billion impacted share owner value—$2.8 billion of it in dividends, and $3.1 billion supporting the equity by stock repurchase.

As the millennium approaches, we will pick up the pace as we bring to bear our enormous financial, technical, and human resources in support of our big businesses as they move to seize some of the biggest growth opportunities in our history.

Our globalization is accelerating as we approach joint venture partners, and even sovereign states, as multi-business teams, share country knowledge, and are capable of assembling supportive financing packages from GE Capital. Global revenues over the last 10 years have increased from 20 percent of the company's total to 38 percent today—and, somewhere around the millennium, we expect the majority of GE revenue to come from outside the United States.

• *New products.* The enormous leverage of information technology, combined with our culture of learning and sharing, creates a tremendous opportunity, both internally—with better inventory control and shorter order-to-remittance cycles, for example—and externally—with remote diagnostics in medical imaging and just-in-time inventory replenishment for our customers.

• *Service.* Improving the profitability of our customers through technology upgrades of the enormous installed base of GE equipment—scores of thousands of jet engines, locomotives, turbines, and CT scanners, for instance—is an enormous growth opportunity for us and a profit opportunity for our customers.

• *Quality.* Already equal to or better than our competitors, quality at GE will be taken to world-leading levels, providing us with yet another competitive differentiator. Our openness to learning, our ability to share across the company, and our bias for speed, as well as the generosity of Motorola and others in sharing their techniques with us, will bring GE to a whole new level of quality in a fraction of the time it would have taken to climb the learning curve on our own.

This is a company focusing on huge growth opportunities as we look to the millennium—a GE that renews itself constantly, exhilarates itself with speed, and freshens itself by constant learning.

SECTION II

Qualities of Leadership

THE KEY TO LEADERSHIP is the quality of leadership. Certain leadership qualities endure despite setbacks, cutbacks, reengineering, downsizing, limited resources, and changing times.

Tom Peters reminds us that there is no substitute for a great leader. Great systems, great organizations, can't last when their leaders aren't good. When a torrent of management fads rushes through corporations, the demand has been, and will continue to be, for brave leaders.

Changing times can produce crises. **Eileen McDargh** believes that captains who get us through the storm engender trust. And trust seems to be missing in many of our downsized, fear-racked businesses.

One leadership quality worth having is bringing out the best in others. **Lou Tice** notes that leaders can improve productivity and profitability by making "a positive difference in the lives of other people"—by becoming servant leaders, or limitless leaders.

Stephen R. Covey writes that one quality essential to leadership—if leaders don't want to lose their way—is to follow the way the compass points. If we know how to read and implement correct principles, "we won't get lost, confused, or fooled by conflicting voices and values."

Leaders ultimately become what they think. **Joe Batten** reminds us of the connection between attitude and leadership success. Toughminded leaders provide "transcendent purpose, direction, macro vision, and magnetic lift and pull." **Michael E. Quigley** suggests that leaders must acquire "the habit of personal intellectual development, and be able to analyze, interpret, and assimilate information for purposes of strategic decision-making."

Peter Senge believes that the challenges of the 21st century cannot merely "be met by isolated heroic leaders. They require a unique mix of different people, in different positions, who lead in different ways." Leaders need "imagination, perseverance, dialogue, and deep caring."

Francis Hesselbein notes that what drives strategic leadership are ten common elements, and says, "Our times require driving strategic leadership through mission, vision, and goals." **Michael Eisner** recommends that the way not only to grow, but to avoid the pitfalls, is to have creative leadership. Leaders must keep their "eye on the ball," fail a few times, follow through, synergize, and rejuvenate. **James M. Kouzes** and **Barry Z. Posner** urge that credibility is an essential quality of leadership. "Credible leaders are trustworthy, honest, competent, dynamic, inspiring, and forward-looking. Credibility is the foundation of leadership."

Gifford Pinchot III and **Elizabeth Pinchot** write that quality leaders have hidden reserves "of entrepreneurial spirit to meet the challenges of an increasingly turbulent environment." Leaders can "refocus people's energy with direct interventions or do so indirectly by adjusting the system so people naturally gravitate toward what needs to be done."

W. Edwards Deming suggests that in order for leaders to make the "transformation from present to better practices," they must "take the rugged route of profound knowledge." They must be quality leaders. **Hugh Nibley** warns that if there is one thing that clearly marks the rise and fall of corporations, "it is the fatal shift from leadership to management. Excellence is the mark of leadership; mediocrity a sign of management."

CHAPTER 13

Brave Leadership

by Tom Peters, President of the Tom Peters Group

WHILE A TORRENT of management fads rushes through corporations, a few truths emerge—but all demand brave leaders.

In recent years, we have seen Total Quality Management, reengineering, the flat organization, the virtual corporation, customer-is-king, the learning organization, third-wave management, empowerment, teams for all seasons and all reasons, and open-book management. What is a manager supposed to make of it? Is it all hype?

A friend of mine thinks it is. "Leadership," she says, "that's it. Give me a rotten school system, a decrepit schoolhouse, a school-budget crisis but a great principal, and you've got a good-to-great school. Give me a 'great' system and facility, but a rotten principal, and you've got a poor-to-awful school."

Jim O'Toole of the Aspen Institute says the same thing in *Leading Change:* Most "salvation-through-quality and reengineering" programs fail; the only constant that correlates with success is over-the-top leadership.

My own take is as follows. There is usually gold in "them thar hills" of fad, even if most "programs" do fail; leadership is a *sine qua non* for standout performance; there are indeed some constants; and a new, if still inchoate, paradigm is emerging.

1. Gold in fad hills. The date is 1980: Japan, Inc. is kicking Detroit's butt. The date is 1995: Detroit is more or less roaring back, and the yen at 85 yen-to-the-dollar is far from the whole story. Net: America had no quality tradition. Fad or not, high program failure rate or not, the "quality thing" is real, firmly embedded in the American managerial psyche, and has improved national competitiveness.

Deming's 14 steps, Crosby's "Quality Is Free," and the Malcolm Baldrige National Quality Award Criteria are not the point. And who cares if 90 percent of balloon-launched programs don't amount to a hill of beans? The best are showing the way. The tide is rising. And laundromat owners as well as jet-engine makers now speak the language of quality.

The date is 1985: Thanks to Mike Milken and international competition, our corporate giants are forced to get lean and flat. How do you manage these newly shaped buggers? Late 1995: The answer is reengineering.

Sure, reengineering can be a cover for mindless middle-management genocide, but the idea stands. Repeat of TQM: Most reengineering programs fail. The hype nauseates. But the tide is rising, true-believer stars are showing the way, and we are learning to manage "horizontally."

The "fad" stories are repeated chapter and verse for virtual organizations, empowerment, and so on: a lot of smoke, numerous fires, a handful of bonfires, and a slowly rising tide. In fact, most of the grand fads are rooted in good sense. Peter Drucker's mid '50s management by objectives, though perverted into bureaucratic gobbledygook, was perfect for the disorganized times. Message: Just because it's faddish, just because it's hyped and poorly executed, don't write it off.

2. It's leadership, meathead. I agree with psychologist James Hillman: Leaders are more or less born, not made. Leadership training can lead to awareness, but some folks have the touch, a lot don't. If the "got its" aren't born to it, they certainly are well on their way to it by age 10. And I believe that inspired leadership can turn sows' ears (rotten circumstances) into silk purses (great schools, great factories, etc.).

Witness, again, the quality "revolution." Exemplary companies have all the charts, all the graphs, use the language. But the magic factor is, pure and simple, "Rushmorean leadership," to steal a phrase from Jim O'Toole. Roger Milliken at Milliken & Co. lives, sleeps, eats, breathes, sweats quality. Go to Germany, as I did a couple of years ago to study stellar middle-sized companies (members of the *Mittelstand*). No quality circles. No statistical process-control charts. But talk, even for a few minutes, with Siegfried Meister, boss of the high-end stove-maker Rational, and you will begin to understand what it means when the quality is in the genes. The passion is there. The integrity is there. In a word, *leadership!*

3. Truth is, there's truth to be had. I'm convinced, after watching and working in organizations for three decades, that there are five success sustainers:

• *Decentralization.* A lot of the *In Search of Excellence* companies let me down. But three still inspire me: Hewlett-Packard, Johnson & Johnson, and 3M. Their businesses are different. All are participants in intense global horse races. But, year in and year out, they deliver and reinvent. The common core: *an amazingly high level of entrepreneur-ship*, in monster-sized institutions. You can get decentralization very wrong, but granting astonishing degrees of unit autonomy, encouraging entrepreneurship, and more or less letting the chips fall where they may tends to be the No. 1 key to sustained vitality.

• *Empowerment.* No word has been so overused, and abused, in the last few years. Nonetheless, giving everyone a piece of the action, fiscally and psychologically, and letting them by and large do their own thing . . . well, that is the ticket.

The empowerment "thing" can be screwed up to a fare-thee-well, but immeasurable energy is unleashed when it's done right.

• *A passion for product.* Button-down strategy researcher Michael Porter sounds more like Elmer Gantry when he says, "You almost have to be a true believer to be competitive. Of the hundreds of world-class companies that I studied, an enormous proportion were run by some maniac who had spent the last 20 years of his life on a crusade to produce the best product."

There are two sorts of corporate bosses: Those who are gung-ho about management *per se*, and those who are obsessed with the product or service they deliver. Talk with the former for an hour, and you may still have no idea of what they make. Hang around the others for 15 seconds, and you'll hear talk of the product, how it's being improved and changed, why it's great, and so on.

• *Great systems.* There's still lots of room for great systems. Pittsburgh-based K. Barchetti Shops has won accolades as an awesome retailer, and boss Katherine Barchetti's secret is aimed totally at the customer systems (and the most sophisticated application of information technology I've seen in a small firm). Research by McKinsey & Co.'s Global Institute suggests that methods of organization (such as the Japanese automakers' lean production system) contribute more to national productivity than any other factor. Bottom line: Svelte, focused systems are priceless.

• *Paranoia.* "Only the paranoid survive," claims ever-paranoid Intel chief Andy Grove in an oft-quoted line. "The new code of conduct," Dartmouth business school professor Rich D'Aveni writes in *Hypercompetition*, "is an active strategy of disrupting the status quo to create a series of unsustainable advantages." Today's winners will have a penchant for disruption, a love of disorder—and even a willingness to throw baby parts (e.g., cherished "core competencies") out with the bathwater. . . again and again.

4. *Something big is going down.* Canadian researcher Henry Mintzberg chides us for our arrogance. Every generation, he says, claims the old days were simple, while today is fraught with peril and unprecedented change. There's some truth to Mintzberg's rap. In a sense, the five verities cited above are for the ages: decentralize, empower people, love that product, and so on.

Nonetheless, it is a spanking new world. The information systems/information technology revolution is real, and still in its infancy! One result: My five constants have been the trademark of big-time winners; now they are the minimum requirements for running info-tech-rich, dispersed "empires" in which no one works for a particular company, which is going to be everybody's game, or else. Going global at birth will also become commonplace. . . for the one-person professional-service firm run out of the spare bedroom as well as for the big guys.

So listen to the fads (with two, not only one, grains of salt). Insist on demonstrated leadership potential in every new hire. Understand that some things (radical decentralization and paranoia, for instance) are eternal. And believe Bob Dylan when he says *the times they are a-changin'*. And a-changin' damn near everything.

CHAPTER 14

Leading in Crises

 by Eileen McDargh, President of McDargh
Communications

SUNNY SKIES, light winds, and gentle surf started yet another lovely spring day in Southern California. Full of optimism, I boarded a flight bound for New Orleans by way of Denver and a major speaking engagement.

I never made it. Snow intervened in Denver, delaying our 747 while nozzles spewed chemicals onto the wings. The co-pilot explained the procedure and how she had walked back into the cabin to visually inspect the coating. Once airborne, she told us we'd hear the landing gear go down a second time as they checked the mechanics. Finally off to New Orleans on Flight #1180.

Not. A freak series of severe thunderstorms blew in from Texas, causing considerable jolting and bucking. The captain, a voice calm and deliberate, explained each deviation as he attempted to discover a better routing. We couldn't even get close. "I'm an old captain, not a bold captain," he explained when he announced we'd be diverting to Birmingham, Alabama. The passengers applauded his honesty with our safety while we all silently and not-so-silently moaned our fate. Cockpit voices told us we'd be informed as soon as the captain landed, walked through the jet, and called base operations. Birmingham was not this carrier's hub.

One hundred-fifty people, many with small children, listened patiently when he returned and explained the exiting procedure from the aircraft, where we'd lodge, and when we'd meet and "have another go at it" in the morning. Not one whimper or angry outburst arose. And true to his word, we all assembled after little sleep, no food, and for many, no change of clothes. We had now bonded in the experience and called out to one another, laughing and sometimes gasping as the still rocky air finally parted enough to bring us into New Orleans.

I lost income on that flight, but I gained a strong metaphor for leadership principles in times of crisis and change. What the captain and crew engendered that is missing in so many of our downsized, fear-racked businesses was TRUST.

Let's use this word as an acronym for understanding what all leaders must do in today's whitewater world.

T: Tell the truth and reveal feelings. Information abounded on Flight #1180. People deserve and need plenty of information about what's happening, why it's happening, and what the next steps are—even if those next steps are to stop, take stock, and develop the next plan of attack. And the information has to be immediate. Waiting while the rumor mill churns out various versions of "the truth" creates anxiety, second-guessing, and sometimes panic. Notice that the captain also admitted that he was "old, not bold." Since leaders are not invincible they should not do anything foolhardy to jeopardize the organization and its people.

R: Respond consistently. Once the captain and crew established a reporting method, they continued with the updates. Voices never changed. A pattern of zigzagging to avoid storms was followed.

U: Understand your role. Be competent. Be visible. With voice as well as physical presence, the captain and crew were "out and about." In times of change and crisis, seeing and hearing the leader is important. By walking through the cabin and putting a hand on different people's shoulders, he reassured passengers. The captain also invited people to stay with him and talk about the flight if anyone was concerned. In times of change and crisis, it is vital that leaders be seen and available for questions and feedback. Too often, the leader meets only with senior people or disappears behind closed doors.

S: See people as trustworthy. The captain stated what he would do and that he expected us to follow his instructions. He basically said, "I trust you to do what is right for yourselves and each other." If a leader wants to be trusted, that presumption must also be present.

T: Take action. Tickle funny bones. On Flight #1180, passengers were kept appraised of each action step and the results of that step, both positive and negative. Whether in the board room, the marketing department, or the cockpit, an action followed by course correction is a wise mode for handling any change or crisis. Lastly, the captain and the crew managed to find humor in the situation. "Laughter," as Victor Borge used to say, "is the shortest distance between people." Laughing over what cannot be controlled creates that element of bonding which is fundamental in maintaining trust.

A self-litmus trust test would benefit us all. What would people say about our behaviors during change or crisis? Would there be mutiny and fleeing the ship? Or would people stick with us to the next destination in the organization's journey? Let's *trust* they would.

CHAPTER 15

Limitless Leadership

by Lou Tice, Founder and Chairman of The Pacific Institute

USE YOUR LEADERSHIP skills not only to improve productivity and profitability, but also to bring out the best in others.

These days I find myself deeply concerned with questions that held only passing interest for me a decade ago, such as, *What sort of leader have I been? What legacy will I leave behind when I step down? Who have I helped to grow in the past? Who am I helping now? Where is more development desirable for me?* and *For what will I be remembered?*

Because of the pressures and expediencies of the day, we seldom address such questions. We're too busy dealing with bottom-line concerns, quarterly profits, day-to-day crises, and trying to keep up with rapidly changing markets, technology, and methods. We become highly adept at fixing the bicycle while we're riding it, but we sometimes neglect to consider where we want to end up in this race that has no finish line and what the process of getting there means. But I believe that taking time to think about these things is one of the factors that sets limitless leaders apart from the rest.

Several times a year, my wife, Diane, and I host a three-day retreat for top-level leaders and their spouses. These men and women come from a variety of organizations. Their nationalities, backgrounds, and experience are often extremely diverse, but their concerns, we have found, are remarkably similar. They want to discuss not just how to increase profits and productivity, but also how to take their leadership abilities to a higher level. They want to make a positive difference in the lives of other people. They hope to mentor and bring out the best in those who will someday take their place. They also want to trade ideas about how to personify and perpetuate a philosophy of servant leadership in every area of life—family, community, personal, professional, and spiritual.

Servant leadership is a concept advanced and championed by the late Robert Greenleaf. As the term suggests, servant leaders see their primary responsibility as one of service to those within their sphere of influence. Greenleaf proposed that if you could answer the following four questions in the affirmative, you were on the right path: *As a result of your leadership, are those whom you serve growing as persons? Are they, while being served, becoming healthier? Are they becoming more autonomous, freer, wiser, more capable? Are they, themselves, more likely to become servant leaders?*

In addition to simply saying "yes" to these questions, it's important to understand how we need to think to arrive at those answers. *What* we think inevitably flows from *how* we think.

The concepts of limitless leadership and servant leadership are closely aligned, though I prefer the term "limitless," because it comes closer to reflecting the essential nature of our existence as leaders and as human beings: an unending chain of generations, each supported by and building on the legacy of the last, each handing down a new legacy to those who follow.

FIVE TRAITS OF LIMITLESS LEADERS

There is much we can learn from great leaders:

1. Limitless leaders are learned optimists. They look for reasons to say yes and are careful about how they say no, because they understand that keeping hope alive and morale high is crucial. They can see the opportunity that exists within every crisis and the possibility for increased growth and confidence within every problem; more importantly, they help us to see things that way, too. Limitless leaders view failures as valuable learning experiences, not as blots on their personal record. When setbacks, mistakes, or failures occur, they invariably separate the performance from the performer. They refuse to play the blame game. They keep their focus on solutions rather than problems, because they know that their present thoughts determine their future.

2. Limitless leaders occasionally go down in the trenches and get their hands dirty, because they don't hold themselves aloof from the folks who do the real work. One of the most influential leaders I've ever known is Major General Bernie Loeffke (ret.), a highly decorated ex-ranger who speaks six languages and was once responsible for more than 15,000 servicemen. In 1992, he was brought out of retirement to direct our investigation into MIAs within the Soviet Union. But when Bernie was introduced at our International Conference last summer, he told the audience that the accomplishment of which he was most proud was his certification as a midwife. During a break, I overheard him offer to lend a hand to one of our staff who was clearing dirty dishes from the tables, because the facility's service personnel hadn't shown up.

3. Limitless leaders are both results and process-oriented. They can create and articulate a clear vision of a goal that inspires us to invent the means to achieve it, and at the same time they help us realize that the quality of what we ultimately achieve is directly related to how we have gone about achieving it. They encourage us to seek continual improvement in every aspect of our lives, they believe in our ability to improve, and they notice and applaud our efforts. They build our self-esteem and self-efficacy in innumerable ways, and see more in us than we ourselves can sometimes see. One evening when General Loeffke and I were having dinner, an Army colonel walked by. Bernie reached out and snagged him, saying, "Lou, I want you to meet Colonel Nick Rowe, one of the bravest men I know." How proud Colonel Rowe must have felt, having his courage affirmed to another person by General Loeffke! And how much more powerful that affirmation is than saying the same thing when no one is present.

4. Limitless leaders don't have all the answers, but they ask great questions and listen carefully to the responses. In fact, the ability to question adroitly, listen attentively to what is and is not being said, and connect bits of information creatively are among the most powerful tools any leader can have. Certainly, leaders must often make decisions based on incomplete or insufficient data, and they accept full accountability for it. They don't make excuses for themselves or anyone else, and they keep their commitments. They practice what they preach and consciously set themselves the task of being role models and mentors without losing their humility.

5. Finally, limitless leaders have a powerful sense of the interconnectedness of all living things, so they refuse to enter into adversarial relationships with others or with themselves. They believe that what hurts one, hurts all, whether we're talking about a family, community, corporation, nation, or planet. They are accomplished mediators who can help us see that compromise and consensus-building are necessary to promote collective efficacy. Operating from an "I'm up, you're down" power position has no place in their scheme of things. They aren't interested in commanding or controlling situations or people. Instead, they strive to understand, and they share the information-gathering and decision-making processes with others who can bring to the table many different points of view.

What they *are* in control of, however, is themselves—their time, energy, resources, communication, and imagination are used deliberately, thoughtfully, and consistently to achieve worthwhile goals and to further causes in which they believe. Do they ever lose control, waste time, or veer off course? You bet they do. One of the most endearing things about limitless leaders is that they don't try to hide their clay feet or appear to be perfect. They accept their own short-comings, flaws, and imperfections with a sense of humor and equanimity, while constantly and visibly working to improve. In so doing they tacitly give us permission to do the same.

I challenge you to pass on what you've learned about using your talents in productive, profitable, and virtuous ways; and to step down or move on when it's time, knowing that you've had a positive and lasting influence.

CHAPTER 16

Leading by Compass

by Stephen R. Covey, Co-Chairman of Franklin Covey Co.

WE WILL NOT lose our way, even in the fog of Europe or the bog of the Far East, if we lead our people and organizations by compass.

Correct principles are like compasses: They are always pointing the way. And if we know how to read them, we won't get lost, confused, or fooled by conflicting voices and values.

Principles are self-evident, self-validating natural laws. They don't change or shift. They provide "true north" direction to our lives when navigating the "streams" of our environments.

We often think of change and improvement coming from the outside in rather than from the inside out. Even if we recognize the need for change within, we usually think in terms of learning new skills, rather than showing more integrity to basic principles. But significant breakthroughs often represent internal breaks with traditional ways of thinking. I refer to these as *paradigm shifts*.

Principle-centered leadership introduces a new paradigm—that we center our lives and our leadership of organizations and people on certain principles. Principle-centered leadership is based on the reality that we cannot violate natural laws with impunity. Whether or not we believe in these laws, they continue to operate because they are universal, self-validating, self-evident, timeless, basic principles of effective human interaction and performance that have been proven effective throughout centuries of human history. They are not easy, quick-fix solutions to personal and interpersonal problems. But when applied consistently, they become behavioral habits, enabling the transformation of individuals, relationships, and organizations.

Practices are the *what-to-dos*, specific applications that fit specific circumstances. Principles are the *why-to-dos*, the elements upon which applications or practices are built. Individuals are more effective and organizations more empowered when they are guided and governed by principles that have filtered through every great society, every responsible civilization, over the centuries. Principles apply at all time in all places. They surface in the form of values, ideas, norms, mores, and teachings that uplift, ennoble, fulfill, empower, and inspire people. The lesson of history is that to the degree people and civilizations have operated in harmony with correct principles, they have prospered. At the root of societal declines are foolish practices that represent violations of correct principles. How many economic disasters, intercultural conflicts, revolutions, and wars could have been avoided had there been greater social commitment to correct principles?

Principle-centered leaders are men and women who have worked "on farms" with "seed and soil" on the basis of natural principles and have built those principles into the center of their lives, their relationships, their agreements, their management processes, and their mission statements.

When we provide training in skills and practices without also teaching principles, we tend to make people dependent on others for further instruction and direction. Without understanding the principles of a given task, people become incapacitated when the situation changes and different practices are required to be successful. Real empowerment is having both the principles *and* the skills for the job.

VALUES (MAPS) VERSUS PRINCIPLES (COMPASS)

Principles, unlike values, are objective and external. They operate in obedience to natural laws, regardless of conditions. Values are subjective and internal. Values are like maps. Maps are not the territories; they are only subjective attempts to describe or represent the territory. The more closely our values or maps are aligned with correct principles—with the realities of the territory, with things as they really are—the more accurate and useful they will be. However, when the territory is constantly changing, when markets are constantly shifting, any map is soon obsolete.

A value-based map may provide some description, but the principle-centered compass provides vision and direction. An accurate map is a good management tool, but a compass set on "true north" principles is a leadership and empowerment tool. When pointing to "true north," the needle reflects alignment with natural laws. If we are locked into managing by maps, we will waste many resources by wandering aimlessly or by squandering opportunity.

Our values often reflect the beliefs of our cultural background. From childhood, we develop a value system that represents a combination of cultural influences, personal discoveries, and family scripts. These become the "glasses" through which we see the world. We evaluate, prioritize, judge, and behave based on how we see life through these glasses.

One common reactive pattern is to live life in compartments, where one's behavior is largely the product of expectations built into certain roles: spouse, parent, child, business executive, community leader, and so on. But because each of these compartments carries its own value system, people often find themselves trying to meet conflicting expectations and values according to the role or the environment they are in at the time.

When people align their personal values with correct principles, they are liberated from old perceptions or paradigms. One of the characteristics of authentic leaders is their humility and ability to take off their glasses and closely examine the lens, analyzing how well their values, perceptions, beliefs, and behaviors align with "true north" principles. Where there are discrepancies (prejudice, ignorance, or error), they make adjustments to realign with greater wisdom. Centering on unchanging principles brings permanency and power into their lives.

FOUR DIMENSIONS

Centering our lives on correct principles is the key to developing this rich internal power, and with this power we can realize many of our dreams. Whatever lies at the center of our lives becomes the primary source of our life-support system. In large measure, that system is represented by four fundamental dimensions: security, guidance, wisdom, and power. Principle-centered leadership and living cultivates these four internal sources of strength.

An analysis of several alternative centers—work, pleasure, friends, enemies, spouse, family, self, church, possessions, money, etc.—shows why this is so and, further, why centering on a set of proven principles provides sufficient *security* to not be threatened by change, comparisons, or criticisms; *guidance* to make *wise* decisions; and *power* to communicate and cooperate under conditions of stress and fatigue.

1. Security. Security represents our sense of worth, identity, emotional anchorage, self-esteem, and personal strength. Of course, we see various degrees of security—on a continuum between a deep sense of high intrinsic worth on one end, and on the other, an extreme insecurity, wherein a person's life is buffeted by all the fickle forces that play upon it.

2. Guidance. Guidance is the direction we receive in life. Encompassed by our map—our internal frame of reference that interprets what is happening "out there"—are standards or criteria that govern decision making and doing. Over time, this internal monitor becomes our source of guidance, our conscience. On the low end of the guidance continuum, we see strong addictions and dependencies, conditioned by centering on selfish, sensual, or subsistence living. The middle of the continuum represents development of the social conscience, the conscience that has been educated and cultivated by centering on human institutions, traditions, and relationships. On the high end of the continuum is the spiritual conscience, wherein guidance comes from inspired or inspiring sources—a compass centered on true principles.

3. Wisdom. Wisdom suggests a sage perspective on life, a sense of balance, a keen understanding of how the various parts and principles apply and relate to each other. It embraces judgment, discernment, comprehension. It is a oneness, an integrated wholeness. The low end of the wisdom continuum are inaccurate maps which cause people to base their thinking on distorted, discordant principles. The high end represents an accurate and complete compass of life wherein all the parts and principles are properly related to each other. As we move toward the high end, we have an increasing sense of the ideal (things as they should be), as well as a sensitive, practical approach to realities (things as they are). Wisdom also includes the ability to discern pure joy as distinct from temporary pleasure.

4. Power. Power is the capacity to act, the strength and courage to accomplish something. It is the vital energy to make choices and decisions. It also represents the capacity to overcome deeply embedded habits and to cultivate higher, more effective habits. At the low end of the power continuum, we see people who are essentially powerless, insecure, products of what happens or has happened to them. They are dependent on circumstances and on others. They are reflections of other people's opinions and directions; they have no real comprehension of what true joy and happiness is. At the high end of the continuum, we see people with vision and discipline, whose lives are functional products of personal decisions rather than of external conditions. These people make things happen; they are proactive; they choose their responses to situations based upon timeless principles and universal standards. They take responsibility for their feelings and moods and attitudes as well as their thoughts and actions.

These four factors—*security, guidance, wisdom,* and *power*—are interdependent. Security and well-founded guidance bring true wisdom, and wisdom becomes the spark or catalyst to release and direct power within us. When these four factors are harmonized, they create the great force, a noble personality, a balanced character, a beautifully integrated individual.

When we center our lives on correct principles, we become more balanced, unified, organized, anchored, rooted. We find a foundation and cornerstone of all our activities, relationships, and decisions. We will have a sense of stewardship about everything in our lives, including time, talents, money, possessions, relationships, our families, and our bodies. We recognize the need to use them for good purposes and, as stewards, to be accountable for their use.

If we are anchored to social mirrors and models, we empower circumstances to guide and control us. We become reactive rather than proactive; we reflect what happens to us; we react to external conditions and stimuli rather than choose our own response and cause things to happen.

Because of a lack of wisdom, our reactions will often tend to be either overreactive or underreactive instead of appropriately proactive. A proactive stance means that we act on the basis of our own decisions and values and not our external conditions or internal moods. We subordinate moods and feelings to higher values and commitments.

ORGANIZATIONAL APPLICATIONS

Once you get principles at the center of your organization, you realize that the only way to treat your employees is how you want them to treat your customers. You see your competition as a learning source, as friends who can keep you sharp and teach you where your weaknesses are. Your identity is not threatened by them or by other external conditions and competencies because you have an anchor and a compass. Even in a sea of turbulent change, you maintain perspective and judgment. And you are always empowered from within.

A center secures, guides, empowers. Like the hub of a wheel, it unifies, integrates. It's the core of personal missions and organizational constitutions. It's the foundation of culture. It aligns shared values, structure, and systems.

Alternate organizational centers (profit, supplier, employee, owner, customer, program, policy, competition, image, and technology) are flawed compared with a principle-centered paradigm. Principle-centered people and companies enjoy a greater degree of security, guidance, wisdom, and power.

When our security or image comes from external comparisons or the opinions of others, we tend to see life and business as a zero-sum game; to be threatened by the success and recognition of others; and to delight secretly in their misfortunes. If we focus our emotional life on the weaknesses of others, we actually empower those weaknesses to control us. The challenge is to be a light, not a judge; be a model, not a critic.

PERSONAL REENGINEERING

Rather than place blame, executives need to undergo personal reengineering to accommodate the new reality. I'm thinking of three things in particular.

1. They need a sense of what "true north" is to them. They must develop a personal mission statement based on a vision that contributes to the organization and based on a value system that is principle-centered, that will not change. Otherwise, they'll be buffeted by all these powerful forces, the megatrends, and they'll end up being reactive—blaming others for their problems and causing their circle of influence to shrink.

2. They must be willing to carry risk. They have got to be at risk in three basic ways in their cultures:

• *In the way they speak.* They need to show both courage and consideration in the way they speak to their bosses, to their co-workers, and to other stakeholders.

• *In the way they listen.* They need to listen with empathy to learn what's happening in the organization, even though that may dishevel their entire world.

• *In the way they act.* They must be willing to carry the risk of being creative, of teaching, and of leaving their comfort zones so that they can adapt to the new reality and experiment to determine if there are new ways of doing things that work better. Risk-taking will be the prime characteristic of the leaders of the future. In a sense, leaders must get into business for themselves and become entrepreneurs. They will be moved inside network organizations or massive matrix organizations from one project to another—and they've got to add value each time they have a new assignment. The new psychological agreements will be project-focused. People will be less focused on lifelong careers with one organization; they will be more focused on getting a job done, on meeting needs, on adding value, and on documenting the value they add.

3. They must make and keep a commitment to lifelong learning. People must accept the personal responsibility to upgrade their knowledge and skills, to become computer literate or gain advanced computer literacy, to read widely, and to be aware of the powerful forces that are operating in their environments. They may need to gain or regain a liberal and fine arts education, in addition to keeping up on what is happening in the world of technology and science, because the arts and sciences create the capacity of the mind to keep learning. They also need to develop a value system that supersedes technology and science so that we live well with the spiritual side of our nature.

Those who do these three things will find that their circle of influence will expand far beyond their immediate vision and beyond their business and impact their family, their children, and their community.

CHAPTER 17

Tough-Minded Leaders

by Joe Batten, Chairman of The Batten Group and Chairman of the International Management Task Force for the Society of Advancement of Management

THE CONNECTION between attitude and leadership success is absolute. All of us ultimately become what we think!

Outstanding leaders differ from each other greatly. There is, however, a similarity in attitudes, beliefs, and values. When I speak on innovative, cutting-edge leadership, I learn from these champions who are on the line every day "doing it."

When we think of leadership greats who are "getting it done," we think of superstars such as Lee Iacocca, Fred Smith, Andrew Grove, J. W. Marriott, Ross Perot, and others who are legends in their own time.

Ross Perot's attitude illustrates superbly the power of tough-minded commitment. When he started Electronic Data Systems (EDS), he had been the number one salesperson at IBM; however, many people were quick to tell him he made a mistake leaving a secure and famous corporation to launch an entrepreneurial effort. Ross, however, was guided, challenged, and stretched by a dream—a vision of what could be. He dreamed of excellence before it was a buzzword. He became what he thought. His success clearly demonstrates that importance of attitude; physical size notwithstanding, he is one of the giants of our time.

TOUGH-MINDED LEADERS

The following traits characterize tough-minded leaders who achieve unusual entrepreneurial and managerial success.

• *Expect the best*. Believe there are strengths, possibilities, and latent richness in all situations, people, and events.

• *Develop an action plan* and target all key wants and needs each week in advance and list priorities under each. Then make sure you accomplish all needed actions before you undertake any wanted actions. In addition to accomplishing more, you'll relish the enjoyment of your wants more when you get to them.

• *Share, care, and dare to be aware.* Cultivate a curious and zestful interest in the uniqueness of your team members. Ask, listen, and really hear. Focus on their strengths to defuse, diffuse, and dissolve their defenses. Defensive people seldom make effective decisions. Help them feel good about you and your vision, mission, and goals. Provide assurance and reassurance, affirmation, and reaffirmation by what you think, say, and are.

• *Think through and write down your dream.* Once you have sculpted a dream—a stretching and transcendent expectation—it becomes possible with some hard work to develop specific goals, objectives, action plans, accountability, and timetables that are then fueled and guided by that dream. It subtly conditions everything you do.

• *Prospect for gold.* The average leader perceives "average" potential in each team member. The "excellent" executive looks for and expects to find new strengths in his or her team members. The great leaders incessantly mine new possibilities in people. They help their team members visualize possibilities, benefits, and applications that they would never think of otherwise.

• *Seek knowledge and growth.* Master your knowledge of the features, benefits, and uniqueness of your product or service. Visualize your team members as walking bundles of strengths and possibilities. Resolve to learn more and more about their strengths, dreams and motives. This not only builds relaxed and zestful relationships, it maximizes productivity, satisfaction, and profit.

• *Resolve to provide unusual and unparalleled service.* The second of the three basic beliefs of IBM reads: "We want to give the best customer service of any company in the world." The secret of the success of IBM is that they are committed to these basic beliefs and, above all, to service. Champions outserve all "competitors."

• *Commit to the fulfillment of positive prophecy.* Firmly commit yourself to the belief that your hoped-for goal is already reality, as this deeply conditions mind, body, spirit. And it becomes fact! Again, I quote Watson of IBM: "We constantly acted as though we were much bigger, much more sophisticated, much more successful than any balance sheet might bear out." IBM illustrates "the magic of believing."

• *Radiate energy and joy.* Continuously search for new strengths in you. Recognize that a "weakness" is only an indication of a missing or insufficiently developed strength. Then, you'll find it much easier and more zestful to look for and relate to the strengths of your team members. Develop your own strength notebook and write down every strength you can think of. Then, add one new strength each week for a year. If you will do this year after year, it will stimulate amazing growth and change and build confidence, purpose, and direction.

• *Harness the power of love.* Love is, indeed, the toughest-minded emotion in the world. An out-glowing of care, service, and commitment to the customer's desires is a common denominator in the tool kit of the leadership artist. Love is the finest mental and spiritual nutrient one can possess for a total life of fulfillment and actualization. Vince Lombardi explained the secret of the success of the Green Bay Packers by saying, "These guys love each other." Ross Perot often says, "I love the members of my team."

Tough-minded leaders become rich in their wallets as they become rich in their minds; they are curious, have a disciplined sense of humor, and are eager for new knowledge and experiences. They are never dissatisfied, which is to be preoccupied with yesterday's failures, but they do expect the best.

Their daily thoughts, actions, and attitudes are fueled by a stretching and constant dream of what is possible. They know that you must always compete with yourself and your possibilities, rather than with others. They are committed to integrity. Their enthusiasm is discernible by others virtually all the time. They let their light shine! They are certain they can become whatever they decide to be. They savor expressing gratitude to other people. They believe there are positive strengths in everyone. They are go-givers rather than go-getters and know that the more they give the more they get. They cultivate a flexible, open, growing, changing mind. They are committed to relationships that are synergistic where the whole is greater than the sum of parts. They have the strength, insight, and wisdom to recognize the power of the following: ask, listen, and hear to determine the wants, needs, and possibilities of all people—particularly their team members. They perceive every person as a bundle, rather a beautiful system, of present and potential strengths. They are ardently committed to the need, power, and profitability of asking. They build a powerful team and constantly search for new opportunities.

These attitudes, values and practices will take you to the top where fulfillment, stimulation, riches, and joy await you. Leading, managing, and selling are the greatest of all professions, and the future is virtually unlimited for those who truly master the art of persuasion.

We must change what we say because of its certain impact on what we then do. We not only become what we think, we become what we say. Think about retooling your lexicon of leadership from the negatively focused management vocabulary of the past. Some of the worst offenders are overworked words like *drive, driven, push, compress, force, tell, get, take, and compete with others.* Worse, our actions are influenced by these words.

Leadership just doesn't exist without followers. And followers are not driven, they are pulled. They are not pushed; they are led! Great power should never be vested in those who compulsively seek it. Life is not for pushing, crowding, insisting, driving, coercing, and directing—the stuff of an addictive society. Rather, we are to lead, to pull, stretch, reach, grow, change, confront and, above all, to expect the best. This is the stuff of true leadership! All the great leaders of history were masters of the art of clarifying and communicating expectations. This professional exercise of power is often an awesome responsibility.

TOUGH-MINDED LEADERSHIP

The tough mind is the opposite of the hard mind. It is open, resilient, growing, reaching, and evergreen. A tough-minded leader provides transcendent purpose, direction, macro vision, and magnetic lift and pull, like a compass. He or she . . .

• *Provides* a crystal-clear focus of all strengths in the organization in order to expect and reinforce the best.

• *Is committed* to service, innovation, quality, and the empowerment of people because this commitment is liberating and enriching to all.

• *Leads* by an inspiring example. Nothing communicates quite like example. A leader is motive-led and value-fed. Perhaps the greatest leadership dictum to ring down through history is "follow me."

• *Ensures* that all compensation is related to results-performance and expects total integrity. A leader is guided in all decisions by these two components.

Will you dare to dream, to etch out your personal vision, to articulate high hopes and then put muscle into those dreams? Will you pursue positive possibilities, expecting the best and daring to become all you can be? Will you dare say, "Follow me"?

CHAPTER 18

Leader as Learner

by Michael E. Quigley, Dean of the Graduate School at Rivier College

IN TURBULENT TIMES, we will find ourselves leading people to resolve matters which might otherwise seem insurmountable.

Any leader today must be in the habit of personal intellectual development, and be able to analyze, interpret, and assimilate information for purposes of strategic decision-making. The wealth of information that is available to us is not the same as the knowledge we must construct for ourselves. Information consists of bits and pieces. Knowledge consists of making connections between those pieces of information and gaining insight and meaning from them. Construction of knowledge requires development of the capacity to discern seemingly unrelated pieces of information, and to gain new and creative insight for achieving the aim of the organization.

CONSTRUCTING KNOWLEDGE

To develop this capacity for constructing knowledge, a leader must think at a theoretical and conceptual level, as well as the concrete, and develop a conceptual framework of reference into which pieces of information can be placed. This activity is like creating a new picture from pieces of a jigsaw puzzle (except in this case, there is no picture on the box). What must exist, however, in the mind of the leader is a theoretical model of the organization. One must have both a vision and a plan for the realization of an idealized state.

Given this mental model, information can be transformed into the knowledge of brainpower, the life-force of innovation shared by individuals, enabling the organization to continuously improve products and services, establish a stable system, and overcome the forces of entropy. The leader must continuously learn the skills of effectiveness to ensure economic survival in a competitive environment. To cease learning and constructing new knowledge is to invite catastrophe at the hands of a competitor who is in a learning mode. A second reason for continuous learning is the transformation of materialistic or mechanistic thinking to quantum thinking, which is non-linear and unpredictable due to the interaction of invisible forces within a system. Quantum thinking requires an entirely new set of skills and the capacity to construct new knowledge.

As managers, we cannot escape our past mechanistic, binary, on-or-off thinking. Such thinking dominates our culture. We even define ourselves in terms of our separateness. And so our thought patterns are revealed in the depiction of our world as management vs. labor, liberal vs. conservative, male vs. female, black vs. white, teacher vs. student, rich vs. poor, engineer vs. sales, and so on. And we find ourselves compelled to live life as a zero-sum game: For one person to win, there must first be a loser.

In a mechanistic world, we define ourselves in terms of what we are not. It is a world devoid of vision, of spiritual purpose, or even human community. Instead, Western culture is becoming accustomed to an atomized existence, preferring the individualistic quest for success to the building of learning communities. The endemic polarization of important facets of life means that in the face of stupendous development of information technology we remain almost incapable of resolving our fundamental human, social, and economic problems.

The reason for this great paradox is not difficult to discern. As machine age thinkers we think only in terms of *convergent problems*, whereas our social problems arise from different states of consciousness and self-awareness, and are therefore *divergent* in nature.

Convergent problems, which arise in designing and improving a product, require quantitative skills. We must be able to measure, quantify, and view an optimal desired state for the product, and arrive at solutions to problems in the design, manufacturing, and marketing stages. Divergent problems arise from ideas in the human mind, from self-awareness, and produce contrary states of mind among people.

Organizations have a need for freedom, but also require order and discipline. An organization requires stability, but also must be able to change. We require tradition, but seek also progress. Both opposites are pursued simultaneously, and give rise to creative tension. But one cannot solve divergent problems by thinking in convergent ways.

Convergent thinking is the method of scientifically inquiring into problems, and through hypothesis and analysis reaching a predictable solution. *Divergent thinking* arises from different states of consciousness and from different states of self-awareness from a multitude of experiences. These perspectives on life tend to diverge, move away, disagree with each other. In convergent thinking, divergent problems cannot be resolved. We will lack the intellectual capacity to do so as long as we fail to hold contrasting truths together in the mind and resolve them at a higher level. Convergent thinking requires logic. Divergent thinking requires supra-logical intelligence and faculties.

Divergent thinking does not lend itself to simple solutions. It requires *transcendent thought*, or the ability to move both views to a level of integration in which win-win thinking is indispensable.

THE WAY OUT

There is a clear need for emergent leaders who develop the capacity for resolving divergent human problems and bring together diverse points of view to achieve a common aim and a shared vision.

How can this be done?

1. Develop spiritual insight and understanding of life which liberate you from materialism and mechanism and focus instead on the realities of the invisible self—the human soul. As Dr. W. Edwards Deming said, the most important things we have to manage in our organizations are invisible. They are unknown, cannot be measured, cannot be quantified, do not show up in the accounting department, and yet they are the essential forces of interaction which provide energy and vitality, and are the source of its innovative spirit.

2. Develop moral values which recognize fundamental principles of nature on which the social order is based, and which keep your eyes focused on the long-term good of the organization and of society. These moral values provide us with a sense of the rightness or wrongness of the direction in which we are headed. Without this moral sense of direction, trust can never become a reality, and hence, agreements and commitments will remain elusive. The moral will translates into shared beliefs and stated values, which leaders express in action daily.

3. Develop an intense intellectual curiosity which enlarges your capability for learning and leads you to learn something new every day of your life, from whatever source, even in the most unlikely places and outside of your field of expertise. Essential to effective leadership is the constant love of learning and the ability to construct knowledge by making connections between seemingly unrelated pieces of information from different disciplines.

4. Develop the capacity for holistic thinking whereby you can see the whole of an entity as greater than the sum of its parts, the result of the interaction of forces, not simply the aggregate of the parts. This thinking involves us in the reintegration of our lives. From the renaissance to the present, Western culture has followed the empirical road and analytical method exclusively; as a result, we have our world compartmentalized. The secret of effective leadership lies in integration so that when we work, we also learn and enjoy doing it.

An excellent example of this integration of life (this higher-order thinking in which opposites are re-integrated at a higher level) is found in this Buddhist text: *The Master in the art of living makes little distinction between his work and his play, his labor and his leisure, his mind and his body, his education and his recreation, his love and his religion. He simply pursues his vision of excellence in whatever he does, leaving others to decide whether he is working or playing. To him he is always doing both.*

If we can achieve this vision of learning for ourselves, we will become increasingly effective leaders, possessing both quantitative skills and the qualitative knowledge and skills characterized by wisdom, prudence, patience, and understanding. We will see a further integration of psychic energy (intellectual curiosity in the cognitive realm), enthusiasm, and inspiration in the affective domain, and joy in working with others in the social realm.

CHAPTER 19

Leading Learning Organizations

by Peter Senge, Senior Lecturer at Massachusetts Institute of Technology

THINK OF THREE types of leaders in learning organizations, roughly corresponding to three positions:

1. Local line leaders, who can undertake meaningful organizational experiments to test whether new learning capabilities lead to improved business results.

2. Executive leaders, who support line leaders, develop learning infrastructures, and lead by example in the gradual process of evolving the norms and behaviors of a learning culture.

3. Internal networkers, or community builders, the "seed carriers" of the new culture, who can move freely about the organization to find those who are predisposed to bringing about change, assist in experiments, and aid in the diffusion of new learning.

I'll sketch what we are learning about these leaders.

LOCAL LINE LEADERS

Nothing can start without committed local line leaders—individuals with significant business responsibility and "bottom-line" focus. They have units that are large enough to be meaningful microcosms, and yet they have enough autonomy to undertake meaningful change.

In effect, they create subcultures that may differ significantly from the mainstream culture. To be useful in creating experimental laboratories, they must also confront issue and business challenges that are seen as both important and recurring.

The key role played by local line leaders is to sanction significant practical experiments. Without serious practical experiments aimed at connecting new learning capabilities to business results, there is no way to assess whether enhancing learning capabilities is just an appealing idea or really makes a difference.

We have seen no examples where significant progress has been made without leadership from local line managers, and many examples where sincerely committed CEOs have failed to generate any significant momentum.

EXECUTIVE LEADERS

Our fervor with practical experiments led by local line managers has frequently made us blind to the necessary, complementary roles played by executive leaders. Local line leaders benefit significantly from "executive champions" who can be protectors, mentors, and thinking partners.

Working in concert with internal networkers, executives can help in connecting innovative local line leaders with other like-minded people. They also play a mentoring role—helping the local line leaders to mature, understand complex political crosscurrents, and communicate their ideas to those who have not been involved.

Part of the problem in appreciating effective executive leadership in learning is that we think of top managers as the key decision makers, the most visible and powerful people. Although undoubtedly some key decisions will always have to be made at the top, cultures are not changed through singular decisions, and decision-making power does not produce new learning capabilities.

When executives lead as teachers, stewards, and designers, they fill roles that are more subtle, contextual, and long term than the traditional model that power-wielding hierarchical leader suggests.

Effective executive leaders build an environment for learning in three ways:

1. Articulating guiding ideas. Guiding ideas are different from slogans or the latest buzzwords. They are arrived at gradually, over many years, through reflection on an organization's history and traditions and on its long-term growth and opportunities.

The power of guiding ideas derives from the energy released when imagination and aspiration come together. Understanding this power has always been a hallmark of great leaders.

2. Attention to learning infrastructure. Executives will increasingly come to realize that, in a world of rapid change and increasing interdependence, learning is too important to be left to chance. "We have plenty of infrastructure for decision making within AT&T," says Chairman Bob Allen. "What we lack is infrastructure for learning."

I have met many CEOs in recent years who have lamented that "we can't learn from ourselves," that significant innovations simply don't spread, or that "we are better at learning from competitors than from our own people." Yet those very same executives rarely recognize that they may be describing their own future job description. When we stop to think, certain questions arise: Why should successful new practices spread in organizations? Who studies these innovations to document why they worked? Where are the learning processes whereby others might follow later in the footsteps of successful innovators? Who is responsible for these learning processes?

3. The executives' own "domain for taking action"—namely, the executive team itself. What is important, first, is that executives see that they, too, must change, and that many of the skills that have made them successful in the past can actively inhibit learning. They are forceful, articulate advocates, but they usually are not very good at inquiring into their own thinking or exposing the areas where their thinking is weak.

"Gradually, I have come to see a whole new model for my role as CEO," says Shell Oil's Phil Carroll. "My real job is to be the ecologist for the organization—to see the company as a living system and to see it as a system within the context of the larger systems of which it is a part. Only then will our vision reliably include return for our shareholders, a productive environment for our employees, and a social vision for the company as a whole."

Achieving such shifts in thinking, values, and behavior among executives is not easy. "The name of the game is giving up power," says Carroll. "Even among 'enlightened' executives, giving up power is difficult. Being the commander in chief is kind of fun."

INTERNAL NETWORKERS

The most unappreciated leadership role is that of the internal networkers, or community builders. Internal networkers are effective for the very reasons that top-management efforts to initiate change can backfire. One paradox may be that "no power is power."

Precisely because they have no positional authority, internal networkers are free to move about a large organization relatively unnoticed. When the CEO visits someone, everyone knows. When the CEO says, "We need to become a learning organization," everyone nods. But when someone with little or no positional authority begins identifying people who are genuinely interested in changing the way they and their teams work, the only ones likely to respond are those who are genuinely interested. And if the internal networker finds one person who is interested and asks, "Who else really cares about these things?" he or she is likely to receive an honest response.

The only authority possessed by internal networkers comes from the strength of their convictions and the clarity of their ideas. This, we find time and again, is the only legitimate authority when deep changes are required, regardless of one's position. The internal networkers have the paradoxical advantage that this is their only source of authority.

It is very difficult to identify the internal networkers because they can be people from many different positions. They might be internal consultants, trainers, or staff in organization development or human resources. They might be front-line workers, engineers, sales representatives, or shop stewards. They might be in senior staff positions.

What is important is that they move freely, with high accessibility. They understand the informal networks, whereby information and stories flow and innovative practices naturally diffuse.

The first vital function played by internal networkers is to identify local line managers who have the power to take action and who are predisposed to developing new learning capabilities. Much time and energy can be wasted working with the wrong people, especially in the early stages of a change process.

The limitations of internal networkers likewise are not difficult to identify. Because they do not have a great deal of formal authority, they can do little to directly counter hierarchical authority. Internal networkers have no authority to institute changes in structures or processes.

The leadership challenges in building learning organizations represent a microcosm of the leadership issue of our times: how communities, be they multinational corporations or societies, productively confront complex, systemic issues where hierarchical authority is inadequate for change. None of today's most pressing issues will be resolved through hierarchical authority.

In all these issues, there are no simple causes, no simple "fixes." There is no one villain to blame. There will be no magic pill. Significant change will require imagination, perseverance, dialogue, deep caring, and a willingness to change on the part of millions of people.

The challenges of systemic change where hierarchy is inadequate will, I believe, push us to new views of leadership based on new principles. These challenges cannot be met by isolated heroic leaders. They will require a unique mix of different people, in different positions, who lead in different ways. Changes will be required in our traditional leadership models.

CHAPTER 20

Strategic Leadership

 by Francis Hesselbein, President and CEO of The Peter F. Drucker Foundation for Nonprofit Management and Chair of the Board of Governors of the Josephson Institute for The Advancement of Ethics

I **RECOMMEND THAT** executives learn to drive strategy and lead people through 10 checkpoints of strategic leadership.

I recently visited with Warren Bennis and the distinguished board of the Leadership Institute at the University of Southern California.

Three of us—Peter Hart, former chairman of MasterCard International; Dick Celeste, former governor of Ohio; and I—were asked to speak on "leadership lessons" learned in our careers. Although we used different examples, there was common language, common philosophy, amazing agreement on basic principles.

I said that my greatest lesson is that "leadership is a matter of *how to be*, not *how to do it,* and that the one indispensable quality of leaders is personal integrity with a sense of ethics that works full time."

When *Business Week* quotes a Harvard Business School professor stating that "the transformation of the Girl Scouts was like turning around a battleship in a small pond," it is clear that the principles of turnaround and driving change are generic, basic, and transferable.

TEN CHECKPOINTS

There are ten common elements to driving strategic leadership through mission and vision. I call these elements the *10 Checkpoints to Strategic Leadership.*

Step 1. Understand the environment. To understand the strategic context for planning, leaders need to understand the environment—global to local—and identify major trends and the implications of those trends for the organization. In 1980, when Peter Drucker published *Managing in Turbulent Times*, he wrote, "A time of turbulence is a dangerous time, but its greatest danger is a temptation to deny reality." He was describing a chronic condition, for we now observe that the turbulent times of the 1980s were simply basic training for managing in the turbulence of the 1990s. The greatest danger still is "a temptation to deny reality."

Step 2. Revisit the mission. In 1976, when I came to New York to become CEO of the largest organization for girls and women in the world—3 million members, with 650,000 men and women in our workforce and fewer than 1 percent of these employed staff—I did not know this country was entering a period of massive historic change that would transform society forever. I just knew that for the work I was immersed in, the patterns of the past were not right for the present I was living and the future I envisioned. So we revisited the mission—affirmed its wonderful 1912 rightness—then distilled it into nine words—"to help each girl reach her own highest potential."

Through a powerful and shared mission, life-shaping values, circular and innovative management systems, and passionate empowerment and high involvement of all our people, board and staff together, we changed—never the values and principles, but we changed the face and the course of a great American institution—an institution that became mission-focused, values-based and demographics-driven, richly diverse, and committed to listening to the customers, some of them five years old.

Step 3. Answer three fundamental Drucker questions: *What is our business? Who is our customer?* and *What does the customer consider value?* In the early 1980s, management audiences generally were not cheering in the aisles when I talked about circular and fluid management systems, dispersed leadership, the excitement of the team approach to management, job rotation, job enrichment, and the high involvement of all workers—about managing for the mission. To some observers this was seen as "soft management," and several writers even described my approach as the ultimate "feminine style of management." (You and I know that management is like money—it has no gender.)

But I could always point to a few spirited models of enlightened corporate leadership—Jim Burke of Johnson & Johnson, David Kearns of Xerox, Max DePree at Herman Miller, Bill Pollard of ServiceMaster, all following their own stars—breaking the paradigms and "changing the rules of the game." And they were real leaders—principled and productive within the corporation and equally visible and effective in the wider community. Their mission statements were clear answers to the classic Drucker question, "What is our business?" And for their corporations they had persuasively answered the question, "Who is the customer?" In their passionate focus on the customer, they had learned the answer to the toughest question, "What does the customer consider value?" I believe if you can answer all three questions, you are well on the way to managing for the mission.

Step 4. Communicate the vision. Burt Nanus, author of *Visionary Leadership*, describes the visionary leader: "Effective leaders have agendas; they are totally results-oriented. They adopt challenging new visions of what is both possible and desirable, communicate their visions, and persuade others to become so committed to these new directions that they are eager to lend their resources and energies to make them happen. In this way, they build lasting institutions that change the world."

Leaders communicate vision until it permeates to the outer edges of the circle of the corporation. Listen to Jack Welch's vision and to his language: "Ten years from now, we want magazines to write about GE as a place where people have the freedom to be creative, a place that brings out the best in everybody. An open, fair place where people have a sense that what they do matters, and where that sense of accomplishment is rewarded in both the pocketbook and the soul. That will be our report card."

Step 5. Ban the hierarchy. I believe that you can't put people in little boxes on a structure chart. Psychologically, you box them in— you contain them. I prefer circles—concentric circles in a staffing design that looks almost organic. Functions and positions are in circles, and job rotation is an enriching reality. Staffing designs are flexible and fluid, people move in circular ways—learning new skills, expanding positions. Using the team approach to management, arcane hierarchy has little relevance to working with today's knowledge workers, "who carry their tool kits in their heads."

For me, "banning the hierarchy" is an essential step to driving change, building high staff morale and high managerial performance, all in a leaner, flatter, circular, cohesive organization.

Step 6. Challenge the gospel. There are no sacred cows. We challenge everything—policies, practices, assumptions, the status quo. For business, government, and nonprofits alike, one of the most difficult tasks is "the planned abandonment" of what works today, but will have little meaning for the future. Periodically we examine the viability of the mission, who the customer is, and what the customer values. Because results are the valid measures of management effectiveness, we vigorously seek innovation that drives us to new levels of performance. In fact, the Drucker Foundation's definition of innovation is Peter's own: "Innovation is change which creates a new dimension of performance."

Recently the *New York Times* quoted the new chairman of Lufthansa as follows: "The old Lufthansa was a surly airline, an inflexible bureaucracy that paid little heed to customer satisfaction, and spent twice as much on each air mile as American, United, and Delta. But the days of administrative bureaucracy are past; everyone understands now that performance counts more than anything."

Step 7. Disperse leadership. The more power you give away, the more you have. Many leaders speak of the empowerment of their people. Jack Welch says, "I don't like the word empowerment. I use, 'the high involvement of people.' " Peter Drucker doesn't use empowerment either. He says that you can't give away power, and that leadership has little to do with power and everything to do with responsibility. You share responsibility, he says.

Step 8. No matter what you call it—just do it. Leaders need to lead by example with clear, consistent messages, great involvement of people in decisions that affect them, and pushing shared decision making across to the outermost circles of the corporation. The mission becomes theirs; the investment is theirs; the energy flows, and dispersed leadership becomes a reality.

Step 9. Tap the power of language. In the 1990s, as we move from "managing things to leading people," even our language is changing. Max DePree writes in *Leadership Is an Art* about the men and women in today's workforce, "People today need a covenant, not a contract." A covenantal relationship with management? This is indeed new language for a new era, a new century, a new generation of leaders. Leaders can be exuberant about language—so much a part of "leading by voice": as in Jack Welch's use of "soul," Max DePree's "frantic learner," or Peter Drucker's "Your mission should fit on a T-shirt."

Let us purge the vocabulary of words that limit and constrict the power of language. I find that when you purge "up and down" from your management vocabulary, and use "moving across," "to and from," there is an amazing difference. We liberate our people with felicitous language.

Step 10. Lead from the front. Great leaders lead from the front—not push from the rear. They are not skillful fence sitters. They walk like they talk; they never break a promise. They believe and demonstrate that their people are the company's greatest asset. They communicate the vision—the star they steer by. They manage for the mission.

Max DePree says, "The first responsibility of a leader is to define reality. The last is to say, 'Thank you.' In between, the leader is a servant."

The indispensable element is a leader who believes leadership is a matter of how to be—not how to do it—and carries forward the vision of what the enterprise could be. Whether these are the best of times or the worst of times is irrelevant—these are our times, the only ones we're going to have. Our times require driving strategic leadership through mission, vision, and goals. As we move toward a new millennium, as leaders, if we do what we do well, we will transform lives—and in doing so, we will transform the enterprise. In the end we ourselves will be transformed. It is called managing the dream.

CHAPTER 21

Creative Leadership

 by Michael Eisner, Chairman and CEO of the Walt
Disney Company

THE CHALLENGE for many executives is how to manage a rapidly growing creative company in a time of accelerated change.

When I joined Disney almost 12 years ago, the company had 35,000 full-time employees. We now have about 117,000. We had about 120,000 stockholders then. We have about 1.3 million today.

I mention these statistics not to prove how majestic we are, but to show how fast we have grown. One danger of such fast growth is that a company can lose its focus, forget its mission, take its eye off of its core competency. Not only is rapid growth a problem, but success, unless properly handled, can be toxic. I have watched other big corporations and have seen what can frequently happen after a long and triumphant run. The mighty stumble and fall.

Some may rise again, Phoenix-like, but others just fade to shadows of their former selves. Too many become self-satisfied, overconfident, arrogant, lazy, restless, or all of the above.

How do you continue to grow and yet avoid these pitfalls? How do you manage a company like Disney, whose principal asset is creativity, and make sure it remains young and vibrant without losing its upward trajectory or its sense of great adventure and without becoming so heavy with bureaucracy and rules that it crashes to the ground?

FIVE RECOMMENDATIONS

I don't have all the answers, but I would like to share with you some of the things we think are necessary.

1. Keep your eye on the ball. A response Babe Ruth once gave to a reporter sticks in my mind. "How is it," he was asked, "that you always come through in the clutch?"

His answer, "I don't know. I just keep my eye on the ball."

Keeping one's eye on the ball is, for me, a metaphor for what we must do as a creative company. At Disney, because of the nature of our business, everything we do is dependent on a steady stream of ideas that can be successfully transformed into film and television and radio and stage and theme park offerings.

Companies like Disney must be open to new ideas from every source, from inside and outside the company. From employees, from free-lance writers, from book and talent agents, from producers and wanna-be's, and yes, even from our children and wives.

But how do you know when you have found a winning idea? It isn't always obvious. And audience research does not help. In fact, it often misleads. I am not a disciple of research—unless of course, it agrees with me. Otherwise, it is useless.

2. Remember that the only way to succeed creatively is to fail. A company like ours must create an atmosphere in which people feel safe to fail. This means forming an organization where failure is not only tolerated, but fear of criticism for submitting a foolish idea is abolished. If not, people become too cautious. They hunker down, afraid to speak up, afraid to rock the boat, afraid of being ridiculed. Potentially brilliant ideas are never uttered, and therefore never heard.

When I came to Disney, a bunch of us would get together with our creative executives for what we called the "Gong Show." We would meet and toss ideas around—mostly ideas for television shows and movies. Anyone who wanted to could present an idea. Rank had no privileges. Kinder, gentler versions of this activity live on.

For example, our flagship, Disney Feature Animation, which has had a string of blockbusters, has its own "Gong Show" three times a year. Anybody who wants to—and I mean anybody—gets a chance to pitch an idea for an animated film to a small group of executives. There usually are about 40 presenters.

For this to work, you must have an environment where people feel safe about giving their ideas. And, while we do not pull our punches when people present their ideas, we create an atmosphere in which each idea can receive full and serious consideration.

If you take the time to listen and be honest in your reactions, and if you create a setting that recognizes that ideas come in all shapes and sizes and are willing to follow the creative mind wherever it goes, people begin to understand a basic fact: If you have an idea you believe in and can express it, it will be considered.

I assure you that this is much more than an exercise in employee relations. Several of our better animated features have come out of the

"Gong Show," and some of our other major winners out of similar programs in the company.

3. Have an organization that can follow through and execute the good ideas. Many people have good ideas, but few do anything about them. At Disney, we follow through.

I'm convinced that all of us can find within ourselves new wellsprings of creativity. Being in connection with our emotional depths is critical to releasing our most powerful and creative forces. Denying this deeper level leads to "disconnection." In effect, people lose touch with aspects of who they are.

The results tend to be vulnerability, fear, and denial, as well as superficiality, falseness, and a mistrust of intuition—all of which can get in the way of deep, creative expression. Fear of criticism and lack of acceptance are primary reasons that people censor their feelings and intuitions and shut down their depths. It explains a lot about the difference between those who are truly creative and those who are somehow blocked, limited, or superficial. Artists produce their best and most creative work when they aren't afraid to take risks, to endure criticism or embarrassment or even failure.

To me, such risk-taking is the primary challenge not just for an artist, but for any truly creative executive. Trusting one's deepest intuitions and instincts may mean overriding contrary research, peer pressure, conventional wisdom, or intimidation. Nothing matters more to me than thinking and talking about new ideas. I spend a lot of my time brainstorming with people in our divisions.

4. Synergy can be the single most important contributor to profit and growth in a creative company. When you embrace a new idea, new business, new product, new film or TV show—you have to make sure that everyone throughout the company knows about it early enough so that every segment of the business can promote or exploit its potential in every other possible market, product, or context.

There is a natural synergy in the normal product cycle of a successful film. If it does well in its initial domestic run, it almost ensures later success in international distribution, home video, network and foreign television, pay-per-view TV, and cable.

In many entertainment companies, that is where the synergy and the story end. At Disney, a well-received film will also provide profitable opportunities in our theme parks, retail stores, even children's radio and television shows for our affiliates and owned stations.

And we go beyond that: The animated feature "Beauty and the Beast" has become a successful stage musical. This is an entirely new business for us—a giant business all by itself—emanating from one successful movie. We now plan to launch one new Broadway show each year beginning in 1997.

This concept of cross-promotion and transformation of popular products into new media is an engine that helps drive our company.

5. Rejuvenation is another key to growth and survival by moving your brightest executives frequently to new responsibilities. A few years back, we decided it was "seven-year itch" time at Disney. No, we were not thinking about the personal lives of our executives. We were concerned about the continued growth of the company. We believed—and I, obviously, still do—that a creatively driven company such as ours has to renew itself constantly, or its ideas will dry and its competitive edge disappear.

So we started moving our most promising executives around, exposing them to other parts of the business, increasing their responsibilities, and bringing new eyes and new ideas to their new operations. All these women and men are the people who make the company work, but it is top management's job to make sure they are excited about that work, constantly renewed in spirit. So don't forget to move them around every seven to ten years. New eyes give rise to new ideas and opportunities.

CHAPTER 22

Credible Leadership

by James M. Kouzes, Chairman and CEO of The Tom Peters Group, and Barry Z. Posner, Professor and Managing Partner of Santa Clara University's Executive Development Center

THERE IS NEED for people to recognize new realities, discard old myths, and seize opportunities to lead us to greatness.

In over 10 years of research, we've heard and read the stories of over 2,500 ordinary people who have led others to get extraordinary things done. The practices revealed in our examination of leadership offer hope for us all.

There's no shortage of opportunities to improve the world in which we live and work. Yet today's challenges seem so daunting. They make us wonder: "Are we up to the task?" Sure, there are some new realities, yet we're convinced that not responding to the call for leadership stems not from a lack of courage or competence, but from insufficient and outdated understanding about today's workplace and the leadership process.

We see that there are countless opportunities to make a difference—opportunities to restore hope, create a sense of meaning in our lives, rebuild a sense of community, increase understanding among diverse peoples, turn information into knowledge, improve the collective standard of living, apply knowledge to products and services, and create extraordinary value for the customer.

Instead of seizing these opportunities, many people seem more reluctant than ever to answer the cry for leadership.

Why? Because we believe just about everything we have been taught by traditional management prevents us from being effective leaders. What's equally unnerving is that nearly every popular notion about leadership is a myth. Far from benign, these misperceptions foster a model of leadership antithetical to the way real-life leaders operate. They also create barriers to revitalization.

DEBUNKING 10 MYTHS

The greatest challenge is to rid ourselves of debilitating traditions and myths.

1. *Leaders are charismatic.* At best this fantasy distorts our appreciation of leaders. At worst it leads to hero worship and cultism. Although leaders must be energetic and enthusiastic, their dynamic approach doesn't come from special powers. It comes from a strong belief in a purpose and a willingness to express that conviction.

2. *The best leaders are renegades who magnetize a band of followers with their courage and daring acts.* In fact, leaders attract constituents not because of their willful defiance, but because of their deep faith in the capacity of the people they would lead to adapt and grow and learn. Leaders develop the capabilities of others not to follow, but to lead for themselves.

3. *Leaders are prescient visionaries.* To be sure, leaders must have a vision, a sense of direction, but their vision need not show any psychic foresight. It can spring from original thinking or represent the inspiration of someone else. What is true is that leaders believe that doing better is always possible, no matter what the probabilities suggest.

4. *Leaders are cool, aloof, and analytical.* Yet when real-life leaders discuss what they're proudest of in their own careers, they describe feelings of inspiration, passion, elation, intensity, challenge, caring, kindness—and yes, even love. Hard work can only be sustained because we care deeply, and heroic acts spring from the heart.

5. *The job of management is primarily one of controlling resources, including time, money, materials, and people.* Flesh-and-blood leaders know, however, that the more they control others, the less likely it is that people will excel. They also know that the more they control, the less they'll be trusted. Leaders don't command and control; they serve and support.

6. *The ideal organization is orderly and stable, and organizational processes can and should be engineered so that things run like clockwork.* Yet when people describe their personal-best leadership achievements, they talk about challenging the process, about changing things, and about shaking up the organization. We don't lead the status quo.

7. *Leaders focus on the short run, the Wall Street analysts, the quarterly statement, and the annual report.* Yet all the effective leaders we've seen had a long-term, future orientation. They looked beyond the horizon of the present. They focused on what was possible to accomplish, broke it down into doable actions, and made it easier for others to enlist.

8. *The job of leaders is to detach themselves from mundane, day-to-day work and invent a grand strategic plan.* Tradition would have us believe that great policy promotes progress. But we know that leaders' deeds are far more important than their words. Credibility of action is the single most significant determinant of whether a leader will be followed over time.

9. Leaders have a superior (hierarchical) position. This perception assumes that leadership starts with a capital L, and that those who are on top are automatically leaders. But leadership isn't a place; it's a process. It involves skills and abilities that are useful whether one is in the executive suite or on the front line, on Wall Street or Main Street.

10. Leadership is reserved for only a very few of us. That myth is perpetuated daily, whenever anyone asks, "Are leaders born or made?" Leadership is certainly not conveyed in a gene, and it's most definitely not a secret code or some mystical or ethereal quality that can't be understood by ordinary people. Our research shows that leadership is an observable, learnable set of practices.

CREDIBLE LEADERS

Over the last 10 years, we have asked more than 10,000 managers from both private and public organizations to tell us what qualities they look for and admire most in a leader. In effect, we ask them, "What makes leaders credible?" The vast majority tell us that they want leaders who are honest, competent, inspiring, and forward-looking. We characterize these leaders as follows:

• *Honest leaders* are truthful, trustworthy, and have integrity. They keep their word and consistently match their actions with their words. Their behaviors are consistent and above board.

• *Competent leaders* are capable, productive, effective, efficient, and thorough. They know how to get the job done. They may have functional or technical expertise, but most importantly, they have the ability to use their knowledge to challenge, inspire, enable, and encourage others. They also set the example by competently modeling exemplary behavior.

• *Inspiring leaders* are uplifting, enthusiastic, energetic, humorous, cheerful, and positive about the future. They communicate a sense of energy and enthusiasm. They are excited about what they are doing, and they share their enthusiasm with others.

• *Forward-looking leaders* are visionary, foresighted, concerned about the future, and have a clear sense of direction and purpose. They know where they are headed and are ready to take others along with them on their journey.

These qualities are strikingly similar to what communication experts define as "source credibility." In assessing the believability of communication sources, researchers typically evaluate people, such as newscasters, salespeople, and leaders, on three criteria: their trustworthiness, expertise, and dynamism.

What we found in our investigation of admired leadership qualities is that, more than anything, people want leaders who are *credible*, meaning trustworthy, honest, competent, dynamic, and inspiring. Credibility is the foundation of leadership. Upon the solid foundation of credibility, leaders build their forward-looking dreams of the future.

WHAT IS CREDIBILITY?

The root word of *credibility* is "*credo,*" which means belief. Credibility is built on a set of beliefs or values. To be credible leaders must first clarify their values. Values are the principles that are most important to us. They are the deep-rooted, pervasive standards that influence every aspect of our lives including our moral judgments, our responses to others, and our commitments to personal and organizational goals. However silently, values give direction to the many decisions we make every day. Values are our personal "bottom line."

Leaders are credible when they act in ways that are consistent with their values. By being true to their values and using them to guide their actions, leaders inspire trust, faith, and confidence. They translate their values into a set of guiding principles for their constituents. First, by communicating their values, leaders let people know what is expected of everyone. Secondly, leaders understand their constituents' values and build consensus based on a set of shared values. These shared values guide the hundreds of decisions that an organization makes every day. When a leader has clearly communicated shared values, the entire organization is able to act consistently and credibly.

When employees believe their managers are highly credible, they feel loyal and committed to their organizations; motivated and willing to make personal sacrifices for the company; proud to tell others they are a part of the organization; and empowered and part of the team. But when people believe their managers are not credible, they feel uncommitted and disenchanted; inclined to leave the organization; more motivated by financial, rather than intrinsic, rewards; and isolated and unsupported.

SIX WAYS TO BECOME A CREDIBLE LEADER

Leadership credibility is earned over time. It is not granted with a title or a position. It must be nurtured and developed. You cannot take it for granted. You must continuously strive to show others that you are worthy of their trust and commitment. Six basic actions can help you build and maintain your credibility.

1. Clarify your values. Values are the social principles that are most important to us, the standards by which we choose to live our lives. They guide how we feel, what we say, what we think, and how we act. Values are our source of energy and purpose. The self-confidence required to lead has at its core two sources: knowledge and integrity. Integrity develops as you learn about yourself and your values. A unifying set of values guides your actions regardless of the situation, which gives you the self-confidence to lead in difficult and stressful situations.

2. Identify what your constituents want. Building any relationship begins with getting to know those we want to lead. Learn their hopes and fears, their values and biases, and what they want. Only in this way can you show them how their interests can be best served by aligning them with yours. If you act only in your self-interest and ignore or not care about the interests of your constituents, people will no longer trust you, and you will lose your credibility with them.

3. Build consensus. Leaders show others how everyone's individual values and interests will be served by coming to consensus on a collective set of common values. Shared values motivate people to work together toward the organization's goals. People feel more personally effective because they care about what they are doing; they feel important because they are making a difference; they are more loyal to their organization when they believe that their values and the company's values are aligned; and they experience less stress and tension because the values provide them with the guidelines for the best actions to take.

While credible leaders honor the diversity of their many constituencies, they also find a common ground of agreement on which everyone can base their interactions. Shared values are the foundation for building a productive and genuine working relationship. They are also the basis for agreements on the "specifications" of products and services. Disagreements over fundamental values lead to conflicts and false expectations.

Use your shared values as a foundation for building a good working relationship. If you make the mistake of guarding control and power and not giving your constituents autonomy to act on the shared values, you are telling them that you don't trust them. By holding on to power, you lose credibility.

4. Communicate shared values with conviction. Enthusiasm, energy, and commitment begin with the leader. To gain the commitment of others you must communicate your values with conviction and in memorable ways. If your commitment doesn't come from the heart, your enthusiasm will be insincere. It will appear that you are trying to sell people something that you do not believe in yourself. If your excitement is not genuine, then you will not be trusted.

5. Stand up for your beliefs. Leaders are people who take a stand. We follow people who have confidence in their decisions. Confusion among your constituents over shared value creates stress; not knowing what you believe leads to conflict, indecision, and rivalry. If you stand up for your beliefs but do not keep an open mind to alternatives and listen carefully to feedback, you will become rigid and autocratic. There have been many famous examples of charismatic leaders who failed because they didn't listen to their constituents.

6. Lead by example. Leadership is not a spectator sport. Leaders don't sit in the stands and watch. Neither are leaders in the game substituting for players. Leaders coach. They demonstrate what is important by how they spend their time, by the priorities on their agenda, by the questions they ask, by the people they see, the places they go, and the behaviors and results they recognize and reward.

Leaders are role models. We look to them for clues to how we should behave. We believe their actions over their words, every time. If you ask people to observe certain standards, then you better live by the same rules. Do what you say you are going to do.

Leaders show others how to behave. Others can see what is expected and required by observing what the leader does, not just from listening to what he or she says. Leaders consciously create opportunities to "walk the talk," to practice what they preach.

If you ask your constituents to observe certain standards and then do not live by the same rules yourself, you will be called a hypocrite. If you are not among the first to show people the way, they will think that you have set a double standard.

A FRAGILE COMMODITY

Credibility is one of the hardest attributes to earn—and it is one of the most fragile. It is earned minute by minute, hour by hour, day by day, year by year. But it can be lost very quickly, if not attended to. You not only have to do the right things to build your reputation, but you must be careful not to do things that could damage or destroy your credibility.

The quest for leadership is first an inner one to discover who you are and what you stand for. As we begin our quest, we must wrestle with some difficult and painful questions. A truly credible person is one who steps out into the unknown, confronts self-doubt, suffers defeat and disappointment, and returns to triumph from the learning. A person who gives us courage is one who risks embarrassment and ruin, and yet succeeds in maintaining the strength of conviction.

Leadership is an affair of the heart and the soul. We encourage you to set an example for others by taking the inner journey into your own heart and soul to explore your values and convictions.

CHAPTER 23

Entrepreneurial Leadership

by Gifford Pinchot III and Elizabeth
Pinchot, authors of *The Intelligent
Organization*

THE DECLINE OF the manager and the rise of the entrepreneurial leader challenges all senior executives to change their ways.

Every executive must look within and ask, "Do I have a hidden reserve of entrepreneurial spirit to meet the challenges of this increasingly turbulent environment?"

Entrepreneurial spirit is buried inside all of us. We may test someone today and find no trace of it, but return five years later and find that a fiery spirit has emerged. Often people find it when they need it. For example, more women today are starting businesses than men. Many women with young children have discovered the entrepreneurial spirit when they see no good choices other than working out of the home. Likewise, early retirements are provoking rapid transitions to entrepreneurial ways. Whether you stay in the increasingly intrapreneurial corporate world or strike out on your own, keep the entrepreneurial side of your nature in good shape.

A DOZEN TIPS

Here are a few hints to keep your dream moving.

1. Find a vision worthy of persistence. To find a dream that turns on your energy and passion, first pay attention to your deeper values and beliefs. Choose your commitments carefully. You can't be the entrepreneurial leader of 10 ideas a year. Pick one dream that is so important, it's worth focusing on.

Your vision should meet three tests: (1) create more value for customers and stockholders; (2) increase the value of the capabilities and assets of the organization; and (3) align with your deepest values and give you a chance to use your greatest talents. Of these, the last is the easiest to test. Ask yourself if you are excited by the possibility of devoting energy to the idea. If not, let it pass for now. You don't have to kill ideas that don't align with your deeper self—just leave the leadership of them to others.

You can only be an effective entrepreneur or intrapreneur for something that so aligns with who you are, new energies are released in abundance. Any lesser alignment will not produce the persistence, creativity, and courage needed.

Once you find something, check it against the needs of customers and core competencies of your organization. If it doesn't fit, you might let it go. You can only be the intrapreneur of a few ideas.

2. Choose a vision of moderate risk. Choose ideas that are trying to happen—that make sense to others—or your battle will be too hard. Successful entrepreneurs are not wild. They choose worthwhile but doable challenges. Having set a challenging objective, they do what they can to reduce the risk. They are moderate risk takers, not gamblers.

3. Seek and use feedback. The entrepreneurial act is a combination of stubborn persistence and flexible responsiveness. The task is to discover a practical route to a new way of doing things. Entrepreneurs are full of false starts and blind alleys. They never abandon the goal, but seek new means after every setback. The more they listen to what the world is telling them about their idea, the faster they learn how to make it work.

4. Develop cross-disciplinary business judgment. Moving from a functional to an entrepreneurial view requires learning the instincts of whole business judgment—answering the question, "What matters most in this situation?" Business judgment is the product of experience, but all experience does not count equally. To acquire business judgment faster, work as a member of a cross-functional team whose results will be judged in the marketplace—or by some other clear and measurable feedback—and participate in key business decisions. Stay with the team long enough to experience results. Think about what worked and what didn't. Change functions—you might begin a project in advanced engineering, follow it into design, stay with it in manufacturing, and finally take time with it in marketing. A person with judgment knows whether the most critical issue is a marketing one or a technical one, whether the effect on morale offsets the cost savings.

For many people, the first chance to take big-picture responsibility will not come at work, but rather in volunteer activities where responsibility goes to those willing to work.

5. Share ownership with the team. You need to think like an owner and get others to own the dream as well. Owners think for the longer run. They focus on making the business work, not on winning internal political battles. When we own something, we share in the outcome. 3M creates a sense of ownership by letting the team that brings an idea forward be the team to commercialize it. They share in any success or failure.

You can increase your own sense of ownership by taking an active part in decisions. You can increase the ownership of your team by encouraging people to participate in decisions, by letting those who believe in the project stay with it, and by giving credit to the team as a whole. Participation doesn't mean abandoning your own point of view. It does mean listening, appreciating others' ideas, using their words rather than yours when both are equivalent, compromising in those things you don't think are critical, while still leading strongly by holding up goals and aspirations and asking others to find ways to achieve them.

6. Never reject help. Intrapreneurs often get top executives excited, and then when they offer help, tell them it is not needed. They are proud of having assembled the resources needed at a lower level. But the quickest way to make enemies is to reject help. If someone offers to help, find a way to say yes. If you don't want their help, don't show them the project. Find ways to accept help without losing control or getting slowed down.

7. Do whatever needs to be done. It is painful to watch managers take early retirement and become entrepreneurs. They have been delegating so long they have forgotten how to do ordinary work. In an entrepreneurial role, you are creating something that doesn't have an organization behind it to take care of the details. You often have to do it yourself.

As Howard Head said of starting the Head ski business, "When the sales force needed a rousing speech, I gave a speech. When the floor needed sweeping, I swept the floor." Intrapreneurial leaders aren't afraid of menial work in the service of a new idea.

The greatest cause of both entrepreneurial and intrapreneurial failure is getting trapped in one's specialty and losing the big picture. The technical type builds a perfect technological solution but neglects to market it. Marketing genius identifies the need and writes great copy but neglects to control costs. Don't let the fact that you don't know how to do something keep you from taking it on. Get help if you can. Even if you are not an expert, do the best you can. Ignoring the parts of business you know least leads directly to failure.

8. It's easier to ask for forgiveness than permission. If you ask, they might say no. If you just do it, you can apologize later. Most of the time when you go ahead and do what needs to be done, there are few repercussions. You will be surprised by how often no one objects to your bold actions. When they do get riled, ask for forgiveness. And, if possible, promise never to do it again.

9. Come to work willing to be fired. Fear of authority makes us do what we think those in power want rather than what we believe is right. Too much fear of authority is incompatible with good entrepreneurial leadership, but fear of authority seems to be inborn. Successful intrapreneurs find the courage to keep their fear of authority under control so they can do what needs to be done.

When we ask intrapreneurial leaders what makes them different the most common answer is, "I come to work every day willing to be fired. I do what I believe is right without fearing the consequences." As Chuck House, legendary Hewlett-Packard intrapreneur, put it: "I don't see that I am taking any risk. I came here to do innovative things. If they want me innovating, then I want this job. If not, the sooner I find out the better."

You can gain the courage to do what is right by trusting that you can always find a way to make a living. Keep your connections alive. It also helps to have some savings: Living beneath your means may be the first step toward intrapreneurial courage.

10. Know where the waterline is. Asking for forgiveness rather than permission works well when you are "boring holes above the waterline." That means that even if it goes wrong the consequences are affordable. Taking chances then makes sense. If you are "boring holes below the waterline," in other words, if the consequences of something going wrong are catastrophic, then ask for permission first. A successful intrapreneurial leader has to cultivate a good intuitive grasp of which risks are catastrophic and which are affordable.

11. Never show fools unfinished work. Buckminster Fuller once said, "Never show fools unfinished work." When you are building your dream, don't rush off and show it to enemies. Work the bugs out of it in conversation with your friends and allies.

This advice conflicts with another valid principle: early involvement of all parties affected. People best implement ideas they have a hand in developing. People support projects they help create. Don't leave key collaborators out of the loop so long that they have no role in developing the plan. Think it through, anticipate objections, and then incorporate their creativity and help.

12. Balance reality and the dream. The role of the entrepreneurial leader is a continual dance between the dream and reality. You can cleave so strongly to current reality that you abandon the dream. Your life will turn gray. You can abandon reality and indulge yourself in fantasy. After a brief period of giddy satisfaction your dream will be dashed to pieces. The challenge is to succumb to neither the false security of accepting reality as it is nor the temptation to indulge in wishful thinking. The successful leader grasps reality in one hand and the dream in the other, refusing to rest until the two are brought together.

Effective leaders today use the tools of community building to create an environment in which many leaders can emerge. They contribute inspiring descriptions of shared vision to align everyone's energies. They care for and protect their employees. They listen and do their best to accept the contributions and divergent ideas of employees as honest attempts to help. They give thanks for the gifts of ideas, courage, and self-appointed leadership that employees bring to the community. They discourage backbiting and politics. They do their best to treat each member as a spiritual equal worthy of respect. They share information so everyone can see how the whole organization works and how it is doing. They publicly celebrate the community's successes. In tragedy they mourn the community's losses.

We've watched Jack Ward Thomas, chief of the U.S. Forest Service, cry in public over the loss of firefighters. Community occurs most easily when free people with some sense of equal worth join together voluntarily for a common enterprise. Great leaders create the sense of freedom, voluntarism, and common worth, but do so most easily in smaller organizations with face-to-face contact. As organizations become larger, more complex, and more geographically distributed, it becomes harder to create enough common vision and community spirit to guide the actions without increasing reliance on the chain of command.

We are reaching a time when every employee will take turns leading. All employees will find circumstances when they see what must be done and must influence others to make their vision of a better way a reality. To create room for everyone to lead when their special knowledge provides the key to the right action, we must move beyond traditional concepts of hierarchy. To become lean and mean is not enough. In the times to come, leaders must find ways to replace hierarchy with indirect methods of leadership that allow greater freedom, lead to more accurate allocation of resources, and focus on the common good.

FREE INTRAPRISE

Learning from the success of free enterprise, leaders will change the terms of the debate from centralization vs. decentralization to monopoly vs. user choice.

We call the system based on free choices between alternative internal suppliers the *free intraprise system* (short for intracorporate free enterprise).

An advanced free intraprise organization has a structure much like that of a virtual organization. Both have a small hierarchy responsible to the top leaders for accomplishing the mission. The main businesses buy the bulk of the components and services that create value for their customers from suppliers. The difference is this: In a virtual organization those suppliers are outside firms, and in a free intraprise organization many are internal "intraprises" (intra corporate enterprises), controlled by the free internal market but still part of the firm.

Most everyone at work provides a service. The advantage of outsourcing is dealing with resources through a market with choice rather than the monopoly structures of a chain of command.

In future organizations, most employees will work in intraprises that provide services to the core businesses. The core businesses will be run by small groups of line managers who buy much of the value that is added by their businesses from internal intraprises.

Free intraprise provides the core discipline for the horizontal networked organization, allowing senior leaders to project strategic intent through a small hierarchy without creating much bureaucracy.

If you tried to enliven a command economy, you would get nowhere by telling local party leaders to take more risks or by training the managers to be more empowering. To crack that bureaucracy, the leaders must allow entrepreneurs to compete with monopolies.

Similarly, to cure corporate bureaucracy, training managers in empowerment is not sufficient. Intrapreneurial teams must be developed to offer services that compete with the functional and staff monopolies. Free choice between different providers will sort out what works to serve the mission and values.

Leaders can use free market choice inside to achieve many of the benefits nations achieve when they liberate the entrepreneurial spirit of their people by creating free market institutions. They can create a self-organizing network that spreads learning and capabilities across divides without the need for direct senior leadership intervention or even direct inspiration. They can create a feedback system that sorts out what internal services are effective without having to evaluate and decide themselves.

To establish a free intraprise system, leaders allow choice between several internal suppliers of services and components; establish right of employees and teams to form an intraprise; protect intraprises against the efforts of former bureaucrats to reestablish their monopolies by political means; and establish accounting systems that support free intraprise.

Internal markets provide a way to be sure everyone's contributions to that mission are cost effective without relying on appraisal from above. For many leaders it is difficult to turn from direct intervention to creating conditions which empower others. But what greater legacy can you leave than the liberation of an organization to a higher level of productivity, innovation, and service?

CHAPTER 24

Quality Leaders

 by the late W. Edwards Deming, an independent consultant for 45 years

TO MAKE THE TRANSFORMATION from present to better practices, we must take the rugged route of profound knowledge.

A good question for anybody in business to ask is: *What business are we in?* To do well, what we are doing? Yes, but this is not enough. We must keep asking: *What product or service would help our customers more?* We must think about the future. What will we be making five years from now? Ten years from now?

The absence of defects does not necessarily build business. Something more is required. In the case of automobiles, for example, the customer may be interested in performance. He or she might include under performance not just acceleration, but also how the car behaves on ice, how the car steers at high speed, how it rides over bumps. Performance and style, whatever these words mean in the minds of customers, must show constant improvement.

Everyone is in favor of improving quality, but many people misunderstand quality, as evident by looking at some of their suggestions for improving quality: automation, new machinery, more computers, gadgets, hard work, best efforts, merit system, MBO, MBR, rankings, inspections, incentive pay, work standards, specifications, motivation.

What's wrong with these suggestions? Every one of them ducks the responsibility of management. Quality is determined by top management. It can't be delegated. An essential ingredient that I call *profound knowledge* is missing. There is no substitute for knowledge. Hard work, best efforts, and best intentions will not by themselves produce quality nor a market. Transformation of management is required—learning and applying profound knowledge.

The quality of the output of a company can't be better than the quality at the top. Quality is made by top management. Job security and jobs are dependent on management's foresight to design products and services that will entice customers and build a market; and their foresight to be ready, ahead of the customer, to modify products and services.

PRESENT PRACTICE VS. BETTER PRACTICE

The prevailing practices of management cause huge monetary losses and huge waste whose magnitudes can neither be evaluated nor measured. These losses must be managed by replacing faulty present practices with better practices.

Present: Have no constancy of purpose. Engage in short-term thinking with emphasis on immediate results. Think only in the present tense. Keep up the price of the company's stock. Maintain dividends. Fail to optimize over time. Make this quarter look good. Ship everything on hand at the end of the month (or quarter). Never mind its quality. Show it as accounts receivable. Defer till next quarter repairs, maintenance, and orders for material. *Better:* Adopt and publish constancy of purpose. Do some long-term planning. Ask this question: Where do we wish to be in five years from now? Then, by what method?

Present: Rank people, sales staff, teams, divisions; reward at the top, punish at the bottom. Have a merit system with annual appraisal of people, a form of ranking. Compensate people with incentive pay and pay based on performance. *Better:* Abolish ranking. Manage the whole company as a system. Make every component and every division contribute toward optimization of the system. Abolish the merit system in your company. Study the capability of the system. Study the management of people. Abolish incentive pay and pay based on performance. Give everyone a chance to take pride in his or her work.

Present: Fail to manage the organization as a system. Think of the components as individual profit centers. Everybody loses when individuals, teams, and divisions in the company work as individual profit centers, not for optimization of the aim of the whole organization. The various components thus rob themselves of long-term profit, joy in work, and other desirable measures of quality of life. People lose hope of ever understanding the relationship of their work to the work of others; they do not talk with each other. *Better:* Manage the company as a system. Enlarge judiciously the boundaries of the system. See that the system includes the future. Encourage communication. Make physical arrangements for informal dialogue between people in the various components of the company, regardless of level or position. Encourage continual learning and advancement. Form groups for comradeship in athletics, music, history, a language, etc., and provide facilities for study groups.

Present: Manage by objective (MBO). Set numerical goals. Manage by results (MBR). Take immediate action on any fault, complaint, delay, accident, breakdown. *Better:* Study the theory of a system. Manage the components for optimization of the aim of the system. Work on a method for improving a process. Understand and improve the processes that produce defects, or faults. Understand the distinction between common causes of variation and special causes to understand the kind of action to take.

Present: Delegate quality to someone or some group. Buy materials and services at lowest bid. *Better:* Keep accountability for quality with the top management. Estimate the total cost of use of materials and services—first cost (purchase price) plus predicted cost of problems in use of them, their effect on the quality of final product.

TRANSFORMATION REQUIRED

Ninety-five percent of changes made in management today make no improvement. Transformation to a new style of management is required to achieve optimization—a process of orchestrating the efforts of all components to achieve the stated aim. Optimization is management's job. Everybody wins with optimization. Anything less than optimization of the whole system brings eventual loss to every component in the system.

Time will bring changes that must be managed and predicted so far as possible. Management of a system may require imagination. An added responsibility of management is to be ready to change the boundary of the system to better serve the aim. Changes may require redefining components.

Management and leaders have still another job—to govern their own future, not to be victims of circumstance. For example, management may change the course of the company and the industry by anticipating the needs of customers for new products or new services. Preparing for the future includes lifelong learning for employees. It includes constant scanning of the environment (technical, social, economic) to perceive need for innovation, new product, new service, or innovation of method.

The components of a system could, in principle, manage themselves. A possible example is a string quartet. Each member supports the other three. None of them is there to attract individual attention. Four simultaneous solos do not make a string quartet. The four players practice singly and together to accomplish their aim—self-satisfaction and pleasure to listeners.

An important job of management is to recognize and manage the interdependence between components. Resolution of conflicts and removal of barriers to cooperation are responsibilities of management.

A job description must do more than prescribe motions: do this, do that; this way, that way. It must tell what the work will be used for, how the work contributes to the aim of the system. Harm comes from internal competition and conflict, and from the fear that is generated.

Competition leads to loss. People pulling in opposite directions on a rope only exhaust themselves: They go nowhere. What we need is cooperation. Every example of cooperation is one of benefit and gains to those who cooperate. Cooperation is especially productive in a well-managed system. The individual components of the system, instead of being competitive, will reinforce each other for optimization and accomplishment of the aim of the system.

We have grown up in a climate of competition between people, teams, departments, divisions, pupils, schools, universities. We have been taught by economists that competition will solve our problems. Actually, competition is destructive. It would be better if everyone would work together as a system, with the aim for everybody to win. What we need is cooperation and transformation to a new style of management.

ROUTE TO TRANSFORMATION

The route to take is what I call *profound knowledge*. The first step, transformation of the individual, comes from understanding the system of profound knowledge. Once the individual understands the system, he or she will apply its principles in every relationship with other people. The person will perceive new meaning to life, to events, to numbers, to interactions between people. The individual will have a basis for judgment of personal decisions and for transformation of the organizations that he or she belongs to.

The system is composed of four interrelated parts.

1. Appreciation for a system. A system is a network of interdependent components that work together to accomplish the aim of the system. Without an aim, there is no system. The aim proposed here for any organization is for everybody to gain—stockholders, employees, suppliers, customers, community, the environment—over the long term. The performance of anyone is governed largely by the system that he or she works in. The greater the independence between components, the greater will be the need for communication and cooperation between them. Also, the greater will be the need for overall management. The obligation of any component is to contribute its best to the system, not to maximize its own production, profit, or sales, nor any other competitive measure. Optimization for everyone concerned should be the basis for negotiation between any two people, between divisions, between union and management, between companies, between competitors, between countries.

2. Knowledge of variation. There will always be variation between people, in output, in service, in product. What is the variation trying to tell us about a process and about the people who work in it? Management requires knowledge about interaction of forces and about the effect of the system on the performance of people. Knowledge of dependence and interdependence between people, groups, divisions, companies, and countries is helpful.

3. Theory of knowledge. The theory of knowledge helps us to understand that management in any form is prediction and that a statement, if it conveys knowledge, predicts future outcomes with risk of being wrong, and that it fits without failure observations of the past. Rational prediction requires theory and builds knowledge through systematic revision and extension of theory based on comparison of prediction with observation. Information, no matter how complete and speedy, is not knowledge.

4. Psychology. Psychology helps us to understand people, interaction between people and circumstances, interaction between customer and supplier, interaction between teacher and pupil, interaction between managers and employees and any system of management. People are born with intrinsic motivation, with a need for relationships with others, with a need for love and esteem, with a natural inclination to learn, and with a right to enjoy their work. Good management preserves these positive innate attributes.

LEADING AND MANAGING PEOPLE

Transformation will take place under a leader. It will not be spontaneous. The job of a leader is to accomplish transformation of the organization.

How can this transformation be accomplished? First, by understanding why the transformation would bring gains. Second, by feeling compelled to accomplish the transformation. Third, by having a plan, step by step. But what is in the leader's own head is not enough. Using persuasive power, he or she must convince and change enough people in power to make it happen.

The role of the leader after transformation has fourteen components. The leader—

1. Understands and conveys to others the meaning of a system. He or she teaches people how the work of the group supports the aims of the system.

2. Helps people to see themselves as components in a system. The leader helps them work in cooperation toward optimizing the efforts of all stages to achieve the aim.

3. Understands that people are different from each other. The leader tries to create interest, challenge, and joy for everybody. He of she tries to optimize the education, skills, hopes, and abilities of everyone.

4. *Learns unceasingly.* The leader encourages people to study and provides, when possible, courses for advancement of learning. He or she encourages continued education.

5. *Is a coach and counsel, not a judge.*

6. *Understands a stable system.* The leader knows that in the stable state, it is distracting to tell the worker about a mistake.

7. *Has three sources of power: authority of office; knowledge; and personality (persuasive power and tact).* The leader develops the second and third, rarely relies on number one. However, he or she has an obligation to use authority of office to change the process to bring improvement.

8. *Studies results with the aim to improve his or her performance as a manager of people.*

9. *Tries to discover who, if anybody, is outside the system, in need of special help.* The person in need of special help is not in the bottom five percent of the distribution of others; he or she is clean outside that distribution.

10. *Creates an environment that encourages trust, freedom, and innovation.*

11. *Does not expect perfection.*

12. *Listens and learns without passing judgment.*

13. *Holds informal, unhurried conversations with every employee at least once a year, not for judgment, merely to listen.* The purpose is to develop understanding of the leader's people, their aims, hopes, and fears. The meeting is spontaneous, not planned ahead.

14. *Understands the benefits of cooperation and the losses from competition between people and between groups.*

One is born with intrinsic motivation, self-esteem, dignity, cooperation, curiosity, joy in learning. These attributes are high at the beginning of life, but are gradually crushed by the forces of destruction. These forces cause humiliation, fear, self-defense, competition for gold stars, high grades, high ratings on the job. They lead anyone to play to win, not for fun. They crush out joy in learning, joy on the job, innovation. Extrinsic motivation (complete resignation to external pressures) gradually replaces intrinsic motivation, self-esteem, dignity.

Instead of judging people, ranking them, and putting them into slots, leaders should help people to optimize the system so that everybody will gain.

CHAPTER 25

Management Versus Leadership

by Hugh Nibley, Professor-Emeritus of Ancient Studies
at Brigham Young University

IF THERE IS ONE thing that clearly marks the decline and fall of civilizations and corporations, it is the fatal shift from leadership to management. Excellence is a mark of leadership; mediocrity a sign of management.

Captain Grace Hopper, that grand old lady of the Navy, has recently called our attention to the contrasting and conflicting natures of management and leadership. No one, she says, ever managed men into battle. She wants more emphasis on teaching leadership. But leadership can no more be taught than creativity or how to be a genius.

The *Generalstab* tried desperately for a hundred years to train up a generation of leaders for the German army, but it never worked, because the men who delighted their superiors, (i.e., the managers), got the high commands, while the men who delighted the lower ranks (i.e., the leaders), got the reprimands.

Leaders are movers and shakers, original, inventive, unpredictable, imaginative, full of surprises that discomfit the enemy in war and the main office in peace. Managers are safe, conservative, predictable, conforming organization men and team players, dedicated to the establishment.

Great leaders have a passion for equality. We think of great generals from David and Alexander on down, sharing their beans or masa with their men, calling them by their first names, marching along with them in the heat, sleeping on the ground, and being the first over the wall. A famous ode by a long-suffering Greek soldier, Archilochus, reminds us that the men in the ranks are not fooled for an instant by the executive type who thinks he is a leader.

For managers, on the other hand, the idea of equality is repugnant and, indeed, counterproductive. Where promotion, perks, privilege, and power are the name of the game, awe and reverence for rank are everything, the inspiration and motivation of all good men and women. Where would management be without the inflexible paper processing, codes of conduct, attention to proper social, political and religious affiliation, vigilant watch over habits and attitudes, etc., that gratify the stock-holders and satisfy security?

"If you love me," said the greatest of all leaders, "you will keep my commandments." "If you know what is good for you," says the manager, "you will keep my commandments, and not make waves."

That is why the rise of management always marks the decline of culture. If the management does not go for Bach, very well, there will be no Bach; if management favors sentimental, doggerel verse extolling the qualities that make for success, young people everywhere will be spouting long trade-journal jingles; if the management's taste in art is what will sell—trite, insipid, folksy kitsch—that is what we will get; if management finds maudlin, saccharine commercials appealing, that is what the public will get; if management must reflect the corporate image in tasteless, trendy new buildings, down come the fine old monuments.

To Parkinson's Law, which shows how management gobbles up everything else, he added what he calls the "Law of Injelitance": *Managers do not promote individuals whose competence might threaten their own position*; and so, as the power of management spreads ever wider, the quality of company products and services deteriorates ever more, if that is possible. In short, while management shuns *equality*, it feeds on *mediocrity*.

On the other hand, leadership is escape from mediocrity. All the great deposits of art, science, and literature from the past—on which all civilization must feed—come to us from a mere handful of leaders. For the qualities of leadership are the same in all fields, the leader being simply the one who sets the highest example; and to do that and open the way to greater light and knowledge, the leader must break the mold. "A ship in port is safe," says Captain Hopper speaking of management, "but that is not what ships were built for," she adds, calling for leadership. True leaders are inspiring because they are inspired, caught up in a higher purpose, devoid of personal ambition, idealistic, and incorruptible.

There is, necessarily, some of the manager in every leader, as there should be some of the leader in every manager. The trick is to achieve balance, along with a sense of priority. In the New Testament, the Scribes and Pharisees are chided for their one-sidedness: They kept careful accounts of the most trivial things, but in their dealings with people they neglected fair play, compassion, and good faith, which happen to be prime qualities of leadership. The Master insisted that *both* states of mind are necessary: "This ye must do (speaking of the bookkeeping) but not neglect the other." But it is the "blind leading the blind," he continues, who reverse priorities, who "choke on a gnat and gulp down a camel." So vast is the discrepancy between management and leadership that only a blind man would get them backwards. Yet that is what we do.

Of course, that is what's been done for centuries. In the time of Socrates, the Sophists were making a big thing of their special manner of dress and delivery. It was all for show, of course; it was "dressing for success" with a vengeance, for the whole purpose of the rhetorical brand of education which they inaugurated and sold at top prices to the ambitious youth was to make the student successful as a paid advocate in the courts of law, a commanding figure in the public assemblies, or a successful promoter of daring business enterprises by mastering the irresistible techniques of persuasion and salesmanship which the Sophists had to offer.

That was the classical education which Christianity embraced at the urging of St. Augustine. He had learned by hard experience that you can't trust revelation because you can't control it, and what the Church needed was something "handier and more reliable for the public" than revelation or even reason, and that is exactly what the rhetorical education had to offer.

And down through the centuries, academic robes and diplomas have never failed to keep the public at a respectful distance, inspire a decent awe for the professions, and impart an air of solemnity and mystery that has been as good as money in the bank. The four faculties of Theology, Philosophy, Medicine, and Law have been the perennial seed-beds not only of professional wisdom, but also of the quackery and venality so generously exposed to public view by Plato, Rabelais, Moliere, Swift, Gibbon, A. E. Housman, H. L. Mencken, and others.

It seems that managers "knows the price of everything and the value of nothing," because for them the value is the price. And to them, money is what makes business *manageable*—money is pure numbers; by converting all values to numbers, everything can be fed into the computer and handled with ease and efficiency. "How much?" becomes the only question we need to ask.

Of course, to "seek ye first financial independence and all other things shall be added" is recognized as a rank *per*version of scripture and an immoral *in*version of values.

To question that "sovereign maxim," one need only consider what strenuous efforts of wit, will, and imagination have been required to defend it. I have never heard, for example, of artists, astronomers, naturalists, poets, athletes, musicians, scholars, or even politicians coming together in high-priced institutes, therapy groups, lecture series, outreach programs, or clinics to get themselves psyched up with slogans, moralizing cliches, or the spiritual exercises of a careful dialectic, to give themselves what is called a "wealth mindset."

Nor do those ancient disciplines lean upon lawyers, those managers of managers, to prove to the world that they are not cheating. Those who have something to give to humanity revel in their work, and do not have to rationalize, advertise, or evangelize to make themselves feel good about what they are doing.

In my latest class, a graduating honors student in business management wrote an interesting paper, full of healthy introspection. "Many times I wonder if my desires are too self-centered," wrote the student. "Basically, my desire to succeed in business is to get personal gain, not necessarily to serve other people. Maybe I am pessimistic, but I feel that most businessmen first seek personal gratification. As a business major, I wonder about the ethics of business—'charge as much as possible for a product which was made by someone else who was paid as little as possible. You live on the difference.' As a business manager, will I be living on someone's industry and not my own? Will I be contributing to society, or will I receive something for nothing? These are difficult questions for me."

These questions have been made more difficult by the rhetoric of our times. Our present society, like the materialistic societies of the past, is full of people who teach that "gain is godliness." But don't blame the College of Commerce! The Sophists, those shrewd businessmen and showmen, started that game 2,500 years ago, and you can't blame others for wanting to get in on something so profitable. The learned doctors and masters have always known which side their bread was buttered on, and taken their place in the line. And be not alarmed that management is running the show—they always have.

Most of our youth come to our schools of management only because they believe that this charade will help them get ahead in the world. And in the last few years, things have gotten out of hand. The economy, once the most important thing in our materialistic lives, has become the *only* thing. We have been swept up in a total dedication to "the Economy" which, like a massive mudslide, is rapidly engulfing and suffocating everything.

Who can halt this slide, correct this course, stop this shift? Only the enlightened leader.

SECTION III

Leaders and Followers

GREAT LEADERS are also great followers. Being both a leader and a follower is mandatory in the 21st century.

John Naisbitt and *Patricia Aburdene* believe that "the effective leader wins commitment by setting an example of excellence: being ethical, open, empowering, and inspiring." Effective leaders, according to *Eric Stephan* and *R. Wayne Pace*, "treat others as friends, are positive, attract followers, empower them, and renew themselves." The world needs "selfless leadership at every level of organization."

J. Oliver Crom notes that principles of leadership age well "because the basic principles and skills don't change. . . Leadership skills are not, and never were, a management monopoly. Nor are they gender exclusive." Today's business slogan should be "Every employee a leader."

Leaders let their followers know that they are one of them. *Daniel I. Kaplan* reminds us that "every moment of the day, the leader sends out messages that set the tone and the level of excellence of the enterprise." *Kenneth Blanchard* helps us understand that "successful leaders adapt their leadership style to the needs of the situation." They also "serve their people, not be served by them."

Leaders especially need to be followers in a team environment. *Jeanne M. Wilson* and *Richard S. Wellins* write that "moving to a team-based culture isn't so difficult if leaders learn new tactical and strategic skills." Above all, leaders need to admit and learn from mistakes. *John H. Zenger* notes that "executives at every level need five new skills to manage people effectively in a full-scale team environment."

Ann Howard writes that "the traditional functions of leaders are diminishing. As employees take more responsibility, leaders must learn new roles"—especially high involvement. Another way of looking at high-involvement leadership is stewardship. **Peter Block** alerts us that stewardship is "an entryway into exploring change and creating strategies to change." It is "the choice to be deeply accountable for the outcomes of an institution without acting to control others."

Ken Melrose advises that "the servant-leader model is not easy to embrace, but it permits the greatest number of people to experience the greatest good. . . . Servant leaders serve people not to get more out of them, but because they want to boost people's self-worth and dignity."

For **Peter F. Drucker** leaders are, above all, doers. They show results. Moreover, they have followers who "do the right thing," "are highly visible," and concentrate on "one thing they can do with excellence to make a difference."

Paul Hersey notes that "today's leaders need to develop four qualities to empower people: vision, a new deal, owned readiness, and paying dues." He continues, "In new organizations, new leaders and followers will incur costs up front, but they will realize big returns down the road."

Kevin Cashman and **Sidney Reisberg** see "self-knowledge to be the most direct route" to leadership. True leaders know themselves. As well as knowing themselves, leaders, according to **Ira Chaleff**, must know "a lot about followers." He adds, "Leadership and followership are two sides of the same process. One can't exist without the other. You can lead in many ways, and you can follow in many ways."

CHAPTER 26

New Leadership

by John Naisbitt and Patricia Aburdene, leading trend forecasters and Presidents of Megatrends, Limited

THE NEW LEADERS recruit, motivate, manage, and lead in better ways.

Male or female, the effective leader wins commitment by setting an example of excellence: being ethical, open, empowering, and inspiring.

The simplest, most straightforward way to earn loyalty is through honest, ethical management. A Lou Harris poll sponsored by Steelcase, Inc. asked office workers what they most valued at work. The answer: "Management that is honest, upright, and ethical" in its dealings with employees and the community. It was considered "very important" by 81 percent of those polled, but only 41 percent said it was "very true" of their employer.

It is your "management" that counts toward your being a good manager. It is you who matters as a leader. You are always leading by example. People want to know what is going on in their company. In the same Steelcase poll, 76 percent rated "free exchange of information among employees and departments" very important; only 35 percent said it described their office.

• ***Training and retraining people.*** Today we are replacing the manager as order-giver with the manager as teacher, facilitator, and coach. The order-giver has all the answers and tells everyone what to do; the facilitator knows how to draw the answers out of those who know them best—the people doing the job. The leader as facilitator asks questions, guides a group to consensus, uses information to demonstrate the need for action.

Terry Armstrong, an associate management professor at the University of West Florida, has been studying the character traits of successful CEOs, presumably leaders whom managers would seek to emulate. "They are more like coaches than quarterbacks," says Armstrong. "They are really very conscious about their organization winning and not necessarily their own success."

The primary challenge of leadership in the next century is to encourage the new, better-educated worker to be more entrepreneurial, self-managing, and oriented toward lifelong meaning. The company most committed to the task of lifelong learning is arguably Motorola, Inc., which has undertaken the immense task of training all its 99,000 employees—one third each year. "Just as when you buy a piece of capital equipment you put aside money to maintain that equipment, we require that 1.5 percent of payroll be put aside to maintain the competency level of the employees," says Bill Wiggenhorn, head of Motorola's training. Over the course of seven to ten years, every Motorola employee will be retrained.

• *Motivating people.* Any successful leader will tell you it is a lot easier to hire people who are already motivated. "Leaders who believe they must continuously scurry about motivating everyone are destined to a fatiguing, ulcerating career," says Robert Wright, a professor of organization theory at California's Pepperdine University.

"I don't look for either youth or experience," says J. William Grimes, head of ESPN, the all-sports cable network. "I want intelligence and, primarily, motivation. I want people who are very eager to accomplish a task, who can't wait to get something done and will always look to do it in new ways."

A good product or a brilliant founder alone does not make a company, says Michael Cooper, president of the Hay Group's Research for Management. Success comes when leaders have "managed their people in ways that keep their involvement and sense of partnership high."

Keeping people excited is the leader's job. In this regard, small business has a great competitive advantage over large companies. People in smaller companies are able to maintain a more positive attitude, says Cooper. "If I were a *Fortune* 500 CEO, I'd be worried."

• *Recruiting people.* To attract and keep good people, flexibility must become the watchword of leadership. "We survey all of our employees, and there's a message that comes in loud and clear," says Mike Shore, a spokesman for IBM. "And that's flexibility."

Corporations will have to recruit the "undiscovered" sources of people, like the estimated 3.3 million people who have taken early retirement, those handicapped people who are now unemployed, and new immigrants who will inevitably enter the United States when labor shortages get so bad that Congress will be required to liberalize immigration quotas, perhaps even child labor laws. What's so terrible about a 14-year-old working limited hours after school?

• *Offering people flexible work arrangements.* But the largest potential source of all is the estimated 14 million nonworking women caring for their families at home. The only chance of coaxing millions of these women back into the work force is company-subsidized day care and flexible work arrangements in the whole range of professional, technical, clerical, manufacturing jobs—part-time, job-sharing, contract work, and home-work arrangements. That is why flexibility should become the motto for personnel policies in the next century. Such arrangements will also help your company keep or recruit women—already in the work force or expected to enter—and retirees.

Day care. The majority of women with children work outside the home. More than 75 percent of working women are in prime child-bearing years, and most women either have children already or will have them at some point in their career lives. In the next century day care will become a common employee benefit.

Eldercare. If business and society can master the challenge of day care, we will be one step closer to confronting the next great care-giving task of the next century—eldercare. Eldercare will affect a wider segment of employees than child care, from CEOs to secretaries, according to "Employers and Eldercare: A New Benefit Coming of Age," a report by the Bureau of National Affairs, a private research group in Washington, D.C. Almost one-third of all working adults are responsible for providing some care for an elderly person. Three quarters of those who care for the elderly in a family are women.

As the parents of the baby boom generation require increased help, more pioneering companies will build on the precedent of day care and begin offering partial reimbursement for eldercare costs as part of the overall trend toward cafeteria plans in which employees select from a menu of different benefits according to their needs.

"We're trying to deal with the whole concept of the balance between work and family life," says Mike Shore of IBM, which grants unpaid leave with benefits of up to three years to give people time to care for children or sick relatives or pursue "once-in-a-lifetime" personal opportunities.

Creative leave policies. The opportunities of the information age, the demands of an established career, or the simple need to make money are luring women back into the work force almost immediately after giving birth. In the labor market of the next century creative leave policies will help employers keep seasoned employees, who would otherwise have to be replaced from a dwindling labor supply.

Full-time/part-time. Retirees and mothers, the two untapped groups where new workers of the next century will be found, are known to favor part-time employment. Part-timers represent 17.4 percent of the U.S. work force, according to the National Planning Association. Labor shortages will actually increase productivity, by forcing corporations to deploy existing labor in more creative, efficient ways.

Job-sharing programs are offered by about 16 percent of U.S. companies, including Quaker Oats and Levi Strauss, according to the American Society for Personnel Administration. These programs will increase, along with other part-time arrangements, as employers are compelled to restructure empty, full-time positions into part-time jobs. In addition, the reverse, making part-timers permanent, is another effective approach.

FROM MANAGEMENT TO LEADERSHIP

The dominant principle of organization has shifted, from management in order to control an enterprise to leadership in order to bring out the best in people and to respond quickly to change.

This is not the "leadership" individuals and groups so often call for when they really want a father figure to take care of all their problems. It is a democratic yet demanding leadership that respects people and encourages self-management, autonomous teams, and entrepreneurial units.

There is a big difference between management and leadership. Leaders and managers differ in orientation, mission, assumptions, behaviors, organizational environments, and ultimately results. Leadership is the process of moving people in some direction mostly through "noncoercive means," says John P. Kotter of the Harvard Business School, who is author of *The Leadership Factor*.

"We have a lot of managers—short-term, control-oriented, report-oriented," says Russell E. Palmer, dean of the University of Pennsylvania's Wharton School of Business. "Leaders think longer term, grasp the relationship of larger realities, think in terms of renewal, have political skills, cause change, affirm values, achieve unity."

Leaders recognize that while capital and technology are important resources, people make or break a company. To harness their power, leaders inspire commitment and empower people by sharing authority. Responding to labor shortages with flexibility, they enable their firms to attract, reward, and motivate the best people. But effective leadership must also monitor the external environment, tracking trends, markets, technological change, and product cycles in an increasingly global era.

The major themes of the 21st century—technological change, compressed product cycles, and global competition—require a leader to scan the global environment and organize the internal tasks, while remaining market-sensitive.

The challenge for individual managers in the next century is to evolve their own personal leadership styles to bring out the best in people.

CHAPTER 27

Five Keys to Effective Leadership

by Eric Stephan and R. Wayne Pace, Professors at the Marriott School of Management, Brigham Young University

EFFECTIVE EXECUTIVES use five simple yet powerful leadership keys, and the first key is to treat others as friends.

1. Treat others as friends. Leadership as the creation of friends turns ordinary definitions of leadership on their heads. Contrast the meaning of friend with the popular meaning of leader. Friends have an abiding, mature love for one another. They sacrifice for one another; they do for one another what each would do for the other. One is not superior nor the other subordinate; one is not the leader while the other follows; they are true and authentic equals in each other's sight. Friends are generous and hospitable, devoted and genial, happy to be in the presence of each other. They are willing to place the needs of the other ahead of their own. They are willing to accept the burdens of others.

In one of our leadership seminars, an executive asked, "But how do you treat someone as a friend?" We answered the question by asking everyone to close their eyes and imagine a long hallway. "Now imagine that one of your good friends has been away on a trip for two weeks. Imagine that your friend has just come into view. See yourself and your friend walking toward each other and stopping next to each other. Watch what you do and say."

We then asked people to explain what they said and did when they met their friends in the hallway. "I smiled and talked enthusiastically about where she had been and what she had been doing," said one woman. "We laughed and hugged," said another. "I asked if he needed any help and suggested that he come to dinner so we could talk longer," said a man.

The message is clear: treat others as you treat your best friends. Say hello. Smile. Ask questions that express your interest in them. Ask what they are doing. Express appreciation for them. Be of service. Encourage them. And don't be afraid to walk, work, eat, and dream together.

Being a friend is the simpler, easier, more effective way to achieve leadership. Being a friend opens the door to exciting, moving, powerful leadership, without the use of complex strategies for winning and influencing people.

2. Create a positive force. Good leaders are rarely negative and never dull. They create a feeling that things are moving in a positive way. They demonstrate by their walk and talk that they are filled with quiet confidence and great strength. They unleash the total power of their personalities.

When leaders fail to create a strong force, lethargy sets in among followers, as people follow the path of least resistance, slow down, and quickly become disenchanted. Being positive and encouraging when things are not going well is difficult. Effective leaders, however, have no other choice.

Great leaders produce a dynamic inner force that influences followers to act. Their energetic, incisive leadership style is characterized by three attributes:

• *Strong commitment to the task at hand.* All leaders commit themselves to a cause, but that is not enough. Effective leaders commit themselves to a purpose beyond everyday activities; great causes become the focus of their constant devotion.

We might ask ourselves, "Am I going to allow daily activities to govern my life, or am I going to live my life according to noble principles?" Unless we consciously decide to do more than engage in routines, our lives will become shallow.

• *Compassion for the people we lead.* A leader's boldness and directness in leading people are tempered by his or her genuine concern for their feelings and needs.

It is easy to be critical and judgmental. We fail to show compassion when we use tactless and offensive ways of saying things. Such verbal abuse must be guarded against every hour of the day if we hope to lead with compassion.

Our mouths get us into more trouble than any other part of us. When we are tired or in a hurry, we say things that threaten and undermine our relationships with others. Compassionate leaders are concerned not only with the ways in which they communicate, but also with the personal and physical needs of their followers. Adequate food, clothing, shelter, transportation, or health care are often the unexpressed but real needs of our friends and co-workers.

- *Cheerful encouragement of those we lead.* One simple way to encourage others is to recognize their talent and potential. We can lead in the same manner, giving encouragement and lifting our associates with words and actions that suggest they have unlimited potential.

3. Invite others to follow. We all like to follow leaders who have made achievements we would like to make. If there are no followers, there is no leader. A leader may want to lead and even be appointed to lead, but the ability to attract followers initially determines whether the leader will be successful.

If we want to attract followers, we must inspire them by creating an attractive vision of what can be achieved and then motivate them by continually and vividly showing that vision. The leader confidently invites others to unite in achieving the vision.

As leaders, we are responsible for our followers, and unless we know where we are going, we will not get there nor will our followers. Goals help us implement our vision. Goals are statements of what needs to be done to achieve the vision. One way to create a goal is to identify a concern that is bothersome or uncomfortable. Next, turn your concern into a goal by deciding with your people what each individual can do to help achieve the goal.

You might say to yourself, "Right now, my main concern with the company is that we are not providing adequate customer service." Decide with others how to overcome your concern. Set a goal that will eliminate the concern and lead the company to achieve the vision. The goal might read: "Each employee will perform one or more acts of customer service each day."

Next, invite as many people as possible to be involved in achieving the goal. Patiently speak of the vision and goal until everyone understands. Ask questions to confirm their understanding and listen to questions to confirm your own understanding. If our goals, dreams, and visions are attractive to people, they will want to join in and reap the rewards.

4. Empower followers to act. Lofty goals without ways to achieve them are not useful. Involve people in setting goals and then instruct them how to achieve the goals. First, delegate activities that lead to the accomplishment of the goals. Give each person a specific assignment. Discuss the best ways to do the assignment so that it will most likely be completed. Ask each individual to describe what should be done and when.

Second, invite all persons, individually, to begin. Express your appreciation for their involvement and willingness to accept the assignment. Indicate how soon the assignment needs to be completed and have them give you a progress report. Encourage them to take full responsibility for seeing that the assignment is completed on time.

When disapproval needs to be expressed, do it with charity, clarity, and specificity. Focus on aspects of the assignment that were not completed rather than on the person.

Effective leaders do not delegate just tasks. Sometimes it is more encouraging and exciting for an individual to research an idea and write a report. If the person looks bored, we can ask the person to explore a new approach and to make a recommendation.

Leaders need to keep people moving and contributing. Once followers feel a lack of forward motion, they quickly become bored and less productive. Leaders cannot afford to wait around until followers energize themselves. They must use every means possible to keep followers involved and on fire.

5. Strengthen yourself. Before we can lead others effectively, we must strengthen ourselves. To lead others tirelessly, patiently, and effectively, through periods of disappointment and fatigue, requires that we master the principles of personal regeneration and self-renewal. It's hard to imagine a great leader who is sad, gloomy, fatigued, depressed, disheveled, and overburdened—rushing thither and yon, helter-skelter, trying to accomplish twenty-one things at once. Leaders should not only get appropriate exercise, rest, and nutrition, but also develop a balanced pattern of living. Hypertense people and workaholics tend to have more health and heart problems.

Though a leader's life may be dedicated to serving and leading people, great leaders take time to relax with friends, eat nourishing food, or sleep after a day of work. They observe the laws of health, find joy in attending to the needs of others, resist the appearance of busyness, and concentrate on one thing at a time to renew their inner strength.

MEETING THE CHALLENGE

Whenever we influence others to move toward a goal, we are acting as leaders. Leadership is not necessarily a function of a specific work position, family role or service assignment. It is a way of getting work done and handling responsibilities. Indeed, leadership may even be considered a way of life.

Our challenge is to continue to assimilate into our own lives the attributes and activities that characterize great leaders. Today, the world is desperately in need of selfless leadership at every level of organization. Exemplary leadership in business, industry, and government is sought after and generously rewarded. Families need to be unified and people strengthened against unscrupulous enticements.

We challenge you to add to your present leadership abilities, following the five keys to leadership success.

CHAPTER 28

Principles of Leadership

by J. Oliver Crom, President and CEO of Dale Carnegie & Associates, Inc., specialists in developing business and personal relations skills

DALE CARNEGIE and his principles of leadership are aging well because the basic principles and skills don't change.

As we race into the battle for business in the new decade and the new century, *leadership* is one of the busiest buzzwords. It's as if leadership skills were a revolutionary new discovery.

New they are not. More than seventy-five years ago, Dale Carnegie, our company founder, recognized the seeds of leadership when he observed that it "usually gravitates to the man (business women were in short supply at the time) who can get up and say what he thinks." To that ability to communicate, he linked the practice of good human relations in the leadership training he pioneered.

LEADERSHIP AND PRODUCTIVITY

Leadership has become the talk of the business world today for several clear reasons:

• *Powerful market factors, such as globalization, have propelled it into new prominence.* Unrelenting international competition has focused attention on the direct relationship between good leadership and greater productivity. Further, the explosion of information and rapid development and widespread acceptance of technology have put added responsibility on sustained leadership skills.

• *Creative managers and executives are taking a new look at their most important asset—their people.* They are seeing a wealth of untapped potential, just waiting to be brought out and put to positive purpose. They are realizing the dollar-and-cents value of providing employees, highly skilled in some areas but lacking in leadership skills, the opportunity to develop them.

• *Business is confronting the need to fill gaps in academic training, gaps that reach as high as the graduate level.* It is now common to find men and women with advanced degrees enrolled in leadership classes—some to learn better human relations, others to develop the ability to listen and communicate effectively. Skills basic to good leadership. Skills frequently neglected or overlooked on campus.

• *Demand for leadership training is coming from ambitious, upwardly mobile young men and women, already expert in their fields but committed to the goal of becoming even better.*

These and other dynamic forces are making leadership training an exciting and exhilarating experience for those who offer it and those who take it. Enrollments in leadership training outside the U.S. are increasing at an even faster rate than record-setting enrollments within the U.S.

LEADERS ARE MADE

Until recently, leadership was often regarded as an inherited talent or a natural accompaniment of unbridled wealth and position. Leadership development has moved into a new and vigorous stage of enlightenment and sophistication. Today we know that good leaders are made, seldom born, seldom produced by wealth and position alone.

By sending thousands of employees each year to leadership training, companies are supporting the idea that leaders can be and are being made, every day. While participants attain varying degrees of leadership excellence, virtually all experience value, including those few who are hesitant or skeptical at first.

Leadership skills are not, and never were, a management monopoly. Nor are they gender exclusive. For maximum profitability and a healthy corporate culture, every employee should be familiar with and practice sound leadership skills. "Every employee a leader" might well be today's business slogan.

DEFINING AND MAKING LEADERS

Since leadership has become so attractive to the business and academic worlds, countless definitions—some more amorphous than others—have been spun out and held up for examination. I offer the following clear-cut definition of leadership:

A leader is a confident, positive person with vision and high ethical values, with the skills for communicating ideas and the ability to motivate and relate well to others.

Some people, both in and out of business, may not readily embrace our concept of trained leadership or the idea of leadership at every level, predicting only chaos and confusion as a result.

But we constantly see examples of people who, through training, develop leadership skills far beyond their expectations. One man recently reported that what he'd learned in our course in communication and human relations helped him turn his business around. His newly acquired leadership skills made the dramatic difference.

Our leadership training concentrates on four stages of development:

* *Overcoming fear.* Fear of speaking up, of being wrong, of failure, of new ideas and new ways of doing things—all are fears that prevent people from growing.

* *Building self-confidence.* As self-confidence replaces fear, people accept greater challenges and experience new successes. These, in turn, inspire more self-confidence.

* *Relating to others.* People share similar feelings and experiences. Each co-worker has a point of view to be considered as they interact.

* *Communicating effectively.* Communication is a two-way process that involves empathic listening as well as expressing ideas well.

MOST IMPORTANT SKILLS

What, you may ask, is the most important leadership skill? Dale Carnegie probably—and we certainly—would give prime importance to the ability to achieve results through people.

In his best-seller, *How to Win Friends and Influence People*, Dale Carnegie wrote: "Dealing with people is probably the biggest problem you face, especially if you are in business."

With this thought in mind, he devoted his entire career to helping would-be leaders develop *people skills*. Drawing on his remarkable insights and study of human needs and human potential, he formulated succinct and memorable guidelines or principles that may be even more viable and potent in today's complex world than when he first presented them.

For example, he wrote about the three Cs: "Don't criticize, condemn, or complain." This principle works wonders superior-to-subordinate, colleague-to-colleague, people-to-people.

FACING UP TO FAULTS

Of course, situations arise that demand intervention and correction. A good leader employs a constructive approach that neither offends nor arouses resentment.

Dale Carnegie advised: "Make the fault seem easy to correct. Praise the slightest improvement." Praise, honest and sincere, will encourage a person to keep improving. "In our interpersonal relations we should never forget," Dale Carnegie said, "that all our associates are human beings and hunger for appreciation."

The practice of taking time to notice and praise encourages the recipient to seek more responsibility, to become more productive, more valuable to the company. And such praise enhances the spirit of the work environment.

In a sampling of people skills, one common factor stands out—attitude. How important is attitude? One of today's most prominent business leaders and authors credits our training with "having a profound influence on my thinking." He wouldn't, in his words, have written his current bestseller "if it weren't for Dale Carnegie."

Under what conditions are leadership skills acquired? Ideally, through practice and coaching by a well-trained instructor. Some may choose short, concentrated periods of training, but we believe that training sessions should be spaced over a number of weeks to provide opportunity between sessions for participants to apply their newly gained knowledge. That way, skills become second nature.

Although our training methods may change to meet new leadership needs brought on by the new decade and new century, we see no need to revise or tamper with the basic principles. They have proved their "right-ness" through the years.

CHAPTER 29

Leader as Model and Mentor

 by Daniel I. Kaplan, President of Hertz Equipment Rental Corporation and Executive Vice President of The Hertz Corporation

EVERY MOMENT of the day, the leader sends out messages that set the tone and the level of excellence of the enterprise.

Nothing a leader can do or say escapes notice. Every action and response, even a chance remark, gives out some signal that will be picked up by someone and passed on to others. From the leader's actions and responses to various situations, people form ideas of what is expected of them and what the leader expects of himself. This message either validates or undermines all other signals that the leader sends out because it tells people whether he or she is for real or for show.

My leadership style is proactive, but still very taxing on my time, energy, and patience. I call it "touching the iron." I learned this style not from any book, but from on-the-job training beginning in 1982 when I was assigned to lead the Hertz Equipment Rental Corporation, with the mission of turning it around from a poorly performing business into a thriving, profitable business.

My background was in purchasing. I had a reputation as a troubleshooter, but I knew next to nothing about the rental equipment business. This meant immersing myself in every detail of the company. This intense style has worked for me and the company, as today we are the industry leader. But I have refined and altered my style as I have achieved greater mastery over the strategy and details of the business.

BUILDING TRUST

The big challenge from the start was building trust. When a new leader is brought in to turn around a troubled company, people want to know whether the newcomer is committed and will stay for the long haul. Never underestimate people's intelligence. If you are just there for show, everybody will sense it, and the response will be cynicism and indifference. Since I was asking our people to work hard and make sacrifices to help turn the company around, there was no room for what I call "corner-office thinking." I went out and "touched the iron," putting in long hours, visiting every location, and then going around the circuit again, doubling back when there was need. I made myself visible to show our employees that I was on the front lines with them, that I wouldn't ask them to do more than I was willing to do.

I looked for chances to show my personal commitment. In the South, there are often sudden downpours that can dampen your ardor to work around a lot of wet, muddy bulldozers and backhoes. You want to linger under the eaves of the shop. But I made it a practice to march out there, putting my clothing at risk, as though there was nothing but blue sky and dry ground. I was driving home a point: *I valued the business and our people more than my clothing.* In short, I was committed.

I make it a practice to shake hands with everyone—managers, secretaries, salespeople, and shop mechanics—even if their hands are greasy. I want that person to know that I recognize his or her personal contribution to the company.

Talking with people and asking a few questions about what they are doing, I hope to show a genuine interest in them and their work. This also gives me valuable new ideas, and when some useful innovation has results that are applicable elsewhere, I make sure that person gets public recognition for his or her contribution.

Admittedly, the early years were tough for me as I struggled to turn the company around and build a new corporate culture. I often felt as though I were carrying the whole load on my shoulders, a feeling that fortunately lightened as the many reforms we launched finally began to yield real success and profits. My overall business strategy was a simple one that I identify as "hitting 1,000 singles," which meant that the way to win games consistently is not to depend on slamming home runs, but to keep the players moving around the bases by hitting well-placed singles. The basic policy is to make continuous improvement through small incremental gains, and learn how to measure every gain. For me, consistency is the name of the game.

I agree wholeheartedly with Peter F. Drucker when he says that leadership "is not based on being clever; it is based primarily on being consistent." Trust comes about when people become convinced that the leader means what he or she says because every statement is backed by the record of performance.

My experience suggests that *trust lies at the heart of all genuine leadership, and consistency is the path that gets you there.*

Setting standards and making them stick means that the leader has to obey them just like everyone else. On the workshop floor, everybody must wear hard hats and safety glasses—and so must I. Not to do so would send out a message either that some rules aren't important or that I am somehow above them. We have gasoline pumps out in the yard for fueling our fleet. When I drive into one of our locations after a long trip and see the tank of my car is nearly empty, I am tempted to fill up at one of these handy pumps. But I never do. If I were seen filling up the tank of my car at the company pump, that would send the wrong signal. If the president of the company crosses over the line, even once, why shouldn't Joe or Mary or anybody else? The invariable rule: one standard for everybody.

When you witness an abuse, you can't turn a blind eye to it, because that, too, shakes your credibility as a leader and devalues ethical standards.

RULES OF MENTORING

I never lose a chance to play the role of mentor, Dutch uncle, cheerleader, and salesman for the corporate culture. I feel that I can't turn away or be aloof. I get involved in five ways.

1. I level with people about company problems, changes, hopes, fears, and prospects and how all this affects them. At our regional meetings, I talk informally for 15 to 30 minutes to bring people up to date on what is going on in the company.

2. When I visit the branches, I have informal sessions with the salespeople, the sales coordinator, and the manager and share certain confidential information with them. My purpose is to draw them into my confidence by treating them as mature, responsible people who have a voice in the decisions we make as a firm. I address each person by his or her first name and try to draw him or her into the discussion.

3. I search for the hot button—the consuming interest, idea, or dream with meaning—for each manager. Sometimes the hot button is hard to locate, but I look for the breakthrough that will help us to understand one another better. A manager on the West Coast eluded me until we had lunch together. He suggested we take the leftover pizza back to the fellows in the shop. I called over the waitress and ordered three large pizzas to go. The man's face lit up. The $20 worth of pizzas made a vital connection with him.

4. I always show up for an appointment unless I am too ill to get out of bed. I am always aware that although it is just another meeting for me, it may be for the employee the most important one he or she will have this year—because it is with the president of the company. On trips to visit European subsidiaries, I often have to fly all night, take a shower, and show up at the branch early in the morning looking bright and fresh, no matter how I feel. People have been waiting for me; they expect my full attention and interest. But deep down, they know that I flew all night and will be on the job all day. You don't talk about it; you don't look for sympathy; your actions speak for you.

5. *I believe in moderation in everything.* If I'm having a late dinner with other company people, I may be dead tired and out of sorts and want a second drink, but I don't order it. I insist on a strict separation between private and business entertaining. When I'm in the latter mode, I'm representing the company at all times. If I order a second drink, I give a wrong signal. Standards are a two-way street, and if I don't treat them that way, I can kiss them off—especially in view of the human tendency to follow the leader.

Being a leader and setting a standard is a job that requires effort and consistency. You have to live it, breathe it, sell it all the time. Does it ever get easier? Yes, as one gets more on top of one's job. It also becomes more rewarding. At least, that's my experience.

CHAPTER 30

Situational Leadership

by Kenneth Blanchard, Chairman of Blanchard
Training & Development

EFFECTIVE LEADERS adapt their style according to the development level
of the people they are managing.

In my first management job, I had an employee named Laurie who
was a problem for me. I never got the kind of productivity I should
have—particularly in the paperwork area of her job performance.

As soon as I realized there was a problem, I lavished my attention
on Laurie. I devoted more time to her than to all my other employees
combined. It never worked, however—my style was ineffective at getting her to improve. When I finally left that job, she had not improved
in this area.

I thought I knew how to manage—at least I was getting good
results from other people and even from Laurie on other tasks. I have
since come to realize that the problem really wasn't her. It was me.

It would be nice if I could tell you that there is a single solution
to handling the Lauries of the world—that there is one best leadership
style. Regrettably, that's not the case.

Although there isn't a single style for handling every employee
you will ever manage, there is a practical, easy-to-understand
approach that can greatly help. I call it *Situational Leadership*.

NO ONE "BEST" LEADERSHIP STYLE

Successful leaders adapt their leadership style to the needs of the
situation. They recognize that there is no one best style. In *Situational
Leadership*, there are four leadership styles representing different combinations of directive and supportive leader behaviors from which to
choose for any given situation.

Directive behavior is defined as the extent to which a leader engages in one-way communication; spells out the employee's role, and tells the employee what to do, where to do it, when to do it, and how to do it; and then closely supervises performance. Three words can be used to define directive behavior: *structure, control,* and *supervise.*

Supportive behavior is defined as the extent to which a leader engages in two-way communication, listens, provides support and encouragement, facilitates interaction, and involves the employee in decision making. Three words can be used to define supportive behavior: *praise, listen,* and *facilitate.*

*1. **Directing**.* High directive/low supportive leader behavior is referred to as *Directing.* The leader tells the subordinate what, how, when, and where to do various tasks.

*2. **Coaching**.* High directive/high supportive behavior is referred to as *Coaching.* In this style the leader still provides a great deal of direction, but he or she also attempts to hear the employees' feelings about decisions as well as their ideas and suggestions.

*3. **Supporting**.* High supportive/low directive leader behavior is called *Supporting.* In this style the leader's role is to provide recognition and to actively listen and facilitate problem solving/decision making on the part of employees.

*4. **Delegating**.* Low supportive/low directive leader behavior is labeled *Delegating.* In this style employees are allowed greater autonomy because they have both the competence and confidence to do the task on their own.

WHEN TO USE EACH STYLE

The key to being a situational leader is knowing when to use each style. The right style is primarily a function of two variables: the degree of difficulty of the task and the developmental level of the person doing the task.

Developmental level is the degree of *competence* and *commitment* an employee has to perform a particular task without supervision. Competence is a function of knowledge or skills which can be gained from education, training, or experience. Commitment is a combination of confidence (self-assuredness) and motivation (interest and enthusiasm).

The amount of direction or support that a leader should provide depends on the development level of the employee for the task at hand. There are four development levels:

1. When beginning a new task where they have had little, if any, prior knowledge or experience, most individuals are enthusiastic and ready to learn, but at a low development level for the task. Such a staff member can be led by a *Directing* style. You need to let him or her know what to expect and how to do the task at hand.

2. As the development level of an employee increases, his or her competence and commitment fluctuate. When people begin to learn a task, they find it is either more difficult to learn to do it than they thought it was going to be or less interesting. Thus, they get disillusioned, which decreases their commitment. People who are disillusioned need *Coaching*—high direction to continue to build skills, as well as high support to address their low commitment.

3. As competence continues to improve, most individuals then go through a self-doubt stage where they question whether they can perform the task on their own. Their boss says they're competent but they're not so sure. These alternating feelings of competence and self-doubt are indicative of a higher level of development. Here a *Supporting* style is most appropriate. The person needs to be listened to and encouraged, but they don't need much direction since they have demonstrated competence to do the task.

4. Finally, in the highest level of development, employees usually demonstrate high levels of competence and commitment. The corresponding leadership style to use is *Delegating*—giving the employee increased autonomy for doing the job they've demonstrated both competence and commitment in doing.

A HIRING SITUATION

When hiring a new manager, the first thing you have to decide is whether you need to hire a "winner" or a "potential winner." Winners are people who have demonstrated that they can do the exact job you need done. They are hard to find, and they cost money—but they are easy to supervise. All they need to know is what the goals are. Potential winners are people who have promise but have not demonstrated that they can do the specific job you need done. They are "cheaper," but they require time and training to develop. When you interview applicants, find out as much about them as you can. As they review their backgrounds, probe with questions along the way to learn why they have done what they have in life and to gain a sense of the quality of people you are dealing with.

Next, share with them the key responsibilities of the job. Be as detailed as you possibly can, including what some of your main concerns and expectations are.

Now, invite people to write down a strategy they would follow if they got the job. That is, what would they do first, followed by what they might do the next three, six, and nine months. Give them an hour to prepare a statement and then ask them to present it. This will give you a sense of their ability to think and plan and communicate their ideas as well as their level of initiative, organization, and creativity.

Next, ask them to indicate in each of their major performance areas what kind of supervision they would need from you—*directing, coaching, supporting,* or *delegating.* Suggest that the direction they need will depend on their sense (and your sense) of their competency in their areas of responsibility, and that the support and involvement you provide will depend on their confidence (and your confidence) in what they are being asked to do. Share your perceptions and come to some agreement on the kind of supervision they would need.

In using this approach, you are essentially contracting for a leadership style with the person before they have even been hired. You will make smarter hiring decisions and quickly find out whether this person is a winner who you will support in delegated responsibilities or if he or she is a potential winner who will require more directing and coaching from you.

There are still people out there who think there is only one best way of leading people. Research and practice indicate, however, that this is not the case. Laurie needed (and deserved) more than the one style of leadership I provided. Your employees do, too!

SERVANT LEADERSHIP

Another style of leadership that can be used to adapt to the needs of the situation is servant leadership. When I first began to teach and train managers some twenty-five years ago, I met Bob Greenleaf, who was just retiring as a top AT&T executive. Bob talked about *servant leadership*—the concept that effective leaders and managers needed to serve their people, not be served by them. It was entirely new thinking then, and in many ways, Bob is considered the father of that term.

Today it is much easier for people to see the importance of servant leadership. Leaders have two basic roles in business: one of *vision* and the other of *implementation.*

In the visionary role, leaders define direction. They communicate mission, values, and beliefs; they communicate what the organization stands for and how shared values encompass the individual values of members.

I once asked Max DePree, who wrote the fabulous book *Leadership Is an Art,* what he felt was the most important role of a leader. He compared the role to that of a third-grade teacher who keeps repeating the basics. "When it comes to vision and values, you have to say it over and over again until people get it right."

In the implementation role, leaders help people implement their goals, skills, and activities. The traditional way of managing people is to direct, control, and supervise their activities and to play the role of judge, critic, and evaluator. Today when people see you as a judge and critic, they spend most of their time trying to please you rather than to accomplish goals and move in the direction of the desired vision.

"Boss watching" becomes a popular sport and people get promoted on their upward influencing skills. All people try to do is protect themselves rather than help move the organization in its desired direction.

The servant leader feels that once the direction is clear, his or her role is to help people achieve their goals. The servant leader seeks to help people win through teaching and coaching so that they can do their best. Servant leaders listen to their people, praise them, support them, and redirect them when they deviate from goals.

Servant leaders constantly try to find out what their people need to be successful. They are interested in making a difference in the lives of their people and in impacting the organization.

They do whatever is necessary to help people win. If the person is in a position that doesn't match his or her skills, they, in a kind way, redirect the person's efforts where his or her talents may be better used.

What do managers need to become servant leaders? The biggest thing they need is to get their egos out of the way. Managers who have themselves as the center of the universe and think everything needs to rotate around them are really covering up "not okay" feelings about themselves. When you don't feel good about yourself, you have two choices: either hide and hope nobody notices you, or overcompensate and try to control your environment. Such people who need to control their environment are acting as if inside they are scared little kids.

Servant leadership is easy for people with high self-esteem. Such people have no problem giving credit to others, listening to other people for ideas, or building other people up. They don't think that building other people up is threatening in any way. They buy into the old Eastern philosophy of an effective leader: *When the job is done the people say they have done it themselves.*

To me, servant leadership is a good way to describe the coaching role that managers are expected to play today to help their people win. Judging and evaluating people erodes their self-esteem; servant leadership builds self-esteem and encourages individual growth while obtaining the organization's objectives.

Servant leadership is a wonderful symbol of what management must be to be successful.

CHAPTER 31

Leading Teams

by Jeanne M. Wilson, Project
Manager, and Richard S. Wellins,
Senior Vice President, Development
Dimensions International

MOVING TO a team-based culture isn't so difficult if leaders learn the new skills.

Many leaders today feel like novice trapeze artists: Their organizations are moving to teams, and they're being asked to leap from the comfort and safety of one platform (the traditional culture) to another (self-directed teams). In the process, they must let go of their old autocratic style and grasp a more empowering approach.

Unfortunately, rather than being an exhilarating experience, this leap causes much anxiety and heartburn. Why? Because leaders often don't know what to do, and others don't know how to help.

FIVE NEW REALITIES

Our experience is that the fear and frustration experienced by teams increase in direct proportion to misinformation circulating about the changing role of leaders. Obviously, then, we need to expose the myths and sort out fact from fancy. We see five new realities:

1. Empowered teams need good leaders. Teams need more coaching, guidance, and attention in their early stages than the same individual contributors would need in a traditional structure. Teams need to get this help from their leaders. If we arbitrarily strip out layers of supervision and support, we'll almost certainly wind up with floundering teams.

In the move toward empowered teams, many leaders' routine or reactive tasks are eliminated or transferred to the team. In most successful cases, leaders are left with reshaped but still substantial roles.

Usually these new roles lean more toward proactive tasks that add significant value to the organization and its customers.

2. Leaders gain power in the transition to teams. Power need not be a zero-sum proposition. Power and influence are expandable resources. It doesn't necessarily follow that the more power team members have, the less their leader has. In fact, the more power and influence a leader has, the better off the teams will be. Traditionally, leaders exert their power internally by controlling subordinates. With the move to teams, though, most of that power needs to be exercised externally to influence support departments, suppliers, and others. A leader's real power comes from the ability to enable process improvements, attract resources, remove barriers, make things happen outside the team, and help team members realize their full potential.

3. Most leaders are capable of making the transition successfully. As is the case with MASH units, organizations must focus their immediate development efforts on the 60 percent who will live or die, depending on the help they receive. Most current leaders will succeed in the new role once they get "medical attention."

4. New leaders must be direct. Successful team leaders loosen the reins; they don't drop them. In a team situation, the leader's role moves from giving directions (telling people what to do or issuing orders) to providing direction (creating a vision of shared goals). Once everyone is committed to a common vision, the leader no longer has to sweat the small stuff. In this scenario, everyone wins.

5. Leaders need to relax—it's okay to make mistakes. To ease the transition, leaders must relinquish two beliefs:

• *When you don't know, don't ask.* It's virtually impossible for leaders to understand everything they need to know about leading teams before making the transition. It will save considerable time and frustration if leaders consult trainers, facilitators, other team leaders, and even their bosses.

• *Don't look vulnerable (weak).* Almost all leaders feel vulnerable sometimes, so it takes significant energy to maintain a facade to the contrary. Why not just admit that the transition is a challenge and go on from there? Revealing your personal feelings to team members helps to build trust and improve relationships.

Admitting and learning from mistakes will earn leaders the respect of team members faster than any other behavior. This is hard for managers to believe—especially those who've spent years trying to hide, deny, or blame others for mistakes.

NEW SKILLS AND MOTIVATIONS

Once leaders have discarded the myths and embraced the new realities, they still find that becoming a high-involvement leader is a whole new game. And playing a new game means mastering a new set of skills and motivations.

These new skills fall into two categories: (1) tactical skills that must be mastered by participative leaders; and (2) strategic skills essential for leading in high-involvement, team-based organizations.

1. Tactical Skills. Tactical skills are the fundamentals of day-to-day leadership needed in high-involvement organizations. Tactical skills include the following:

• *Communication.* Effective communication, both oral and written, remains a key leadership responsibility. Although today's leaders need not be first-class orators or write elegant prose, they must communicate information and ideas clearly and effectively.

• *Managing the performance of others.* Effective leadership involves knowing how to manage individual and team performance. Leaders need to work regularly with team members to set performance goals and boundaries, evaluate performance, and provide feedback.

• *Analysis and judgment.* Analysis refers to a person's ability to gather relevant facts, organize the information in a meaningful fashion, and look for cause-and-effect relationships. A counterpart to analysis, judgment involves making logical and effective decisions based on the analysis conducted. Effective leaders exhibit sound analysis and judgment.

• *Coaching.* Successful team leaders are noted for their coaching ability. While coaching for performance improvement is crucial, most coaching should be proactive. This means that effective leaders coach before the fact, helping to ensure their team members' success.

• *Championing continuous improvement and empowerment.* Responsibility for service excellence and product quality has moved from the domain of management to the domain of all employees. A major role of team leaders is to foster an environment that respects and encourages people's ideas and contributions and to ensure that the team has the support and resources necessary to turn their ideas into action.

2. Strategic Skills. Strategic skills account for the differences between average, middle-of-the-road, participative managers with lingering autocratic tendencies and those who've mastered the ability to lead effectively in high-involvement, team-oriented environments. Strategic skills include the following:

• *Leading through vision and values.* A vision is an end goal that helps paint a picture of where we want to go, while values help define the means by which we hope to achieve the vision. Although the concept of leading through vision and values is difficult to grasp and even more difficult to practice, it is essential to the success of team-based organizations.

• *Building trust.* While it is relatively simple to understand the practical importance of trust, trust can be difficult to achieve and very easy to violate. Nothing violates trust more than saying one thing and doing another. If leaders can't "walk the talk," they're better off not saying anything at all.

• *Facilitating team performance.* This is far more complex than simply managing meetings effectively. Effective leaders also know how to help get teams off to a good start, tie in team goals to the overall vision of the organization, and keep the team going—perhaps the most challenging skill of all.

• *Facilitating learning.* Helping people learn and develop is essential to a high-involvement team. The critical job of team leaders, then, is to create an environment and culture that support ongoing learning and growth. Facilitating learning means building a culture where risk taking is encouraged, failure is seen as a positive experience, and people are open to others' thoughts and ideas.

• *Building partnerships.* Because the complexity of today's work world means that we do little alone, building partnerships is an important leadership skill. Leaders must give up the idea that their success and job security depend on how well they protect their turf. The new "turf" is the entire organization working together to achieve mutual goals.

CHAPTER 32

Leading in a Team Environment

by John H. Zenger, President of Zenger-Miller, Inc., an international training and consulting firm

EXECUTIVES AT EVERY LEVEL need five new skills to manage people effectively in a full-scale team environment.

Many managers pay a punishing price for their aversion to change: declining quality, productivity, morale, and market share. Now they face a declining need for their services as organizations are delayering, downsizing, rightsizing, retiring, pruning, and out-placing in their management ranks. "The massacre of middle managers over the last decade will continue," says Alvin Toffler, prophetic author of *Future Shock* and *Powershift*. "The middle manager's task of collecting information from down below and passing it on upstairs is going to either be automated or vanish." Effective managers are re-integrating work processes and delegating many traditional duties to high-performance teams.

Depending on needs, these teams may be ongoing or temporary; functional or cross-functional; synonymous with or auxiliary to the activities of the natural work group; conventionally supervised or, in various degrees, self-managed. Further, many companies are structuring a full-scale team environment—involving a thorough redesign of work processes, work systems, front-line jobs, and management roles.

Still, the well-documented vitality of teams in no way devalues the need for skilled managers. What's called for now is a different kind of manager—more strategic, collaborative, facilitative, and responsive to customers, employees, and organizational imperatives. "A new breed of managers is emerging," explains the recent national policy study from the Work in America Institute. "This new breed has discovered and applied a form of management which is responsive to the changing nature of the work force and to the pressures of competition. This is a social invention of such significance that it cannot be ignored by any organization interested in its own long-term survival and growth." So, how is it that old-style managers now face a rapidly shrinking need for their services? Because teams of their subordinates—and, unfortunately for many managers, teams of their former subordinates—are acquiring the skills to carry out the duties that these managers previously performed.

But they can make themselves vital once again to companies whose primary goal is continuously improving performance through teams. To do so, they must master the skills and muster a personal commitment to lead effectively in a team environment.

Today's manager must respond to a new environment by adding new layers of leadership skills. When used alone, the following skills are suited only to a rigidly traditional workplace.

- *Direct people.*
- *Get people to understand ideas.*
- *Manage one-on-one.*
- *Maximize the performance of the department.*
- *Implement changes imposed from above.*

The following skills are needed in today's workplace.

- *Involve people.*
- *Get people to generate ideas.*
- *Encourage teamwork.*
- *Build relationships with other departments.*
- *Initiate changes within the department.*

FIVE STRATEGIC SKILLS

To build and maintain a full-scale team environment, five additional strategic skills are needed.

1. Develop self-motivated people who set their own ambitious goals and evaluate their own efforts. In a team environment, employees don't rely on managers to map out their every move. Team members must be self-starters, highly motivated to achieve team goals and capable of solving operational and interpersonal problems.

But how do you "develop" such people? By building team members' skills and confidence, by gradually delegating new tasks, and by helping employees set goals, evaluate performance, and take corrective action, today's manager must turn mere "workers" into true owners of a piece of the business. That done, what "self-motivates" employees is what motivates anyone else who owns a business: pride in a job well done and desire to achieve tangible results.

Remarkably—and here's the major paradox of managing in a team environment—these new managers do not delegate themselves out of a job. Even after a team takes primary control of its day-to-day work, somebody has to reconcile short-term team goals with long-term corporate goals, seek out and pass along timely information, secure necessary resources, and balance the interests of multiple teams—among other activities. So, at bottom, these new managers survive and prosper not by jealously guarding their traditional power, but by giving it away.

2. *Get groups of diverse people to generate and implement their own best ideas.* "Management by fear is out," according to the Work in America study. "Coaching and counseling, group decision making, and group problem solving are in." Why? Because high-performing organizations now charge their teams not just with generating ideas, but with selecting, implementing, and tracking the impact of ideas that pack the biggest punch vis-á-vis team and corporate-wide goals.

Further, the vogue for training in "managing diversity" only foreshadows the transformation that managers and supervisors must undergo in order to capitalize on an increasingly diverse work force. Not that "*e pluribus unum*" is a new idea, but gone is the myth of the melting pot, in which matzo and corn pone, gazpacho and goulash, become white bread and canned tomato soup.

That's why few skills are more vital to the new manager than facilitating group decision making, problem solving, and conflict resolution.

3. *Build teams that manage more of their own day-to-day work.* From the Great Pyramids to the great pyramid companies, a principal measure of leadership was the ability to get people to obey. But Ricardo Semler, president of Brazil's largest builder of marine and food-processing machinery, holds a different view: "Pyramids emphasize power, promote insecurity, distort communications, hobble interaction, and make it very difficult for the people who plan and the people who execute to move in the same direction."

So, to counteract such problems, many managers have recently learned to share decision-making power—a baseline behavior in high-performing companies. In the future, the measure of a leader will be the ability to "build teams that manage more of their own day-to-day work."

Still, as one leading-edge motto decrees: "You can't empower one group by disempowering another," for many managers will clutch their traditional power, at least until they find an alternative. Fortunately, as David C. McClelland points out in his landmark book, *Power: The Inner Experience*, managers do have a choice.

McClelland identifies "two faces" of managerial power: (1) power based on the submission of other people, and (2) power based on "a concern for group goals, for finding those goals that will move [the group], for helping the group to formulate them, for taking initiative in providing means of achieving them, and for giving group members the feeling of competence they need to work hard for them." This second face of power belongs to the manager who learns how to lead in a team environment.

4. Champion cross-functional efforts to improve quality, service, and productivity. Two brutal decades of global competition have taught many U.S. companies that continuous, long-term improvement is the best way to satisfy today's savvy, penny-wise customers. That's why many organizations are now enduring painful changes in a once inviolable feature of American corporate culture: the functional or departmental fiefdom.

Traditional managers act as functional advocates, myopically "maximizing" the short-term performance of their units and treating other units as competitors for resources and information. Today, many managers are learning to see peers and parallel units as internal customers and suppliers, and to concentrate their improvement efforts at the points of overlap among units.

In such a world, a manager must lead and participate on ad hoc and permanent teams for improving processes jointly owned by several functions. As an unwavering example of quality-focused, essentially "boundaryless" behaviors, this manager helps team members make continuous improvement the core of their daily actions.

5. Anticipate, initiate, and respond to changes dictated by forces outside the organization. A common metaphor for team leadership has long been the symphony orchestra. The manager is the conductor, employees are musicians, and together they make beautiful music. But the metaphor fails to apply in at least one respect: While a symphony musician usually plays a single instrument, each work team member performs multiple tasks once assigned to several different people.

These employees have the technical and interpersonal skills to make effective decisions, the flexibility to respond quickly to changing needs, and a pride of ownership that a specialist rarely feels.

In other ways, the symphony metaphor does apply. Although conductors may play an instrument, they rarely do. Instead, they stay more in touch with the music, as a whole, than any musician does. Similarly, today's manager tunes in—and helps employees tune in—to crosscurrents, trends, and evolving customer needs. Then, this manager "cues" the team members, who in turn play the right notes to meet the expectations of paying customers.

Perhaps these five leadership skills are all a manager needs to turn the ore of workers into the bullion of high-performing teams. But let's face facts: Supervisors won't be willing or able to use these skills until middle managers do, and middle managers won't use them until executives do. Every level must delegate significant new responsibilities and commensurate authority to the level below it. To gain real power in today's team environment, managers must learn to help others to use power effectively.

CHAPTER 33

High-Involvement Leadership

by Ann Howard, President of the Leadership Research Institute and Senior Consultant for Development Dimensions International

THE TRADITIONAL FUNCTIONS of leaders are diminishing. As employees take more responsibility, leaders must learn new roles.

High-involvement leadership sounds simple: Organizations empower their employees by pushing down decision-making responsibility to those close to internal and external customers; employees take charge of their own jobs; and leaders have more time on their hands as their traditional functions shrink. In reality, leaders soon discover that they must take on new and more complex roles that they aren't sure they want and don't completely understand. High involvement inevitably requires transforming leadership practices.

A NEW MODEL OF LEADERSHIP

Traditional leadership roles have their roots in turn-of-the-century practices of scientific management overlaid with the confinement of mid-century bureaucracies. The leader maintains strong control over prescribed functions and protects and constrains both the privileges of management and assigned turf.

Traditional roles include: (1) *controller*—enforces a prescribed way of work; (2) *commander*—tells employees what to do and expects obedience; (3) *judge*—sizes up employees' performance and metes out rewards and punishments; (4) *ruler*—harbors decision making as a management privilege; and (5) *guard*—protects turf and hoards resources.

As high-involvement leadership takes hold, these roles become dysfunctional and new ones must be nurtured. Roles that facilitate high-involvement leadership are designed for sleeker organizations— built for the speed, flexibility, quality, and service essential for global competition. Because high involvement begins by pushing decision making down, the role of delegator is a prerequisite. The *delegator* moves decision making to lower levels and sees that responsibility and authority accompany job tasks.

I have identified 10 more empowering leadership roles. Each is associated with a different part of the body—head, mouth, heart, hand, or foot—that symbolizes how the approach is implemented.

These approaches and roles are meant to achieve five outcomes.

1. Discover the way. Enforcing "one best way" of working, the traditional role of the *controller*, is unsuited to an environment of rapid change. The empowering leader seeks new and better ways of accomplishing the mission. Symbolized by the *head*, discovering the way requires mental processes such as conceptualization and imagination, as well as inquiry and judgment. Roles that support this approach include: visionary—one who sees a more perfect future and expresses potential achievements consistent with the vision; and *change agent*—one who looks for better ways to perform work by challenging current paradigms and encouraging improvement ideas from direct reports and external stakeholders.

2. Light the way. In contrast to the traditional, the empowering leader illuminates and illustrates where the work group should be headed and the values that should guide goal accomplishment. Inspiring and influencing are hallmarks of lighting the way; hence its association with the *mouth*. Roles that support this approach include: *inspirer*—communicates the vision and inspires acceptance of and commitment to it; and *model*—personifies priorities and values; is both trusting and trustworthy.

3. Encourage the way. If employees are to assume added risks and responsibilities, the empowering leader must encourage them by offering reassurance, applauding their accomplishments, and taking their interests to *heart*. The leader's objective is to boost their confidence rather than *judge* their incompetence. Roles that support this approach include: *supporter*—constantly expresses confidence in direct reports' self-sufficiency and treats their mistakes as learning opportunities; and *champion*—visibly celebrates their accomplishments; promotes their best ideas to higher management.

4. Enable the way. The empowering leader offers a helping *hand* so that direct reports can make their own decisions and manage their own responsibilities. It is not enough simply to delegate responsibility and decision making; the leader must enable others to handle tasks. Roles that support this approach include: *coach*—helps others learn to be self-sufficient through personal development; and *team builder*—establishes and supports teams that engage in self-managing activities.

5. Smooth the way. The empowering leader seeks and attracts resources from outside the group. Smoothing the way requires *foot-*

work. The leader must bring needed information and materials into the group and build mutually supportive relationships with outsiders. Roles that support this approach include: *facilitator*—provides resources for the work group and removes obstacles that impede progress; and *partner*—builds alliances with and communication bridges to other work units and external partners.

IMPLEMENTING THE NEW MODEL

The new leadership model guided a recent study designed to generate critical information about leaders in high-involvement implementations. Participants evaluated the importance of items representing each of the five traditional leadership roles and the empowering leadership roles. Two traditional leadership roles, *ruler* and *judge*, were particularly unpopular.

By contrast, all of the empowering leadership roles were rated above average in importance. Study participants strongly favored the proposed model of empowering leadership roles. They judged *modeling trust*, represented by the item "be consistent in words and actions," as the most important role.

In business units with high involvement, people expressed greater satisfaction with current leadership practices. Empowering leaders are more committed, more satisfied with their jobs, and have fewer uncertainties about their leadership roles.

Those reporting to empowering leaders are more involved, satisfied, effective, committed, and less stressed.

LEARNING THE NEW RULES

Although progress has been made in the past five years, leaders have not yet mastered high-involvement leadership.

What Hurts

- *Not enough heart.* By neglecting the encouraging roles, leaders might miss many opportunities to enhance their direct reports' feelings about their own worth and their contribution.
- *Overevaluation.* If leaders believe they are better at empowering leadership than they are, this lessens their motivation to change.
- *Misunderstanding.* If high-involvement leadership is to have maximum effect, leaders must ensure that direct reports enjoy the benefits of all roles being performed.
- *Faulty implementation.* Inadequate or unsupported implementations undermine attempts to lead in a high-involvement style. Faced with insufficient support, associates depend on the leader.

What Helps

• *Modeling by higher-level managers.* Role modeling implies that high-involvement leadership will flourish best if installed from the top to the bottom of the managerial hierarchy, because leaders will imitate behaviors of their own leaders.

• *Being female.* The supportiveness emphasized in the new model fits more naturally with the social roles that women traditionally have been expected to fulfill.

• *Skill training.* Without specific attention to skills, training might change leaders' self-images but not their behaviors.

TIPS FOR MASTERING THE NEW ROLES

The pattern of results provides tips for mastery.

Delegator: Find the appropriate balance between not letting go and abandoning your direct reports.

Visionary: Training helps, but be warned that this role requires more effort than others.

Change agent: Solicit ideas from direct reports more often; they don't think leaders do it enough.

Inspirer: It takes effort, but direct reports know when leaders inspire them. Don't get bogged down "fighting fires" when you should be "lighting fires."

Model of trust: Trusted leaders are more effective and their direct reports more satisfied.

Supporter: A sure route to satisfaction with your leadership. Learn not to blame employees for failures; search for contributing circumstances instead.

Champion: Don't be fooled into thinking this isn't important. Direct reports frequently complain of too little recognition, and even little gestures are readily observed and understood.

Coach: Training and good role models offer routes to improvement. Coach your direct reports on decision-making processes and reduce your own workload.

Team builder: Building strong teams helps reduce workload among your direct reports, but it may be tough to find role models higher up in the organization.

Facilitator: Removing obstacles can reduce the workload of your direct reports. One of the most important leadership roles but frequently misunderstood.

Partner: Another misunderstood role, although your boss could be a role model. Partner requires greater effort than many other roles.

Given the potential payoffs of high-involvement leadership, mastering its new roles is definitely worth the effort.

CHAPTER 34

Reassigning Responsibility

by Peter Block, a partner in Designed Learning

THE ALTERNATIVE to leadership is stewardship, an entryway into exploring change and creating strategies conducive to change.

If we are looking for cultural or mythical heroes, let us follow the trail and scent of those in power. If, however, we care about how our institutions serve a citizen, keep a customer, or save a dollar, the attention on right leadership and right sponsorship is misplaced.

Every organization is now engaged in reshaping itself. For these reform efforts to be real rather than rhetorical, something has to shift, not in the leaders, but in the actions of those who deliver an envelope, make a light bulb, and assemble a car. Genuine reform most often boils down to a shift in the depth of ownership and responsibility core workers feel toward the success of their workplace. All of the focus on leaders and leadership has the unintended effect of reducing the ownership and responsibility felt by those close to the work.

There is a growing awareness that our efforts at enlightened leadership are not delivering the results we expect. Even though efforts in total-quality management, empowerment, employee involvement, employment ownership, and reengineering are worthwhile, the day-to-day experience of those who do the work remains relatively unchanged.

THE LEADERSHIP QUESTION

The strength of leadership is that it embraces initiative and responsibility. The underbelly of leadership is that it is inevitably associated with maintaining control, pointing direction, and knowing what is best for others. We expect our leaders to drive cultural change by determining the desired future; defining the path to get there; and establishing rewards for acting appropriately. While we need leaders to define the playing field and make clear the desired results, we do not need them to formulate culture or specify behaviors.

Our search for strong leadership involves a desire for others to assume ownership and responsibility. This desire localizes power, purpose, and privilege in those at the top. Focusing power and purpose at the top undermines community, fosters dependency, and makes partnerships unsustainable.

Keeping the leader at the center of change is incompatible with creating partnerships and widely distributed ownership and responsibility. If, in fact, placing ownership and responsibility close to the core work is the fundamental cultural change we seek, strong leadership does not have within itself the capability to deliver. It is not the fault of the people in these positions; it is a limitation of the way the role is framed.

We have the right language about redistributing ownership and creating partnerships. We know it is a process and not a program. We understand it takes time and training. We realize it requires commitment, not coercion. But when we talk about leadership, we believe that change has to start at the top. We create a vision and enroll others in it. We urge bosses to be role models and to walk their talk. We create a special department to manage the change and design a pay system that reinforces the new direction. All of this is reasonable, but results in high activity and low transformation.

We keep looking to our leaders to provide the hope that sustainable improvement is possible. If hope is contingent on sponsorship and the actions of those in power, then employees will never claim the ownership that is required. The continued belief that top management has the ability to transform whole institutions faces these limitations:

* *The leaders we are looking for are more in the news than in our lives.*

* *Great leaders reinforce the idea that accomplishment in society comes from great individual acts.* We credit individuals for outcomes that required teams and communities to accomplish. Partnership is denied and individualism reaffirmed.

* *Our attention stays fixed on those at the top.* We live the myth that without sponsorship from the top, we cannot realize our intentions.

* *People in power who succeed begin to believe their own press.* They begin to believe that an institution's success was, in fact, their own creation.

THE STEWARDSHIP ANSWER

Stewardship is the choice to be deeply accountable for the outcomes of an institution without acting to control others, define purpose for others, or take care of others. Stewardship puts the spotlight on the people doing the work and focuses on individual and team ownership and responsibility. The strategy is to treat those serving customers as franchise owners and let the change effort center around them. Offer "management" training to workers, and ask core work teams to maintain controls, define the means, and create a caring environment.

We were raised to believe that if we are accountable, we need the authority to go with it. How many times have we heard the cry, "How can you hold me accountable without giving me authority?" Stewardship involves questioning the belief that accountability and control go hand in hand. We can be accountable and give control to those close to the work with the belief that the work is better served.

Instead of top management defining culture and values, we can ask that employee teams decide what operating environment best suits their tasks. Have work teams define the measurements they need for control. This takes leaders out of the control and caretaking business.

For most bosses, caretaking is the hardest thing to give up. We have been told from day one that the morale, emotional well-being, and performance of our subordinates are in our hands. This is true for parents, but not for partners. We do not serve other adults when we take responsibility for their well-being. We continue to care, but when we care take, we treat others as if they were not able to provide for themselves.

Stewardship supports the belief that we can care for our organization and not have to control it. This connection between accountability and caretaking needs to be broken. There needs to be a way for us to be accountable for outcomes of an organization without feeling we must control the people in it.

Setting goals for people, defining the measures of progress toward those goals, and then rewarding them for reaching those goals does not honor their capabilities. This is the form our control has taken. This is not stewardship; it is patriarchy.

Stewardship affirms the spiritual meaning of the idea: to honor what has been given to us, to use power with a sense of grace, and to pursue purposes that transcend short-term self-interest. Retaining accountability, but surrendering control, creates conditions for ownership and responsibility.

GETTING PRACTICAL

Four elements are required for reforms that have lasting impact on customers, costs, and quality:

1. Reframe supervision toward partnership and away from parenting. Partners have a right to say no to each other. They tell the truth to each other, neither protecting the other from bad news. They are jointly accountable for outcomes, and each is responsible for his or her own future. Caretaking and control are minimized, only coming to play in extreme situations.

2. Localize choice and power close to the product and customer. This means re-integrating the managing and the doing of the work. Individuals and work teams with training and full information should be making the decisions that under "leadership" environments were once held to be the prerogative of the boss.

3. Recognize, reward, and write about the value of labor. Connect the pay systems for core workers to real business outcomes and success in their marketplace. The heroism and value of low-power people taking care of customers day after day too easily gets lost.

4. Hold the expectation that local franchises of core work teams will build the institution. Genuine, sustainable change will come from small, manageable units achieving high performance. A group of classrooms in a school building delivers education; a district, a superintendent's office, the state legislature do not. In business, a district office delivers high-quality sales and service, not the regional office or headquarters. Regional and corporate staff are support services to the local unit in building the business. Focus improvement efforts on local units. Involve units with the business literacy, training, and latitude to reshape themselves in response to the markets they serve.

Real change in performance comes from a shared sense of stewardship and accountability. This comes from creating real partnership with people doing the work.

CHAPTER 35

Leader as Servant

 by Ken Melrose, Chariman and CEO of The Toro Company

THE SERVANT-LEADER model is not easy to embrace, but it permits the greatest number of people to experience the greatest good.

Over the years at Toro, I've learned a few things about managing the turf. If you think of your turf as your domain—as the environment you operate in—then your turf becomes your area of influence. Turf may also refer to your organization, your work area, your home, garden, or domain.

The Master of Men fittingly expressed the ideal of leadership when he said, "Whosoever wants to be great among you must be your servant." These few words stand up against all the management books on the shelves today. The great leader is a great servant.

Although the model of the leader as servant has been in the canons of management for years, in practice it's still rare. I believe that without strong models of servant leaders, a person is hard pressed to put the principles of servant leadership into practice.

Fortunately, I had great models. Early in my career, when I was working for The Pillsbury Company as a marketing manager, my boss used to tell me, "Realize that you are the flexible resource, and the other person is the fixed resource." So I tried to be flexible and relate to other people. That's easier when you care about the other person.

I care deeply about the people of Toro. I try to get to know them personally and let them know they are appreciated. But frankly, showing warmth has not always been easy for me. I have had to work at it. Now I take more time with people who want to talk. I listen to them. What they have to say doesn't have to be earth-shattering. What's important is to take a few minutes out of the day to share one-on-one with another human being. I focus on their eyes and face. I listen to their words and try to understand their emotions. These exchanges keep me informed and remind me what matters most in life: meaningful, caring relationships.

PIE A LA TORO

Since 1985 I've held a monthly meeting with 15 or so employees. We call it "PIE a la Toro." We get together and have lunch; sometimes we even have pie. But the purpose is to allow employees to discuss what is on their minds. It gives me a chance to ask how they feel about Toro, their jobs, and our direction. These get-togethers give us a chance to relate to each other, to break down barriers. The conversation is warm and natural.

I also have informal meetings or lunch in my office with new employees. They experience a sort of pleasant culture shock when they come to Toro. They talk about their sense of belonging, about the company's mission and their role in it, and about their feelings for involvement, commitment, and participation.

The servant-leader model requires a change in attitude more than a structural change. To operate in this mode, leaders have to shed their egos and deeply embrace the belief that people perform best in an atmosphere of freedom and trust.

BECOMING A SERVANT LEADER

Servant leaders serve people not to get more out of them, but because they want to boost people's self-worth and dignity. Leadership is not a position; it's a combination of something you are (character) and some things you do (competence).

Leadership can be coveted by people for the wrong reasons; some seem to thrive on power, others may need to assert control. But if we think of leadership as a position, it's almost impossible to develop an environment of trust.

Whenever we step in front of the crowd and say, "Follow me," the implication is that we know where we're going and what we want to achieve and that we're committed to giving our very best efforts.

Remember: You have it within your power to help your company develop a new culture—with a climate of trust defined by a set of values that stresses the dignity and importance of every employee. This is the service you can best offer your company as a leader.

You don't have to be the perfect example of all the disciplines of excellence. In fact, your imperfections may enhance your humanness and thereby help set the tone for risks, innovation, and trust.

Servant leaders ask, "What does the organization, my stakeholders, need me to be today: a coach, a teacher, a decision maker, a supporter, a listener, a pilgrim, a servant, someone who makes waves?" Since the needs change daily, leaders need to be continually learning. In a sense, every leader is in the discovery and rediscovery business.

CHAPTER 36

Leaders Are Doers

 Peter F. Drucker, Honorary Chairman of The Peter F. Drucker Foundation

ABOVE ALL, leaders are doers—and they do one thing that they can do with excellence to make a difference.

Over the years, I have discussed with scores—perhaps even hundreds—of leaders their roles, their goals, and their performance. I have worked with manufacturing giants and tiny firms, with organizations that span the world. I have worked with some exceedingly bright executives and a few dummies, with people who talk a good deal about leadership and with others who apparently never even think of themselves as leaders and who rarely, if ever, talk about leadership.

The lessons are unambiguous. The first is that there may be "born leaders," but there surely are far too few to depend on them. Leadership must be learned and can be learned. But the second major lesson is that "leadership personality," "leadership style," and "leadership traits" do not exist. Among the most effective leaders I have encountered and worked with in a half century, some locked themselves into their offices and others were ultragregarious. Some (though not many) were "nice guys," and others were stern disciplinarians. Some were quick and impulsive; others studied and studied again, and then took forever to come to a decision. Some were warm; others remained aloof. Some immediately spoke of their families; others never mentioned anything apart from the task at hand.

Some leaders were excruciatingly vain—and it did not affect their performance. Some were self-effacing to a fault—and again it did not affect their performance as leaders. Some were as austere in their private lives as a hermit in the desert; others were ostentatious and pleasure-loving and whooped it up at every opportunity. Some were good listeners, but among the most effective leaders I have worked with were also a few loners who listened only to their own inner voice.

The one and only personality trait the effective ones I have encountered did have in common was something they did not have: they had no "charisma" and little use either for the term or what it signifies.

KNOW FOUR THINGS

All the effective leaders I have encountered—both those I worked with and those I merely watched—knew four simple things:

1. The only definition of a leader is someone who has followers. Some people are thinkers. Some are prophets. Both roles are important. But without followers, there can be no leaders.

2. An effective leader is not someone who is loved or admired. He or she is someone whose followers do the right things. Popularity is not leadership. Results are.

3. Leaders are highly visible. They therefore set examples.

4. Leadership is not rank, privileges, titles, or money—it is responsibility.

Regardless of their almost limitless diversity with respect to personality, style, abilities, and interests, effective leaders behaved much the same way:

• They did not start out with the question "What do I want?" They started out asking, "What needs to be done?"

• Then they asked, "What can and should I do to make a difference?" This has to be something that both needs to be done and fits the leader's strengths and the way she or he is most effective.

• They constantly asked, "What are the organization's mission and goals? What constitutes performance and results in this organization?"

• They were extremely tolerant of diversity in people and did not look for carbon copies of themselves. It rarely even occurred to them to ask, "Do I like or dislike this person?" But they were totally— fiendishly—intolerant when it came to a person's performance, standards, and values.

• They were not afraid of strength in their associates. They gloried in it. Whether they had heard of it or not, their motto was what Andrew Carnegie wanted to have put on his tombstone: "Here lies a man who attracted better people into his service than he was himself."

• One way or another, they submitted themselves to the "mirror test"—that is, they made sure that the person they saw in the mirror in the morning was the kind of person they wanted to be. This way they fortified themselves against the leader's greatest temptations: to do things that are popular rather than right, and to do petty, mean, sleazy things.

• Finally, these effective leaders were not preachers, they were doers. In the mid 1920s, when I was in my final high school years, a whole spate of books on World War I and its campaigns suddenly appeared in English, French, and German. For our term project, our excellent history teacher—himself a badly wounded war veteran—told each of us to pick several of these books, read them carefully, and write a major essay on our selections. When we then discussed these essays in class, one of my fellow students said, "Every one of these books says that the Great War was a war of total military incompetence. Why was it?"

Our teacher did not hesitate a second, but shot right back, "Because not enough generals were killed; they stayed way behind the lines and let others do the fighting and dying."

Effective leaders delegate a good many things; they have to or they drown in trivia. But they do not delegate the one thing that only they can do with excellence, the one thing that will make a difference, the one thing that will set standards, the one thing they want to be remembered for. They do it.

It does not matter what kind of organization you work in; you will find opportunities to learn about leadership from all organizations— public, private, and nonprofit.

I challenge you to ask, "What in my organization could I do that would truly make a difference? How can I truly set an example?" And I hope that you will then do it.

CHAPTER 37

The Toll Road to Empowerment

by Paul Hersey, Chairman and CEO of the Center for Leadership Studies

IN NEW ORGANIZATIONS, new leaders and followers will incur costs up front, but they will realize big returns down the road.

Consider Southern California's first toll road, recently completed in Orange County: The implicit contract guaranteeing a "free way" has been altered; there are fewer ways on and off; we are powerfully induced to travel in "teams" in the carpool lanes, and the landscaping is spartan and none too attractive.

I'm impressed by the parallels between travel on this toll road and the way organizations are changing. I'm struck by the new ways of leading and following, and gaining and giving power—driven by the mandate to remain competitive and the need to do more with less.

Many companies are seeking to improve their competitive stance by developing more self-reliant leaders and followers through an "empowerment" process. Many people likened this experience to having had fairy dust sprinkled on them with the expectation that they would go forward and be more productive. So unsuccessful are most of these "initiatives" that the term *empowerment* is now taboo at some companies!

FOUR TOKENS OF EMPOWERMENT

Today's leaders need to develop four qualities to empower people: *vision, a new deal, owned readiness,* and *paying dues.*

1. Vision. Peter Senge writes: "Empowering people toward personal mastery empowers the organization, but only if individuals are deeply aligned around a common sense of purpose and shared vision." With that wisdom in mind, I'd like to share a story. In San Diego, drivers on

Interstate 8 are credited with being more efficient than those on any other interstate. During rush hour, drivers in three or four densely packed lanes move quickly and relatively safely. These commuters get where they want to be faster than anyone else and in greater numbers.

Why this stretch—and why does this happen only for those driving west in the morning and east in the evening? The answer is literally two kinds of vision: a gentle roll of the landscape gives these drivers an opportunity to see miles ahead. They feel safer, move faster, and move in concert with one another! The other vision is equally important: lighting. The sun in the east creates a brilliant high-contrast image for those traveling west to the coast in the morning. The reverse is true in the evening. What a delight it is to witness competent, cooperative drivers creating a drive-time symphony. For peak performance, the message from Interstate 8 is simple: *Give people the long view down the road and put the sun at their backs, and they will get there faster.* Toll ways ought to take advantage of the lay of the land and the light.

2. The New Deal: Get Ready. With a new landscape created in a large degree by the demise of the "implicit employment contract," this business of people being willing and able to perform a myriad of tasks (do more with less) has become all the more critical. Clearly, this implied contract is not going to be replaced with another similar one. In its stead we have employability. Regardless of restructuring, reengineering, and layoffs, employees know they now need to be ready to move to a new job—quickly. If vision is the way, then readiness is the vehicle, and more employees are providing their own "transportation," meaning they are increasingly self-reliant.

Where is this leading? Ultimately the journey takes us to the interchanges where all the customers are. Leaders and followers are now working with companies but for customers. Fostering positive attitudes and coaching for new behaviors around self-reliance may well be the quickest way to joining the fast pack on the toll way to empowerment and bottom-line results.

3. Owning Readiness. At the core of this body of self-reliant behaviors for followers is what Peter Senge refers to as the state of personal mastery: owning your readiness and taking responsibility for progress. This involves becoming continually more competent at taking charge of your skills and growing progressively more forthright in the communication of the degree of your confidence, commitment, and motivation, back to your leader. By *follower* I don't mean just a subordinate. Anytime somebody attempts to influence your behavior, you become a follower. Regardless of whether that attempt to influence comes from up, down or across, for that task they are in the lead.

Getting people to attain higher levels of readiness for critical tasks serves as the means to generate torque to move quickly down the road and nimbly up the hills.

To achieve empowered followership, we need to understand the four types of relationships that can exist between leader and follower. These correspond with the four readiness levels:

• *The first readiness level is the tell/being told mode.* Followers who disown their inability or insecurity are apt to behave in a frustrated, defensive, argumentative, or complaining manner, and perform only to the exact request. The insecure person is likely to shut down or exhibit discomfort nonverbally through closed body language and convey a sense of confusion and even a fear of failure.

The follower who owns his or her readiness at this level expresses: "Just tell me what, where, how, and when to do it." Providing there is adequate trust between leader and follower, the communication around the unwillingness or insecurity is candid: "I am insecure or unwilling to do this task because. . ." Steps can then be taken to ameliorate the challenges and concerns that exist for the follower around his or her confidence, commitment, and motivation. The job or task then gets completed more quickly and efficiently.

• *The second readiness level is characterized by selling/being sold as leaders to persuade followers and seek "buy-in" for tasks.* Disowners of this readiness level (unable but willing or confident) usually have an inflated sense of their knowledge, experience, and skill around the task. Often characterized as "not knowing what they don't know" or "ignorance on fire" for the task at hand, their high degree of motivation and commitment remains obvious.

Followers owning their inability will ask for specific, structuring information about the task. Ordinarily, they must be given the "gift of feedback" and be clear on what good performance looks like, as the standards rise. Followers owning their inability know to focus on the big picture and seek outcomes rather than incremental successes and to act thoughtfully and judiciously, not spontaneously.

• *The third mode, participating, is characterized by the ability to perform a task, but below-average levels of confidence, commitment, and motivation.* While followers are aware of their skill level and have demonstrated it, they may be hesitant to perform. This hesitancy stems from feelings of being afraid, overwhelmed, confused, or angry and hurt over something like being passed over for promotion. Followers owning the participation process realize that they can ill-afford to linger here in this "needy" mode. They see this place as a quick refueling stop before moving on.

• *People at the fourth level, the delegating mode, own their task readiness by the very nature of being able, willing, or confident.* The follower at this level continues to keep the leader informed. Task readiness in this mode is at its highest level, and self-reliant followers constitute the productive, quality, work force that serve as the power train of an empowered organization. Employees who cluster at this readiness level for most of their tasks are truly independent, responsive, and ready—and remain very employable.

4. Paying Dues. Vision, the new deal, and followers owning their readiness—for these qualities of empowerment to be attained, we need to pause and pay up front. We may want to continue to look for that shortcut, but it just is not there! What does this process of paying dues involve? To begin with it's slow going at the beginning. We can expect the same sort of "bog down" that occurs after we leave toll plaza and jockey for lane position.

Most of the costs are incurred up front. They involve a departure from the way things may have been done before. This includes hiring the right people, training, and working closely with them when necessary to advance their readiness for critical tasks. It also involves investing the time and effort necessary to gain a clear vision of what is ahead. Allocating resources to reward followers who grow to own their readiness can also be associated with the cost of driving this toll way.

Several business leaders have more than made up this outlay just in the returns reaped from their front-line leaders learning when and how to delegate to the willing and able follower. This "found" time has allowed managers and supervisors to engage in the high payoff functions, such as such as planning, networking, and visioning.

GET THE "LEAD" OUT

Leaders must use a judicious mix of structuring and supporting behaviors and become more competent in diagnosing, adapting, and communicating. In effect, they must change fuels. The mix is becoming very different now. At new organizations with new leaders and new self-reliant followers with new deals, the fuel of choice continues to shift from position power to personal power.

Empowered, skillful, willing, highly employable workers do not want or need to be leveraged with top-down power. They can and will go elsewhere. The personal power that is earned by and accorded to competent leaders is what propels the empowered work force. New leaders keep their tanks full by frequently refilling. They know that with fewer ways on and off the toll road, there will certainly be some very long stretches where they need every last drop.

Where are the personal power pumps? They are on the turnouts where leaders and followers pause and trace a route on a map together, at the vistas where they view the span ahead, at the junctions where calculated risks are taken and sound decisions are made, in the bumper-to-bumper traffic where patient and thoughtful leadership is provided, and at all the places we recognize that this drive—this work—is good for you, good for me, and good for the organization.

CHAPTER 38

Road to Leadership

by Kevin Cashman, CEO, and Sidney Reisberg, former Vice President, LeaderSource, an executive coaching firm

MANY ROADS lead to leadership, but we've found self-knowledge to be the most direct route for business executives.

Many people enjoy taking a trip, but not to some strange place called Self-Knowledge. "Why should I go there?"

Throughout the ages, the phrase *nosce teipsum*, know thyself, appears over and over in the writings of Ovid, Cicero, and Socrates, in the sayings of the Seven Sages of Greece, on the entrance to the temple of Apollo, and in Christian writings. One scholar says it was part of Shakespeare's "regular moral and religious diet."

Nosce teipsum threads its way through history as the pre-eminent precept in life. Chaucer: "Full wise is he that can himself know." Browning: "Truth is within ourselves." Pope: "And all our knowledge is, ourselves to know." Montaigne: "If a man does not know himself, how should he know his functions and his powers?" Saint Exupery: "Each man must look to himself to teach him the meaning of life." Lao Tzu: "Knowledge of self is the source of our abilities."

Contemporary thinkers from Ralph Waldo Emerson to Abraham Maslow to Warren Bennis to Stephen R. Covey have carried on the tradition. Emerson wrote, "The purpose of life seems to be to acquaint man with himself." Bennis writes: "Letting the self emerge is the essential task of leaders." Covey says, "Real success is success with self."

TRAVEL TIPS

Executives may be using psychological maps, which are incomplete descriptions of the territory.

• ***Multiple tools and perspectives promote self-knowledge.***
Most executive development programs begin and end with psychological assessment. Although a valuable tool, it's not enough. A person, no less than an elephant, is not understood from one vantage point. To psychology we must add the perspectives of human development, career management, interpersonal influence, and lifestyle balance. There is also the limitation of working with one expert. When a team of coaches with specialties in different disciplines all work together with one executive, the results can be dramatic. Fragmented information integrates into focused powerful leadership, consistent with the uniqueness of the person.

• ***360-degree feedback doesn't reveal the whole horizon.***
When this feedback is the primary source of self-understanding, executives learn how others perceive them, instead of learning about themselves. If a development process is modeled solely around 360-degree feedback, executives principally learn how to create themselves in the image of others. Learning *how to act* instead of learning *how to be* is a direct route to becoming a follower versus a leader.

For 360-degree feedback to be valuable, it needs to be seen in a larger context. What are the development implications of these perceptions? How do leaders reconcile the gap between self-perception and other perceptions to enhance their leadership consistent with who they are? Leaders should use 360-degree feedback to help answer these questions, not to serve as the principal source of self-understanding.

• ***Before driving, be sure to read your owner's manual.***
Trying to change people is a waste of time, energy, and money. Helping people to grow through self-understanding is a great investment. Most executives don't need to change, they just need to understand what they have. It's much like someone who just purchased a high-performance sports car. Although they know how to drive, there is still a crucial question: Do they know how to drive *that* vehicle? Without understanding the owner's manual, are they confident that they can get the highest performance out of that vehicle in all conditions? Like the sports car owner, most executives are driving without their owner's manual and not getting maximum performance out of their "vehicle." They don't need to change vehicles, but they do need to read the fine print.

• ***Pack light.*** Leave your books at home. Most leadership courses deal with skill and strategy development, tools of the leadership trade. They have plenty of "smart books" sitting on "smart bookshelves," and they've heard plenty of "smart consultants." The crucial variable, however, is not more external knowledge. The missing ingredient is self-knowledge and how to use it.

• ***Don't get lost in self-absorption.*** Developing leadership effectiveness from the inside out is preparation for effective action. It is not an end in itself. Gaining heightened self-knowledge is a process of reclaiming ourselves as a pre-condition for more effective performance. It's like an archer pulling the bow back to have a more effective and forceful shot. Most executives are so absorbed in their work and themselves they become less effective as a result. They need to get beyond the pattern of self-absorption to a deeper level of self-understanding. We can only give what we have; and when we have more, we can give more of ourselves as leaders.

• ***Take time to think and reflect.*** Gaining self-knowledge requires being free of distractions for a few days. Immersing oneself in the entire process of self-discovery over a few days has dramatic effects. One hour of coaching here and there has a limited impact; the value of the initial coaching sessions quickly fades as the person arrives back at the office. At the next coaching session, both parties feel like they have to start over.

• ***Adjust your mirrors.*** Keeping yourself and surroundings in clear focus is an ongoing process. Self-knowledge is not a one-time visit. Potential becomes real leadership through application. Drawing on a team of experts regularly can be the difference between having great personal insights and achieving high performance. Ongoing coaching ensures that the leader has objective mirrors to sustain growth.

There are as many ways to lead as there are leaders. Helping leaders to awaken, engage, and deploy their unique capabilities may be the true competitive advantage in today's marketplace.

CHAPTER 39

Effective Followership

by Ira Chaleff, an executive coach

WE READ SCORES of articles about leadership in management magazines, but where are the articles about followership?

A teacher had better know a lot about students, a doctor a lot about patients, and a leader a lot about followers.

How much do you know about followers? If you don't also pay attention to followership you are studying half of a subject; leadership and followership are two parts of one dynamic relationship.

Senior executives are both leaders and followers. Do you report to a chairman, CEO, or VP? If so, you both lead and follow. In this dual role, you may find that you cannot be an effective and ethical leader if you are not first a courageous follower.

For example, suppose you work as a marketing VP. Your organization's mission is clear. You exert strong leadership to implement your piece of the strategy. But the EVP is a micromanager who fires off instructions that distract from the strategy. You are left with three choices: follow the EVP literally; become a chaotic leader who constantly changes your team's priorities (passive followership); or confront the EVP about his or her counterproductive style and be an influence for positive change. The last choice constitutes courageous followership and is necessary if you're going to, in turn, be a good leader.

Or suppose your mission is to develop a highly skilled, motivated, flexible workforce which can help your organization transform itself into the 21st century. You have clear programs in place to achieve this. But the CEO repeatedly insists on further headcount reductions which go well beyond what budget realities demand. You watch morale and motivation plummet as you implement the CEO's dictates. It's clear that repeated downsizing is destructive to the company's well-being. What do you do and how can you do it effectively? This requires a very different model of followership.

I'M NOT A FOLLOWER!

Most "leaders" don't like to think of themselves as followers. In our culture being a follower connotes weakness, passivity, or mindlessness. But this need not be the case. Leaders can empower followers, and followers can empower themselves! Leading isn't strong and good, and following weak and bad; leadership and followership are two sides of the same process. One can't exist without the other. You can lead in many ways, and you can follow in many ways.

I don't believe that followers are passive; I contend that followers don't exist to serve leaders. In healthy organizations, both leaders and followers serve a common purpose. Ultimately, a follower doesn't draw power or authority from a leader, but from the organization's purpose and from the commitment and skills he or she brings to that purpose. An effective follower is supportive, not passive!

THE COURAGE OF FOLLOWERS

Being anything but passive is sometimes easier said than done! We've all been in situations where we thought the leader was off the mark, but we haven't been willing to forcefully speak our minds about it. Warren Bennis observes that 7 out of 10 staff won't say anything when they feel the leader is about to make a mistake. They may speak up once, but if what they say is discounted, either by words or body language, they won't speak up again, sometimes with costly consequences.

Why don't we speak up? We are conditioned from an early age to obey authority, to say "yes sir" or "yes ma'am," to have a "can do" attitude. This conditioning is deep, and most of us have to work to overcome it. We are afraid that if we question authority we will be viewed as a nuisance, pushed out of the loop, overlooked for promotion, even fired. We fear the consequences of speaking up far more than we are afraid of the more serious consequences of not speaking up.

So we don't say what we're really feeling. And if enough people do this we wind up with top management having very little idea of what's really happening in the organization and of how much resistance their actions are generating. Good followership requires courage. It's not enough to believe that we will display courage at a crucial hour. We must display it routinely in our relationships and communications. Courage is a muscle which needs to be exercised or it will atrophy. The rewards of courage are great. Individually we cease to feel victimized by people or events, and collectively we move from a state of alienation to an open and engaged community.

A primary challenge we face as leaders is creating an atmosphere in which people have the courage to tell us what they really think. A primary challenge we face as followers is telling the leaders what we really think, whether or not the atmosphere encourages us to do so.

SUPPORTING LEADERS

Not all leader-follower relationships are based on fear, but there is a layer in our relationships based on intimidation by authority.

The ideal leader-follower dynamic is a healthy relationship between peers, although one party formally possesses ultimate authority. The key is to build mutually supportive relationships. Followers are in just as strong a position as are leaders to initiate this.

Leaders are usually under great pressure. The demands for performance at the top are often brutal. The tolerance in the culture for a senior executive expressing vulnerability is low. It benefits the organization if followers stay alert for ways to support the leader better and reduce the stress the leader is under.

Energetically supporting a leader also builds trust. The more genuine concern we show for our leader's welfare, the more we stand up *for* our leader, the stronger our position will be when we need to stand up *to* our leader.

CHALLENGE THE LEADER

Sometimes, the worst thing we can do is to follow the leader. Sometimes we must challenge the leader's actions or policies. Why is this so?

Because leaders are human:

• *They have strengths and weaknesses.*

• *The higher up they go in an organization the more their flaws are magnified.*

• *The more successful leaders are the more they become convinced that their way of doing things is correct—in effect, they take their strengths to extremes, at which point they become liabilities.*

The result is that leaders can do things which hurt the common purpose rather seriously and squander or misuse the power they have. Most leaders can only use their power well over time if they are surrounded by followers who have the courage and skill to successfully give the leaders honest feedback.

It requires honest feedback for leaders to remain real about the impact of their actions. But how many leaders create an atmosphere which encourages this? If followers are less than forthright, leaders have no way of knowing the consequences of their actions. They feel that they must be doing well as they're so exalted! But these leaders are flying blind.

TRANSFORMING BAD SITUATIONS

What if we muster our courage and give our leaders feedback about their actions and nothing changes? Do we throw up our hands and shed all responsibility for the situation?

Morally we can't just challenge leaders; we must also help them transform situations. This may involve transforming ourselves as well.

If we have given our best effort to bring about transformation without success, then we may have another choice to make which also requires courage—whether to stay or leave. Following is not passive; it is an active choice. As we choose to follow, we may also choose to no longer follow. In certain circumstances, leaving is the only way to keep our personal integrity and professional reputation. We cannot claim we were just "following orders."

Good followership is a series of conscious commitments and courageous acts. As followers we are wise to act courageously towards our leaders. We already have the power we need to do so in either role. It is our choice to exercise this power and develop it further in the service of our common purpose.

SECTION IV

Soul of Leadership

THE SOUL OF LEADERSHIP flows from the soul of the leader. It's not much to be only physically concerned about your business, mission, and vision—where you make sure all of the procedures are in place. You've got to be passionately, emotionally, almost spiritually concerned about your business, your followers, your product.

For **Judith M. Bardwick**, leadership is not intellectual or cognitive, it is emotional: "In war-time conditions, when the world is scary and the future uncertain, when people are experiencing fear, dread, foreboding and exhaustion, they have an emotional need for a leader, a person whom they can trust and to whom they want to make an emotional commitment. Leaders evoke emotional connections in followers only to the extent that followers are emotionally needy." Ultimately, she says, "leaders lead because they create a passionate commitment in other people to pursue the strategy and succeed."

Chip R. Bell notes that leaders are "embraced" when they lead with passion. "Great mentors are not always rational beings. They are often flame seekers. They give passionate birth in the face of threatening circumstances."

For **Everett T. Suters** inspirational leadership is the soul of a leader. "Teams thrive on inspiration, and that comes from hands-off executives who add it to otherwise ho-hum management functions. Real leaders add real value by building companies with common products and services around unique concepts."

Craig R. Hickman writes that "the condition of the heart and soul of the leader is of primary concern to those who are being asked to follow." Leaders need to "give adequate thought and consideration to how and why they lead, the methods and motives behind their leadership actions." Doing so will help leaders achieve "a dynamic balance between managers" and themselves.

D. Kirkwood Hart reminds us that the moral principles of leadership "are the foundation upon which all leadership practices must rest." Incorporating the moral principles of leadership is vital because "an understanding of the ideal must precede the practical." **Robert E. Staub II** believes that "leadership is the critical competency, the crown jewel of all the core competencies needed to have a healthy culture." Leaders must overcome their ego, their fear, and their impatience.

Sheila Murray Bethel says that leaders can make a "big difference in performance" if they possess 12 value-based leadership qualities. For **Blaine N. Lee**, leaders can also make a difference when they base their leadership power on principles. Principle-centered power allows leaders to be followed out of trust, respect, and honor. Along the same lines, **Alexander B. Horniman** believes that leaders "become powerful" when they center their relationships on the rock of moral dimensions. Good leaders are those who create "excellent relationships."

Patrick L. Townsend and **Joan E. Gebhardt** suggest that military leaders "tend to be more people-centered than their business counterparts," because they have been "compelled to trust" their people, and have maintained that trust. **David M. Noer** writes that what we don't trust is "ambiguity, equivocation, systems, and complexity."

H. Ross Perot notes that caring leaders are people "the rest of the team trusts and respects. As a leader, you have to earn that trust every minute of every day."

Jim Shaffer believes that leadership means telling the truth. Leadership needs to be "based on shared interests and partnerships," and telling the truth aids in that process. **Delmar L. Landen** notes that leaders should lead by covenant, and not by contract. "Covenants are shaped by our values, deeds, and convictions. They elevate people to higher levels of achievement." **Bill Westfall** suggests that leaders should care equally for both the spirit and the body of their organization.

CHAPTER 40

Emotional Leadership

by Judith M. Bardwick, President of Bardwick & Associates

ULTIMATELY, leaders lead because they create a passionate commitment in other people to pursue the strategy and succeed.

When life is orderly and tasks are predictable and most things are going well, people neither want nor need much leadership. Comfortable people are not in any state of need that would lead them to embrace a leader and seek change. In those circumstances people want peace-time management and leadership.

Peace-time management involves incremental modification of what exists, without major disruption and without any major emotional consequences.

In peace time, when there's no sense of emergency or urgency, "leaders" don't have to be special, and they don't have to generate an emotional following. Then, "leaders" are simply people who occupy positions of power. Anyone in those positions is seen as a "leader," irrespective of what they do, because there's no need to do very much. And that's fine with their followers as long as life remains comfortable and orderly.

Today, there are few circumstances in which peace-time managers can succeed because, overall, peace-time conditions are over. In this era of globalization, we need to find comfort in endless danger.

Technology has created a borderless world, and a borderless economy. The result is that everyone will lose the protection of distance and time. More and more, it doesn't matter where work is done. This results in increased opportunities and increased competition.

Peace-time managers, people who are most comfortable in static conditions, will have to learn to become war-time leaders, people who embrace major change because they see far more opportunity than threat in turbulence.

In peace time, people don't get honed on a hard stone in which they learn to be unafraid of change, and of making the right but the hard choice.

Emotional neediness, or the desire for leadership, results from conditions of change, crisis, and urgency—what I call *war-time*. In *war-time* conditions, when the world is scary and the future uncertain, when people are experiencing fear, dread, foreboding, and exhaustion, they have an emotional need for a leader, a person whom they can trust and to whom they want to make an emotional commitment. Leaders evoke emotional connections in followers only to the extent that followers are emotionally needy.

WHAT WAR-TIME LEADERS DO

There are six things leaders must do.

1. Define the business of the business. The most important question in any organization has to be, "What is the business of our business?" The answer determines what you should do and shouldn't do (revisit the question often because the answer can change swiftly).

Deciding what's the business of the business is the first step in setting priorities. Setting priorities is a major leadership responsibility because, without priorities, efforts are splintered. Leaders must get people to focus, to be involved only in what matters the most. They must skillfully harness the natural sense of urgency that arises from external threat and use that to focus on doing what counts. Achieving the mission against hard odds, hitting stretch targets in the business of the business, is the glue that holds people together with a commitment to the good of all.

The best leadership frames the organization's mission and values in ways that members find transcendent: The goals of the business are transmuted from the dross of ordinary work into goals that are worthy of heroic efforts and even sacrifices.

2. Create a winning strategy. Leaders create a strategy that causes the organization to succeed, to grow, to prosper, to beat the competition. In a borderless economy, the question "What is our strategy, and what are our competitors' strategies?" must be raised and answered often. A winning strategy must say what the organization will do better than anyone else to be the customer's choice.

For strategy to succeed it must anticipate, create, and guide change—and it must create commitment. It needs to be so plausible, clever, bold, and achievable that it generates a conviction that even if the journey is hard, it's worth taking because the strategy has created a major competitive advantage.

Defining the business of the business shrewdly and wisely, and creating a strategy for winning that is convincing, are critical in terms of getting people convinced that they have real leaders.

3. Communicate persuasively. Leaders know that trust is a competitive advantage. Basically, trust is a matter of predictability. People trust others when they're told something will happen and it does. Major change always threatens trust and, ultimately, confidence in leadership. Ineffective communication results in an enormous increase in mistrust, confusion, and cynicism, and a huge decline in morale and confidence in the leadership. Persuasive communication is critical in periods of major threat and change.

During periods of change, most leaders send out too many communications. When there are too many messages, not much gets through. And, where there's too much anxiety, not much gets through either. Leaders must decide what few pieces of information people really need to know, and simplify the messages they send. And, to reduce anxiety and increase commitment, leaders must communicate in person.

4. Behave with integrity. Without integrity, trust is never achieved. The best leaders are transparent; they do what they say, they walk the talk. People believe them because they act in line with the values they espouse. There are no Machiavellian games of manipulation.

Having integrity rests partly on personal courage. It requires being truthful with one's self as well as with others in terms of what is genuinely valued and considered important. Behaving with integrity also means being consistent in one's choices and actions. Leaders must have some certainty about what direction to take and which path to choose. That requires a clear conviction: a steadfastness of purpose in distinguishing between right and wrong, wise and foolish.

5. Respect others. The best leaders don't waste other people's brains. Leaders need a core sense of confidence which allows them to be comfortable receiving input, including disagreement, from others. They don't experience needing other people's input as demeaning. Effective leaders require input from everyone involved; they prefer spirited debate before decisions are made. Today, subordinates can bring lots of experience, knowledge, and skill to the table, if their leaders are able to "hear." Hearing others, like empowering others, isn't a matter of process; it's a matter of respect.

6. Act. The peace-time manager is great at planning and logistics, tasks in which people work hard but no one gets hurt. In contrast, in war time leaders must consider doing the unbearable.

War-time leadership involves actions in which some may be injured or even die. War-time leadership requires strength of character, self-discipline, courage, and deviance from what's popular.

When conditions are ambiguous and decisions are difficult, leaders must decide, choose, and act. They understand that when leaders don't act, they're perceived as indecisive and weak—and that increases people's sense of anxiety, powerlessness, and insecurity. When people doubt their leaders' ability, confidence, or effectiveness, the mission is sabotaged.

And people need to perceive that leaders believe that change creates more opportunity than threat. Thus, even while leaders must keep contact with reality, they also must be optimists.

Today, leaders must convince people that dealing with unending change will result in something better. Leadership, ultimately, is an emotional bond, sometimes even a passionate commitment between followers and the leader and the leader's goals. Leaders generate hope and conviction in followers.

At the emotional level, leaders create followers because they generate: confidence in people who are frightened, certainty in people who were vacillating, action where there was hesitation, strength where there was weakness, expertise where there was floundering, courage where there were cowards, optimism where there was cynicism, and a conviction that the future will be better.

Leadership is not intellectual or cognitive. Leadership is emotional.

CHAPTER 41

Passionate Leadership

by Chip R. Bell, Senior Partner with Performance Research Associates

WHY ARE SOME leaders embraced while others are rejected? The answer has little to do with reason, but everything to do with passion.

Larry Smith lost it! And, of all places, he lost it in the big-deal quarterly executive meeting. He absolutely went over the edge in his impassioned plea for customer focus.

The "Larry loses his cool" incident led me to reflect on contemporary leadership. I thought about the corporate artifacts of control, consistency, and "keeping one's cool." I thought about how little these artifacts had anything to do with fervor, spirit, and passion in any context of life—except in the corporate world.

People do not brag about their rational marriages, their reasonable hobbies, or their sensible vacations. There is rarely "in control" behavior when Junior is seen rounding third base. Exhortations of ecstasy are never restrained on the fishing bank when the cork suddenly disappears, and with surprising force. Logic is not the tone of retorts when loud-mouthed, red-necked cousin Luther unleashes his hate-filled segregationist views at a family reunion. But, somehow all that ardor is an unwelcome aberration after time has expired. And, the closer one gets to mahogany row, the less tolerance there seems to be for "sounds of the heart."

I also thought about how freeing it is for everyone when a person speaks from the heart. Are we uncomfortable? Yes! Do we wonder: "Where the hell is this going?" Yes! But, we all feel momentarily in kinship with real life. Julia Roberts echoed the theme in "Steel Magnolias" when, as a passionate diabetic expectant mother facing the life-threatening potential of giving birth for the first time, she said: "I would rather have 30 minutes of 'wonderful' than a lifetime of 'nothing special.' "

Great mentors are not always rational beings. They are often flame seekers. They give passionate birth in the face of threatening circumstances.

PASSION IS HONEST

Passion is more honest than reason! To be sure, logic is more elegant, more sensible, and surely more prudent. And, one feels far more secure and calm with the rational. Predictability never makes the heart race. Passion leaves a person feeling fearful of the on-the-edge, unanticipated outcome. It also makes us feel free, alive, and somehow "a real, whole person." And, when leaders surface that feeling in us, we are somehow more energized, more like a knight ready for battle.

When I was an infantry unit commander in Vietnam, young men went into battle with no knowledge of the complex sociopolitical ramifications of the Vietnam war. Yet, these men were ready to die. For what? For "duty, honor, and country." How illogical and amorphous can a cause be? What is the sensibility of courageously charging a well-entrenched sniper with an almost certain potential you will be among his body count—for duty?

What made GIs do it? It was passion, not reason. Action was enticed by the spirit of the day, not the sanity of the moment. What would you die for at work? "Die for?" you ask. Consider this: Is not business welfare as important to our global survival as national pride?

"Whoa!" you say. We can't have the chaos of unbridled emotion and the confusion of out-of-control desire. What would the stockholders say? After all, is it not the role of a leader to bring forth a sense of "grace under pressure"? Should leaders not strive to be more anchor than sail? More rudder than oar?

"No!" We have missed the boat on what it means to be leader. The world, the organization, and the situation offer far more "predictable" than is predictably required. The truth is that rationality oozes from the seams of every business encounter. Leaders do not have to add order, sanity, rationality, or logic. Every dimension of business life reeks with those qualities.

Sane leaders foster "insane" passion. Memorable leaders call up in each of us a visit with the raggedy edge of brilliance and the out-of-the-way corner of genius. When we feel inspired, incensed, or ennobled, we have visited the magical realm of passion. And, we typically return from that realm renewed, revitalized, and slightly revolted. The bittersweet taste of unexplored talent is the by-product of a passion projection into that world. And, when a leader has had a hand in that flight, there is a sense of partnership wedded to an otherwise solitary search.

PASSION IS INVITATIONAL

"There is an energy field between humans," wrote philosopher Rollo May. "And, when a person reaches out in passion, it is usually met with an answering passion." Passionate connections provoke passionate responses. Leadership is fundamentally about influencing.

Ask 20 people to name the greatest leaders of all times. Sure, you might get a military general or two. But, the list will likely be made up more of leaders who stirred their followers with fire than leaders who lectured their followers with reasoning. John Kennedy, Winston Churchill, Martin Luther King, Mother Teresa, and Albert Schweitzer were not famous for their rationalism—nor is Herb Kelleher (Southwest Airlines), Bruce Nordstrom, the late Sam Walton, or the late J. Willard Marriott, Sr. Leaders' invitations to action are embossed on their own yearnings to express their "cause" to others in ways that encourage others to join.

One of my partners and I checked into a mid-town New York hotel one evening. I approached the desk clerk with a mile-wide smile and a jovial disposition. I made 20 seconds of small talk with the desk clerk, making certain to use the clerk's name which I eyeballed on his uniform jacket. Ron, my partner, was at the tail end of a head cold and had just taken an eight-hour flight. He was, to put it diplomatically, in a rather somber mood and said only the minimum to the desk clerk.

Our plan was for us to go to our respective rooms, drop our luggage, and rendezvous in my room to go out for dinner. And, that is what we did.

Ron dropped his luggage in his room and then came across the hall to my suite! "How did you get this suite?" Ron asked with obvious irritation. "My Southern accent!" I quickly replied. The truth obviously lay in the fact that I took the time, just 20 seconds, to connect with the desk clerk.

PASSION IS MAGICAL

Passion takes the plain vanilla out of encounters. It is a leap into relationships. And, it is magical! Goethe called it "boldness" and said: "Whatever you can do, or dream you can, begin in boldness. Boldness has genius, power, and magic in it. Until one is committed, there is hesitancy, the chance to draw back, always ineffectiveness. The moment one definitely commits oneself, then Providence moves, too. All sorts of things occur to help one that would never otherwise have occurred."

Philosopher Hegel wrote, "Nothing great in the world has been accomplished without passion."

Followers need passionate connections. Leaders who come soaring from the heart awaken boldness in others. It builds a relationship platform that raises everyone to a higher level. Civil War Southern general Thomas J. Jackson was never again called "Tom" after someone spotted him on the battlefield and remarked, "There stands General Jackson like a stone wall." His troops developed the reputation of demonstrating the same spirited, "never say die" passion in combat. And, who can forget the same phenomenon among leaders named Martin, Mahatma, and Susan B.? Again, people may be instructed by reason, but they are inspired by passion.

Why are you here, in this role, at this time? What difference will you being here make? What legacy will you leave behind? Will you be forgotten for what you maintained or remembered for what you added? Imposing mountains are climbed, culture-changing movements are started, and breakthrough miracles are sparked by leaders who took the governors off rationalism and prudence, letting their spirit ascend from within.

CHAPTER 42

Inspirational Leadership

by Everett T. Suters, Chairman and CEO of Curry Marketing, Inc., and MDI, Inc.

TEAMS THRIVE on inspiration, and that comes from hands-off executives who add it to otherwise ho-hum management functions. And real leaders add real value by building companies with common products and services around unique concepts.

Our greatest potential threat is not external to our businesses, but is rather an internal threat that is rarely recognized or addressed—and that threat is the *loss of inspiration* within ourselves and our associates.

I define inspiration as that emotion which enhances or intensifies activity by giving life, action, and spirit to the achieving of objectives. The great hidden resource of most companies is the difference between the average jobs that some of our people are doing and the outstanding jobs they would do if they were so inspired.

Why, then, isn't the power of inspiration given more attention by management? Most managers ignore inspiration because it is emotion, intangible and unmeasurable. And yet its presence or absence is quickly felt within the culture of the company; in fact, a low grade atmosphere and attitude might be described as the loss of inspiration.

Inspiration starts or stops at the top. In almost any organization, five to seven people at the top will determine success or failure, and will either inspire or not inspire people. Many enterprises are launched successfully, often against overwhelming odds, grow rapidly to a point, but then begin to fail, just when you would expect them to become even more successful, because of top management's failure to make the transition from "hands-on" perspiration management to "hands-off" inspiration management.

- *"Hands-on" managers* provide leadership by giving direction to their people. Their direction is a course of action that is imposed as authoritative instruction. In other words, these managers tell their people what to do!

- *"Hands-off" managers* provide leadership and guidance for people to generate their own inspiration. Their leadership is described in the writings of Lao-tze, 600 B.C., when he wrote: "To lead the people, get behind them. When the great leader's work is done, the people say, 'We did it ourselves.' " We give advice on courses of action, as opposed to exercising our authority in telling people what to do.

SOME HARD LESSONS

I was very much a "hands-on" manager and went through a painful transition to become a "hands-off" manager. In 1966, eight years after starting my first business, it appeared that I had a very successful, fast-growing company. But I was a terribly overworked, frustrated "hands-on" manager, and was seriously considering selling my business and going back to work for a large corporation.

My once successful "hands-on" style had destroyed my effectiveness. My time, energy, and inspiration became more and more diluted among too many responsibilities. In desperation, I attended a conference for company presidents and sought the advice of other CEOs. I quickly discovered how I could program myself out of my major problems by becoming a "hands-off" manager.

Occasionally, situations occur that demand our "hands-on" attention. We must then be like "bell-cows," leading the way with a high profile, showing and telling people what to do, and perhaps putting in longer hours and directly producing more results than anyone else in our group. However, after our "hands-on" attention is no longer required, we must revert to being "hands-off" managers, or we will become less focused on those few top priorities that represent the greatest potential in results, and we will then be faced with the threat of losing our inspiration.

Management deals simultaneously in two time dimensions: the work of tomorrow and the work of today. Therefore, we'd better keep our jobs in proper perspective when we take a "bifocal" view of the management process. Although the work of today is more immediate and demanding than the work of tomorrow, the work of tomorrow is almost always more important. But many managers are so busy dealing with the work of today that they do not think much about the work of tomorrow.

The work of tomorrow deals with the "hands-off" strategic functions of establishing objectives and planning how to achieve these objectives. These functions are sources of inspiration for managers because the objectives we expect to achieve are more inspiring than those that we have already achieved. The very process of planning is inspirational because we always plan to succeed, and never intentionally plan to fail.

ADD INSPIRATION TO FUNCTIONS

Here's how to add more inspiration using a "hands-off" approach to common management functions.

• *When organizing resources to achieve objectives*, we can show that we believe in and trust our associates by giving them their own responsibilities, and then not looking over their shoulders or second-guessing them while they are doing their own work.

• *In staffing*, we can focus on hiring the right people, retaining the right people, training them to assume more responsibility, rehabilitating those who become counterproductive, and eliminating uninspiring misfits who can't be rehabilitated and any others who do not belong in the organization.

• *When communicating*, we can use words and actions to show we care about and believe in our employees. Caring about and believing in people are two different concepts. People appreciate it when we display that we care about them, and caring about them tends to develop loyalty. This generates some inspiration, but people tend to be more inspired when we display that we believe in them.

We also add inspiration when we *openly communicate* with our people and don't keep them in the dark. What they need to know is irrelevant—they are inspired by being kept informed about what they want to know. In my companies, we are always very open, even to the extent of distributing financial statements to all of our managers, good times or bad. If you don't tell people what is going on, they will guess and guess wrong, usually on the negative side.

• *Monitoring and controlling* can also be inspiring, although they usually are not. I have often heard the expression: "People do what we *inspect*, not what we *expect*." The fallacy of this statement is that we cannot inspect the thinking that takes place in the minds of those very few key people who will determine the success or failure of our companies. We can realize better control of overall results by monitoring the *assumptions* of the major decisions, and subsequent results of those who have "thinking" jobs.

• *When we restructure*, we can add inspiration by adding or subtracting layers of management. It is very popular now to "bash" hierarchy and to extol the virtues of a flat structure. But, in my opinion, management hierarchy is getting a "bum rap." While most *Fortune* 500 companies probably do have too many levels of management, many mid-size organizations have too few.

These are two key questions in determining the right hierarchy: (1) How many levels of management should your organization have? and

(2) How many people should answer to the senior executives in your organization? If you have more than two or three managers answering to any other manager in your top three levels, I suggest that you do some restructuring.

• *When managing your time*, you will be more inspiring if you minimize the distractions that prevent you from focusing on your more important priorities and cause you to deal with matters you neither want nor should be involved with. Turf invaders are those people who invade on your turf, uninvited, unwelcome, and unwanted. To keep them off your turf, you might ask them the magic question: "What do you recommend?" If you ask this question every time they come to you with a problem regarding their responsibilities, you discipline them to think through their own recommendations about how to handle their responsibilities. More often than not, they will come up with their own answers.

If that doesn't work, you might move your office to a more remote location in the company. The symbolism of this move can be very powerful. You might also go to their offices when people need to see you. This conveys an attitude of wanting to support them. When you make them always come to your office, you convey the impression that they are supporting you.

• *You will also be more inspiring if you do not promote a perception that you, or any of your key people, are irreplaceable.* It is a great paradox that managers do not become irreplaceable because of their management skills, but rather because of their non-managerial skills. The value-added of "hands-off" management is in establishing objectives, planning how to achieve these objectives, orchestrating the use of resources, and giving guidance. These are not irreplaceable functions.

Henry David Thoreau wrote: "Most people lead lives of quiet desperation," and unfortunately, I believe he was right. However, all people want to feel better about themselves, and have the expectation of improving the quality of their lives. Executives have an opportunity, if not an obligation, to create an atmosphere and attitude that will inspire people and empower them to improve their lives. Inspiration is contagious and reciprocal. The more your associates become inspired, the more their inspiration, in turn, will inspire you. Our threat is not the loss of the inspiration of our people, but rather the loss of our own inspiration, and our own passion for our work. The greatest chance of this happening is when we are "hands-on" managers.

Thoreau also wrote: "If a man does not keep pace with his companions, perhaps it is because he hears a different drummer." My wish is that you will not allow the louder drumbeats of your "hands-on" demands of today distract you from your less demanding, but more important, drumbeats of tomorrow!

CHAPTER 43

Soul of Leadership

by Craig R. Hickman, President and CEO of
Management Perspective Group, Inc.

THE CONDITION OF the heart and soul of the leader is of primary concern to those who are being asked to follow.

In researching this article, I examined more than a hundred leaders to better understand their methods and motives of leadership.

Among these leaders were business executives, educators, commanders-in-chief, politicians, foreign heads of state, economic theorists, Wall Street power brokers, military dictators, contemporary and classical philosophers, TV evangelists, software developers, bureaucrats, media moguls, sports figures, industrialists, and a host of others.

What I discovered among most leaders was a preoccupation with results and a shallow, superficial regard for issues and situations dealing with morality, ethics, mental-emotional-spiritual health, and the search for deeper meaning in life. In general, few leaders give adequate thought and consideration to how and why they lead, and the methods and motives behind their leadership actions.

The leadership soul cries out for nourishment. But ethics, morals, and a deeper sense of life's meaning can't come back into the equation until we abandon our shallow and superficial approach to leadership. Until then, we'll most likely sit back and wait until something else goes wrong or the results fail to meet our expectations. Then, crying for blood, we'll reach for the first stone, or worse, just chalk up the failure to politics or business as usual.

Many Americans have mastered the results-oriented behavior associated with strong leadership. They have a wide repertoire of dances down pat: flattering speech, administrative know-how, tough-mindedness, gamesmanship, people skills, strategic thinking, image control, and a host of other skills and behaviors. Technically, we can waltz or samba with the best of them, but our dance technique lacks great music and choreography.

The mechanics of leadership provide the pattern and pace of those activities we choose to label "leading," but only the soul of the leader can provide great music and choreography.

Fortunately, there are some recent signs of life in the current leadership landscape. The Yankelovich research firm recently reported increased concern among many Americans about questions of morality, ethics, spirituality, and social well-being. Their report suggests that we seem to be hearing the far-off music and envisioning the choreography.

My own extensive involvement with successful CEOs, ambitious middle managers, and aspiring workers worldwide has convinced me that businesspeople, too, have begun to question the deeper, fundamental methods and motives of their leaders.

I offer a simple approach for assessing fundamental leadership methods and motives—one that examines the choices between controlling or empowering others and between personal or mutual gain. At the most fundamental level, every one of us leads by choosing to control or empower others to one degree or another, and by choosing to seek personal or mutual benefit to one degree or another.

- At the bottom of this leadership ladder, we find "more control of others for more personal gain," in other words, the amount of control is extreme and the desire for personal gain is excessive. These are *oppressors*.

- Up one step, we find "less control of others for less personal benefit," i.e., the amount of control over others and the extent of personal benefit is reduced to some degree in deference to the needs and desires of others. These are *dominators*.

- Moving up another step, we encounter "less empowering of others for less mutual benefit," or, the extent of empowerment is kept within certain bounds and the extent of mutual benefit is limited to particular groups or domains. These are *maximizers*.

- Finally, moving to the last step, we discover "more empowering of others for more mutual benefit," where the extent of empowerment and the extent of mutual benefit are both widespread in their application. These are *orchestrators*.

As you can see, the four leadership styles (combinations of methods and motives) match up with four phases of organizational and societal development: crisis, change, stability, and renewal.

Of the four phases, the first and last occur least frequently, the second and third the most frequently.

Genuine leadership methods and motives will most likely surface during the *transition* from one phase or set of circumstances to another. For example, a leader with entrenched controlling methods and personal gain motives will continue using an oppressive style long after it no longer works constructively.

Having briefly reviewed the hierarchy of leadership methods and motives, styles, and phases, let's now examine the soul of leadership.

SELF-ASSESSMENT

Do you care enough to learn more about yourself, the good and the bad? Do you care enough to change? Do you care enough to examine your own leadership methods and motives?

All of us need to look at ourselves more deeply and honestly and create in ourselves a greater capacity for ethical, moral, and meaningful leadership. We must fully commit ourselves to obtaining a degree of self-knowledge, much deeper and more intimate than most leaders ever try to attain. If, upon self-examination, you find that your problems are related to your natural or preferred leadership style, you must decide whether you can and want to change.

Changing your natural or preferred leadership style means altering the fundamental methods and motives that form the soul of your leadership. Although such fundamentals can be hard to change, you can do a much better job of doing so if you carefully educate your heart. Consider the following insights.

Hearts can be jealous, evil, immoral, and depraved. These hearts are usually unreachable unless they finally see that their actions will eventually destroy themselves as well as others.

Other hearts are proud, impatient, and distrusting. They seal themselves off from efforts at change. Constantly justifying themselves, they most often remain unchanged and hard.

Some hearts are manipulative, exploitative, secretive, insensitive, uncaring, unfeeling, callous, untouched, indifferent, numb, disinterested, and cold. Such hearts could care less about changing except for the most selfish reasons. These hearts resist change as much as the others.

Of course, except in the most severe cases, the hard heart can soften, the cold heart can thaw, and the treacherous heart can forsake evil. Most of us exhibit a little hardness, coldness, or treachery at times in our lives, and we should remain alert for their appearance so we can correct and rebuild.

Not surprisingly, the characteristics of entrenched oppressors, perpetual dominators, and unrelenting maximizers (excessiveness, destructiveness, jealousy, pride, impatience, distrust, manipulativeness, exploitativeness, and secrecy) tend to go hand in hand with such cold, hard, or treacherous hearts. To overcome such characteristics, hearts must be educated.

SELF-MONITORING PROCESS

America's current leadership famine stems from many people adopting other than appropriate leadership styles; but it has been deepened by an insufficient number of leaders striving to become orchestrators. We have become so good at reacting to rapidly changing and increasingly complex situations that we have allowed our deepest motivations to adjust to the circumstances.

We have become a society sadly lacking in clear-cut morality, firm ethical standards, and steadfast spirituality. When we have effectively shifted among oppressive, dominating, maximizing, or orchestrating leadership, we have often done so without a devotion to the higher level, namely orchestration. Some, in fact, have become so effective at switching, they seem to have completely lost their leadership souls.

To combat this tendency, take careful stock of your true, preferred leadership style. In short, you must monitor the soul of your leadership.

Are you committed enough to the orchestrating path to set aside one hour a week to monitor your progress? If so, you might follow this agenda:

1. *Identify* the major leadership acts (decisions, judgments, actions, recommendations, discussions, etc.) you undertook in the past week. List them in order of significance.

2. *Assess,* using the Ladder of Leadership styles, the methods and motives associated with each leadership act by placing the number of the leadership act at the appropriate level on the leadership ladder. Be as discriminating and honest as you can in locating each leadership act.

3. *Write down* in your daily planner or journal any positive or negative comment you (or others) can make about your leadership actions for the past week. Have your methods and motives been consistent? Has any crisis situation caused you to waiver from your normal leadership style? Can you spot any positive or negative trends?

4. *Keep track* of progress on strengthening positive leadership characteristics and eliminating negative ones. Record progress at least weekly in your planner or journal.

By putting yourself through this self-monitoring process once a week, you should begin to understand yourself better as a leader. That understanding can revitalize your life.

To improve your leadership, do all you can to better interpret organizational phases and apply appropriate leadership styles while continually striving to become an orchestrator in renewal organizations. Pay close attention to the fundamental methods and motives of your leadership. Begin to see things as they really are so you can help make things better for everyone, not in a quick-fix, shallow, or short-term way, but through an enduring, constant rediscovery of your leadership soul.

CHAPTER 44

Moral Principles of Leadership

 by D. Kirkwood Hart, the 1996 BYU Alumni Professor, Marriott School of Management, Brigham Young University

WHILE LEADERSHIP is one of our foremost obsessions, we still don't understand it very well.

We know a great deal about hands-on leadership, but we know little about the moral principles of leadership. These are the foundation upon which all leadership practices must rest, and yet they are rarely studied and applied. Because of our collective failure to get at these moral principles, leadership goes astray, management schemes fail, and employees are alienated.

BEGIN WITH THE IDEAL

To be effective, all leadership must begin with a knowledge of, and belief in, certain moral principles: *an understanding of the ideal must precede the practical.* In our time, some people argue that moral values are culturally defined. In their opinion, any principles will do so long as they don't hurt anyone else.

This "I'm OK, you're OK" thinking has caused a lot of individual, social, and political damage—not because it is ill-intentioned, but because it makes leadership criteria dependent upon what is trendy in any given culture, or subculture.

I argue that there are objective moral principles that transcend both cultures and times. They are constant because they emerge from a common and unchanging human nature, and their validity has been consistently demonstrated through the centuries and across cultural boundaries.

There is a fundamental human need for all individuals to be free, to be treated with dignity, to express their own creativity. Therefore, I contend that leaders have the moral obligation to create such conditions for their subordinates for the simple reason that they have power over them: In other words, *the powers of office morally obligate leaders.*

The primary imperative of the leadership orthodoxy is: All loyalty must be directed upward, and no loyalty downward is required. In fact, loyalty downward is considered to be dysfunctional leadership, since it supposedly inhibits leadership flexibility.

At first glance, this may seem to be an overstatement, yet this is one of the most fundamental assumptions of orthodox leadership. This assumption underlies the pernicious waves of downsizing in organizations, both public and private. Leaders claim the right to downsize as a necessity for effective performance, and yet, nearly every study about downsizing demonstrates that the employees who remain tend to be alienated, cynical, unwilling to take any risks, and far less productive.

The steward leadership imperative is that *loyalty downward must always be greater than loyalty upward.* In other words, leaders must be more loyal to their employees than the reverse. Many studies show what this does for the teamwork, and profitability.

Steward leadership is a reasonably straightforward notion. It rests upon the primacy of the moral character of the leader, a character based upon the seven cardinal virtues: courage, temperance, justice, prudence, faith, hope, and charity. However, at a time when good leadership is so desperately needed, too many authors trivialize the subject by reducing it to pure technique.

These individuals are the defenders of the contemporary leadership paradigm: a leadership orthodoxy whose credo rests upon the assumption that all individuals are, by nature, self-interested, and that in the service of that self-interest, we are also malleable—willing to adapt our very personalities to meet the needs of organizations that we hope will reward us. The "practicality" of the leadership orthodoxy, in fact, rests upon a set of value assumptions that are accepted as being morally correct and unquestionable.

Our obsession with technique has led us to neglect the heart and soul of leadership: that moral essence that sets an Abraham Lincoln apart from a Millard Fillmore, or a Harry Truman from a Lyndon Johnson, or a General James Gavin from a General Dwight Eisenhower, or a Max DePree from a Steve Ross.

WHY DO SOME SUCCEED?

I find it helpful to reduce the problem to a simple question: Why do some leaders succeed in a spectacular fashion, while others—in the same circumstances and with similar, or even better, credentials—fall flat on their faces? The answer has been the same in nearly all instances: *Successful leaders, where success is measured over the long haul, understand the principles of steward leadership, and combine them with a congruent technical expertise.*

The argument for steward leadership rests upon three assumptions: first, steward leadership is based upon a relatively few moral principles; second, those principles are constant because they emerge from our common, innate human nature; and, third, a knowledge of, and belief in, the moral principles must precede the techniques of leadership, if the latter are to be successful. Thus, the moral principles of steward leadership are relevant to all leaders.

The moral principles of steward leadership apply across disciplinary and cultural boundaries, because they emerge from our common human nature, just as Deming's moral principles of management emerge from that same common human nature. Industry-specific examples are sometimes useful, but they are not essential. What is essential is that a leader understands and believes in the principles of steward leadership and then applies them to the situation.

Creativity in practical application takes precedence over an obsessive concern with industry-specific rules—but even more important, the good character of the leader must take precedence over technical proficiency. Technical expertise is extremely important, but the imperative to gain such technical knowledge is driven by the prior commitment to the moral principles of steward leadership.

CHAPTER 45

Overcoming Ego

by Robert E. Staub, President of Staub-Peterson
Leadership Consultants

LEADERSHIP IS the critical competency, the crown jewel of all the core competencies needed to have a healthy culture.

For too long, corporate America has been overmanaged and seriously underled. We are now reaping the bitter harvest that comes from forfeiting the future by focusing on the short term. We live in an age of rapid change, competitive challenge, and an emergent global economy. Thriving in such an environment requires powerful and effective leadership at all levels.

The good news is that effective and powerful leadership can be developed. Effective leaders are not born, they are made over time. Leadership is not a mysterious substance. It is a mixture of science and art. In our companies and society, we must learn how to nurture, develop, and support quality leadership. A place to begin is with sound principles of leadership.

OVERCOMING THREE BARRIERS

The greatest barriers to becoming a more effective leader—of being able to achieve long-term, meaningful, and sustainable results while crafting the relationships to accelerate those results—are to be found within the leader. These barriers must be faced if we are to develop the leadership we are crying for. The barriers are: *ego, fear,* and *impatience.*

• *Ego* is that part of us which believes we know it all and makes us unwilling or slow to learn from others or even from our own mistakes. It is the part of our identity which would rather blame others than take a look at what we have done to contribute to the problem. It can also take the path of excusing ourselves by saying that we aren't capable of something, which begs off by deflating our confidence to learn and change the quality of our lives or of our environment. Leaders who make a positive difference have learned to manage their egos and to pursue their vision rather than the dictates of a limited self-definition. They also have a feel for how to manage the egos of others.

• *Fear* is the emotion of paralysis. It forces us to be unduly prudent, holding back and waiting for someone else to act. William Blake said, "Prudence is an old maid, courted by incapacity." Fear can make us incapable of acting while life passes us by. Out of our emotion of fear we can shrink to a tenth of our true size and either engage in actions which of which we are not worthy or refrain from taking the actions which are in keeping with our highest aspirations. Leaders feel fear, but they act on what they most aspire to, using the fear as raw energy to keep them humble but focused. The fear becomes an ally and not a limiting factor.

• *Impatience* is the unwillingness to allow events and processes to mature and unfold. Processes require time and effort. Impatience either destroys or damages the desired results. Impatience can also lead to aborting a process or program because the results are not immediate.

LEADERS ARE LEARNERS

Leaders are learners and curious about the world. They manage their egos, their fears, and their impatience in order to try new things, to achieve better results, and to create stronger relationships. They inspire others to rise above their own issues around ego, fear, and impatience to produce the actions which realize results and make dreams come true.

There are three kinds of people in life: one makes things happen, another watches things happen, and a third wonders what happened. Leaders make things happen. And for them to make things happen, they have to inspire some members of the other two groups to enter the ranks of those who make things happen.

Effective leaders remember that all work is done by people, with people, through people, and for people. Leaders function by creating alignment around tasks, inspiring and relating to people. Leadership is high touch.

In studying effective leaders, I find only one way to define effective leadership and only two ways to measure it: Effective leaders are known solely by the *actions* they take—and these actions are measured by the *results* they achieve and by the *relationships* they forge. We know leaders by the actions that flow from them and by the actions they inspire others to take. We then measure the success of those actions by what they generate in terms of results and relationships.

• *Results* center upon and emerge from the vision or direction set by a leader. These are measured and known by the quality of the services, products, and overall coordination of tasks which shape the work environment.

• *Relationships* center upon cultivating and improving the willingness, commitment, and abilities of those around the leader to keep producing and enhancing the desired results: products and services.

Leaders can't achieve results without forging meaningful, powerful, and ongoing relationships. The actions of effective leaders shape relationships and propel the system and the people within the system to produce meaningful long-term results. Leaders are willing to make mistakes en route to the desired results, and they do not allow their followers to despair on the journey.

To continue to produce results, leaders must envision the desired future outcome, communicate that vision, and build the team to bring the vision to fruition

Successful long-term leadership requires a high level of self-understanding. This great principle of self-relationship is best reflected in the words of Sun Tzu, one of the masters of leadership strategy. In his classic, *The Art of War*, the venerable Chinese general of a thousand years ago says:

> *If you know not yourself and know not your enemy, then you will lose every battle you fight. If you know your enemy but know not yourself, then you will lose every other battle you fight. If you know yourself and know your enemy, you need not fear the outcome of a hundred battles.*

The actions of successful leaders in achieving results and in building relationships are based on a healthy level of self-understanding and empathy with others. This makes for long-term strength and provides a level of strategic insight unmatched by people who are the victims of their drives and ambitions. The capacity for empathy allows for a deeper and more penetrating understanding of human nature. The mistakes of overreaching, of creating scapegoats, of backing down to a bully, of short-term gains at the expense of the future, are those of the individual who lacks insight into his or her own nature and the nature of people.

We all must contribute to the revitalization of our organizations and our society through an intelligent and compassionate focus on results and relationships.

CHAPTER 46

Qualities of Leadership

by Sheila Murray Bethel, Founder and President of
Getting Control, Inc.

YOU CAN MAKE a big difference in performance if you have the mission, mind, and morals of leadership.

Can you train someone to be a leader? Can you develop leadership qualities within yourself? Can you make a difference? The answer is *yes!* We must make a difference as individuals, organizations, and as a nation.

The years leading to and after the turn of the century will be the most challenging the world has ever faced. We need leaders at every level of our society.

The most exciting part of living in these changing times is that, while we still want to be successful, our new definition of success includes the desire to make a contribution—to personally make a difference. That means you and I take responsibility to lead ourselves first, then extend those skills to our families, our jobs, and our communities. This kind of grassroots leadership will make the difference in building our organizations and our country during the next century.

The foundation of effective value-based leadership comes in two parts: (1) the desire to serve—Lao Tzu, ancient Chinese philosopher said, "A leader is one who serves"; and (2) the understanding that we lead first by example. Everything we say or do sends a message, sets a tone, or teaches people what to do or what not to do.

QUALITIES MAKE A DIFFERENCE

With this foundation firmly in place, you can build a structure of the 12 value-based leadership qualities that will help you make a difference by serving more effectively and setting powerful examples that motivate and inspire others.

1. Have a mission that matters. Having a mission that matters, one that makes a difference, is at the very core of a leader. It motivates and inspires followers. It is a powerful leadership quality that builds charisma. It releases the leaders' full potential and is their driving force. A mission acts like a magnet, attracting others. Missions often start small, and their size is not important. The fact that the leader has a mission is the important part. A clear value-based mission is a shining example to followers.

2. Be a big thinker. Robert F. Kennedy, quoting Robert Frost, said, "Some men see things as they are and say, why? I dream of things that never were and say, why not?" Leaders see things on a large perspective; they see things better than they are. Leaders are curious and have what Cavett Roberts calls "Divine Discontent." They challenge tradition, are not afraid of idealism, and are eager to create and bring out the best in others. Big thinkers have a clear definition of their personal goals and have the ability to help others expand their thinking and imagination.

3. Be ethical. Albert Schweitzer said, "Ethics is the maintaining of life at the highest point of development." A leader has clearly defined ethics and is steadfast in upholding them, even in the worst of times. Reaching for the highest point of development is the example leaders set for their followers. Leaders have a keen sense of fairness and justice. They are highly principled and law abiding. They value the rights of others and respect their followers. They have strong convictions and are not afraid to stand and be counted. They know that true success means having high ethics.

4. Be a change master. Rosabeth Moss Kanter calls leaders "prime movers" who move people and things in directions more beneficial to all. Leaders have the ability to create change; to accept it, handle it, and succeed during times of change. They welcome change as the only constant in life. They learn from the past and then let it go. They don't burden themselves with old ideas, prejudices, habits, or processes. Inspired leaders look for opportunity in change. They understand that they don't have to like the change, but they must understand it. They live by the tenet of the Serenity Prayer: "God grant me the serenity to accept the things I cannot change, courage to change the things I can, and wisdom to know the difference."

5. Be sensitive. Sensitivity is a vital quality for leaders. Today's leaders must be sensitive to the needs, values, and perceptions of their followers, because without responsive, productive people, the other considerations quickly become secondary. Sensitivity builds one of the most desirable qualities a follower can have—loyalty. Daniel Yankelovich describes sensitivity as one of the "soft" qualities which is crucial to the leaders effectiveness. At its best, sensitivity is "people building."

6. Be a risk taker. Leaders have the courage to begin while others are waiting for better times, safer situations, and assured results. Leaders are willing to take a risk because they know that overcaution and indecision rob opportunity and success. They are willing to fail in order to succeed. Leaders know that no one wins all the time, and that winning is not always the goal. They take initiative, are independent, and are not unduly influenced by others. Leaders live by the philosophy that "anything worth doing is worth doing poorly at first." They allow themselves and others to grow by making mistakes and not expecting perfection. President Harry Truman said, "Life is risky"; leaders take risks.

7. Be a decision maker. Deciding to decide is often harder than carrying through once the decision has been made. Leaders know that not deciding is a decision. It is letting time, fate, and circumstances make the choices. The leader is vitally aware of this and would rather make a wrong decision than none at all. Few decisions in life are so critical that they cannot be corrected. Leaders know that indecision wastes time, energy, talent, money and opportunity. They make decisions and commitments to avoid future failures. Leaders are willing to make decisions and plans that affect future generations because they know that indecision will forfeit everyone's future.

8. Use power wisely. Leaders do not shrink from power, nor do they seek it unnecessarily. They know that having clout often intimidates others, so they use their power judiciously. They "pull rank" only in emergencies. Leaders know that the "higher up you go—the more gently down you reach." They use their power to direct others and help them achieve their full potential. Leaders take responsibility for themselves, their actions, and the results. They use their power to instill this example in others. They know that power and greatness is not a goal to be sought after, but a by-product of learning how to serve.

9. Be a communicator. The power to communicate is the key to forging productive relationships. Good communication pays off in a leaders ability to: motivate and inspire people, take action, build cooperation and trust, maintain focus on the issues, resolve conflict, provide accurate information, and prevent communication breakdowns. The better the leader communicates, the better the chance to make a difference. "What you are speaks so loudly I cannot hear what you say," wrote Emerson. When the leader's words and actions match, communication becomes the highest form of leading by example.

10. Be a team builder. Team building encompasses all the qualities of a leader. It maximizes the potential of both leader and follower. The team-building leader will be a coach: directing, motivating, training, delegating, and making work enjoyable. Team building is the catalyst of all a leader wants to accomplish. As a servant-leader, there's no better way to make a difference than to create teams of caring, cooperative, committed followers. A leader recently said, "Team building is the most difficult and, at the same time, most rewarding of all the responsibilities I have."

11. Be courageous. "Have the courage of your convictions" is a familiar saying. Easier said than done! Leaders must have a strong belief system to withstand and meet boldly today's challenges and to maintain the courage of their convictions. Believing in their physical, emotional, intellectual, spiritual standards and values enables them to apply all their resources and creative energy when faced with problems of overwhelming odds. General George C. Patton said courage is "fear holding on another minute." Leaders are valiant and undaunted; in their approach to life, they "hold on." They venture forth with faith and stamina and set a courageous example for others to follow.

12. Be committed. Commitment is the primary word for leaders. They realize that without it all else is meaningless. Commitment runs deep in leaders. Their dedication to their mission pulls others to them. Their commitment exudes confidence and hope. Others become committed when they are with an unselfish, committed leader. They commit to high standards of excellence for themselves and others. They know that people grow when striving for excellence. They determine a course, make a plan, and then have the self-discipline to follow through in spite of obstacles.

Leaders stay, long after others give up. They know that life and business are like the seasons, so their commitment is sustained through the good and bad, hot and cold, ups and downs. They know that spring (hope and opportunity) always follows winter (darkness and lack of growth). Leaders are committed to their goals, while living one day at a time, knowing that if they take care of today, tomorrow will take care of itself. Leaders that make a difference are committed.

CHAPTER 47

Leading with Power

by Blaine N. Lee, Vice President, Franklin Covey Co.

LEGITIMATE EXECUTIVE POWER comes from a combination of character and competence—from being honorable and having the skill to exercise certain power principles.

We live in an interconnected world. We work together, shop together, worship together, and play together. In all these settings, we are with other people whose feelings, views, desires, goals, and values may be different from ours. When we come together, it is natural that we influence and are influenced by each other.

So who among us is powerful? How do we define power between individuals? Power is our ability to influence one another. If you're like most people, you know power when you see it, but it is hard to define.

An exercise I often perform with organizations illustrates this point. I ask, "Here's a personnel roster—rank these people in terms of their power." With no more instruction, people have no difficulty completing the task. Although there is some disagreement about the ranking of those in the middle, most people readily agree on who really has power. In fact, what I often find is that everyone agrees who's at the top and bottom of the list. People seem to sense who is powerful.

Do you know a powerful person? This might be someone you have worked with, someone you have lived with, or some historical or current public figure you have read about. However you define power, this person has it. What makes others follow a leader with power?

THREE PATHS TO POWER

Although the reasons why followers follow are varied and complex, there are three basic paths to power.

1. Followers follow out of fear. They are afraid of what might happen to them if they don't do what they are asked to do. This may be called *coercive power.* The leader in this case has created a fear in the follower that either something bad is going to happen to them or something good will be taken away from them, if they do not comply. So out of fear of the aversive potential effects of consequences, they acquiesce and "get along by going along" or by giving "lip service loyalty," at least initially. But their commitment is superficial, and their energies can quickly turn to sabotage and destruction when "no one is looking" or the threat is no longer present. A well-publicized example involved the disgruntled airline clerk who, feeling he had been unjustly manipulated, deftly wiped out the flight schedules stored in computer memories the night he quit. The cost of forced compliance? Well over a million dollars and thousands of work hours were lost, with enormous negative backlash from unhappy passengers.

Coercive power is based on fear in both the leader and the follower. Leaders tend to lean on coercive power when they are afraid they won't get compliance. It is the big stick approach, an approach that few publicly support but many use, either because it seems justified in the face of other, bigger threats hovering over the leader, or it is the expedient thing to do and seems to work at the time. But its effectiveness is an illusion.

The leader who controls others through fear will find that the control is reactive and temporary. It is gone when the leader or the representative or the controlling system is gone. It often mobilizes the creative energies of followers to unite and resist in new, as yet uncontrolled ways. Coercive power imposes a psychological and emotional burden on both leaders and followers. It encourages suspicion, deceit, dishonesty and, in the long run, dissolution. As Alexander Solzhenitsyn has observed, "You only have power over people so long as you don't take everything away from them. But when you've robbed a man of everything, he's no longer in your power—he's free again."

2. Followers follow because of the benefits that come to them if they do. This may be called *utility power* because the power in the relationship is based on the useful exchange of goods and services. The followers have something the leader wants (time, money, energy, personal resources, interest, talent, support, etc.) and the leader has something they want (information, money, promotions, inclusion, camaraderie, security, opportunity, etc.). These followers operate with the belief that the leader can and will do something for them, if they maintain their part of the bargain by doing something for the leader. Much of what happens in the normal operation of organizations, from billion-dollar corporations to daily family living, is fueled by utility power.

Most organizations are held together by utility power. Utility power is based on a sense of equity and fairness. As long as followers feel that they are receiving fairly for what they are giving, the relationship will be sustained. The compliance which is based on utility power tends to look more like influence than control. The agency of the followers is respected and regarded, but from the perspective of "caveat emptor." Leaders are followed because it is functional for the followers. It gives them access to what the leader controls, through position or expertness or charisma. The nature of followership when based on utility power is still reactive, but the reaction tends to be positive rather than negative.

It is being increasingly acknowledged that relationships based on utility power often lead to individualism, rather than teamwork and group effectiveness, as individuals are reinforced for paying attention to their own perspective and desires. Individual players may change as wants and needs fluctuate. Shifting demographics of the workforce indicate that long-term loyalty, by leaders or followers, is the exception. Individuals come and go, from CEOs to clerks, with little repercussion in the marketplace—in a real sense we are all customers who go where we can get what we want the way we want.

In addition, a form of situational ethics is fostered, in which individuals are continually deciding, in the absence of shared organizational values, what is best and right and fair. At its worst, utility power mirrors the elements of justice prominent in a litigious society, with courts of law forcing fairness in takeovers, divorces, and bankruptcies. At its best, utility power reflects a willingness to stay in a relationship, whether business or personal, as long as it has a payoff for both parties.

3. *Followers follow out of trust, respect, and honor.* This kind of power represents an entirely different approach. It is based on the power some people have with others because others tend to believe in them and what they are trying to accomplish. They are trusted. They are respected. They are honored. And they are followed because others want to follow them, want to believe in them and their cause, want to do what the leader wants. This is not blind faith, mindless obedience, or robotic servitude; this is knowledgeable, wholehearted, uninhibited commitment. This is *principle-centered power.*

Nearly every one of us has experienced this type of power. We may have experienced it as followers, in relationships with employers, family members, or friends. It may have been someone who gave us an opportunity to succeed or excel, or encouraged us when things looked bleak, or just been available when needed. Whatever they did, they did it because they believed in us, and we reciprocate with respect, loyalty, commitment, and a willingness to follow, almost without condition or restriction.

THE POWER PROCESS

The power process describes the dynamic relationship between people as they attempt to influence each other. The power process begins with you. When I say you, I'm thinking about you in some very special ways—your skills, your future, your past, and your character. You possess a certain set of skills that enable you to do your job. You have the capacity to acquire new skills in the future. Your past is a record of where you have been and what you have done. Your character is an internal set of beliefs, motivations, desires, and principles that are manifested by your behavior.

Whatever the challenge, we have a choice. Will we choose one of the three types of power, or will we choose to be powerless? Powerful or powerless? That is the fundamental choice we make over and over again in life. Will we choose to act or be acted upon? If we choose to be powerful, which path to power will get us the results we want most? You might ask yourself, "What power base *will* I operate from, or will I choose to be powerless?" If other people are involved, you may be a formal or informal leader, or just a member of a group. In any case, you are in a position to determine and select a base to operate from to accomplish your purposes. The real question is "Which power base *can* I operate from?"

If we doubt our ability to affect others or make things happen the way we want, we back away from situations assuming there is nothing we can do. We choose to be powerless. There are many reasons we may feel this way. We might be ignorant of possibilities and alternatives. We might be frozen emotionally, unable to respond. We might get trapped in our circumstances genuinely believing there is no other way. If, however, we choose to act, even if we are acting in less than optimal ways, we choose to be powerful rather than powerless.

When we are afraid that nothing else will work, or that we won't make the deadline, or that others might not respond, we often resort to coercive power. It is relatively easy when push comes to shove and the pressures are on, to lean on position or status or credentials or affiliations or size to force someone else to follow. In the absence of well-developed interactive skill, or the capacity to remain true to deeply held values under pressure or a history of integrity and trust with others, it is almost impossible not to resort to force when a leader is in the middle of a crisis.

For the leader who wishes to increase principle-centered power, a long-term commitment is required. Trust in relationships cannot be fabricated *ad hoc*. Sincerity cannot be faked for long. Eventually, leaders reveal themselves. And what a leader is, beyond what the leader can do to or do for followers, ultimately determines the depth of principle-centered power.

PRINCIPLE-CENTERED POWER

Principle-centered power is rare. It is a mark of quality, distinction, and excellence in all relationships. It is based on honor, with the leader honoring the follower and the follower choosing to contribute because the leader is also honored. The hallmark of principle-centered power is sustained, proactive influence. Power is sustained because it is not dependent on whether or not something desirable or undesirable happens to the follower. To be proactive is to continually make choices based on deeply held values. And principle-centered power is created when the values of the followers and the values of the leader overlap. Principle-centered power is not forced; it is invited, as the personal agendas of both leader and follower are encompassed by a larger purpose. Principle-centered power occurs when the cause or purpose or goal is believed in as deeply by the followers as by the leaders. Hans Selye commented, "Leaders are leaders only as long as they have the respect and loyalty of their followers."

Principle-centered power is based on honor extended to you from others and by you to others. This leads to influence that lasts over extended periods of time and can even outlive the person from whom it emanates. Principle-centered power leads to the wonderful relationships we experience with close associates, family members, and friends. When people honor each other, trust is established that leads to synergy, interdependence, and deep respect. Both parties make decisions and choices based on what is right, what is best, what is valued most highly. Honor is power. To be honorable is to have power. It is more than appearance or manipulation, more than clever words or egotistical desires.

There is control with principle-centered power, but it is internal; it is self-control. Principle-centered power encourages ethical behavior because followers feel free to choose based on what they want most, what they want in the long term, rather than what they desire now.

You can develop principle-centered power in your life. You can become more influential than you may have thought possible. In ways that endure and perhaps extend beyond your lifetime, you can be as powerful and influential in the lives of others as the most important people in your life have been in yours. Here are ten suggestions for developing principle-centered power:

1. Persuasion, which includes sharing reasons and rationale, making a strong case for your position or desire while maintaining genuine respect for followers' ideas and perspective. Tell why as well as what; commit to stay in the communication process until mutually beneficial and satisfying outcomes are reached.

2. Patience, with the process and the person. In spite of the failings, shortcomings, and inconveniences created by followers, and your own impatience and anticipation for achieving your goals, maintain a long-term perspective, and stay committed to your goals in the face of short-term obstacles and resistance.

3. Gentleness, not harshness, hardness, or forcefulness, when dealing with vulnerabilities, disclosures, and feelings followers might express.

4. Teachableness, which means operating with the assumption that you do not have all the answers, all the insights, and valuing the different viewpoint, judgment, and experience followers may have.

5. Acceptance, withholding judgment, giving the benefit of the doubt, requiring no evidence or specific performance as a condition for sustaining high self-worth, making them your agenda.

6. Kindness, sensitive, caring, thoughtful, remembering the little things (which are the big things) in relationships.

7. Knowledge, acquiring accurate information and perspectives about followers as they can become while being worthy of respect for what they are now, regardless of what they own, control, or do, giving full consideration to their intentions, desires, values, and goals rather than focusing elusively on their behavior.

8. Discipline, compassionate confrontation, acknowledging mistakes and the need for followers to make "course corrections" in a context of genuine care, concern, and warmth, asking if safe for followers to try and to risk.

9. Consistency, so that your leadership style is not a manipulative technique that you bring into play when you don't get your way, are faced with crisis or challenge, or are feeling trapped; rather, this becomes a set of values, a personal code, a manifestation of your character, a reflection of who you are and who you are becoming.

10. Integrity, honestly matching words and feelings and thoughts and actions, with no desire other than for the good of others, without malice or desire to deceive, take advantage, manipulate, or control; constantly reviewing your intent as you strive for congruence.

When you demonstrate principle-centered power through your leadership choice, you may find that you are more careful what you ask of others, but have more confidence in doing so. As your understanding of the relationship between power and leadership increases, your ability to influence and lead others will grow. As the poet Henry Wadsworth Longfellow teaches us in "A Psalm of Life," "Lives of great men all remind us we can make our lives sublime, and, departing, leave behind us footprints on the sands of time."

CHAPTER 48

Moral Dimensions of Leadership

by Alexander B. Horniman, Professor of Business Administration and Senior Fellow at the Olsson Center for Applied Ethics, Darden Graduate School of Business Administration, University of Virginia

ONE WAY TO assess one's leadership is to examine one's relationships—to see if they are founded on rock or sand.

There are many ways to think about leadership. I like to think of leadership as the ability to create opportunities for one's self and for others. Opportunities tend to be about relationships; excellence in relationships, therefore, may be a useful way of describing leadership.

A "good" leader is one who creates excellent relationships. Through these excellent relationships, opportunities are created both for the individual and those with whom their interactions take place. Excellent relationships are based upon several rather simple yet important dimensions. People who do well on these dimensions will, in all probability, create relationships that will lead others to perceive them as powerful people and consequently as leaders. Leadership is therefore a *process* available to everyone, yet seldom achieved.

Excellent relationships are built upon four basic moral dimensions. They may be thought of as "the moral rock," and consist of the following:

    1. Truth telling,

    2. Promise keeping,

    3. Fairly treating others, and

    4. Respecting the individual.

There is nothing new about these dimensions, and yet when relationships are described as "good" or "excellent," one or more of these dimensions is *always* present. When relationships are described as "bad" or "poor," one or more of those dimensions is *always* missing or violated.

Leaders are people who are perceived to be powerful (in the moral sense), and their power is directly related to the extent to which their relationships with others reflect a positive position on these four dimensions.

When relationships are based squarely on "the rock," they create qualitatively different opportunities than when the relationships move off the rock. Once the relationships have left the rock, it is difficult if not impossible to get them back on.

• **Truth Telling.** One of the most important dimensions in any relationship is truth telling. Relationships characterized by truth telling are quite different than those where it is not a consistent dimension. When one or both parties leave the truth-telling rock, the integrity and stability of the relationship suffer. It is also difficult if not impossible to get back on the rock. Leaders are people who are considered powerful, and their power is based on their position or the moral rock of telling their truth and expecting others to do the same.

• **Promise Keeping.** Excellent relationships are squarely anchored on promise keeping. People who do what they say they will do can be depended upon, and this dependability becomes the basis of trust. When promises are kept, the empowerment process begins. When promises are broken by a departure from the rock, the relationship loses integrity, and the irreversible depowerment process begins. Leaders build their moral power by keeping their promises. The opportunities to be a promise keeper are numerous each and every day.

• **Fairness as Justice.** Whereas "truth telling" and "promise keeping" are fairly straightforward, fairness tends to be more subjective in terms of individual perceptions. When relationships are perceived to be fair, a sense of power and empowerment follows. When the relationships are perceived to be "unfair," the consequences to one or more parties are disadvantaging and depowering.

• **Respect for the Individual.** Since relationships are usually, if not always, about people, the degree of respect becomes quite significant. Like fairness, perceptions of respect are quite personal and subjective. When people are treated as "ends of worth and dignity," they act very differently than when they are treated as "mere means." Leaders create moral power to the extent to which they treat others as ends of worth and dignity. Not only are they seen as powerful, they have empowered those who benefit from their relationship.

There are hundreds of opportunities each day to demonstrate respect for the individual. People demonstrate powerful leadership by getting this right.

Leadership is about the moral power that emerges when people build their relationships around and upon "the rock." Leadership is not the exclusive domain of a few, but rather a series of opportunities for all of us.

LEADERSHIP AND THE MORAL ROCK

Business is about relationships. At the enterprise level, business is about relationships with the various stakeholders, including customers, suppliers, employees, regulatory agents, and stockholders. A good enterprise does a "good job" at those relationships. At the personal level, a good relationship can be defined in terms of how well people:

- *Tell the truth,*
- *Keep their promises,*
- *Treat each other fairly, and*
- *Demonstrate mutual respect.*

At first glance, these notions are quite obvious and perhaps simplistic. At second glance, the four items mentioned above provide the moral basis for determining whether relationships are perceived as "good" or "bad," both at the interpersonal and enterprise level. Leaders are people who derive their power by getting these issues right.

When viewed as an interrelated system, the four basic moral dimensions create the underlying value structure for what will be referred to here as the "moral rock."

If a person's relationships are centered on "the rock," they have a higher probability of working well than if they get off "the rock." The interesting issue here is that all relationships are somewhere either on or off "the rock." The question is just, where are they?

- *Truth Telling.* In a relationship, the more frequently and the further away from truth telling the person moves, the more difficult it is to return to the rock. It is often said that a person may not like what another says but can always know they can depend on them to be telling their truth as they understand it. It is difficult to know what the real truth is. It is essential that we tell our truth as we know it. Leaders are people who get this one right, and this may well be the basis of their power. Truth telling may sometimes be painful, but it is always powerful.

- *Promise Keeping.* Relationships are all about promise keeping. Do people do what they say they will do? Can they be depended on? Just as individuals are judged regularly on this criteria, so too, are enterprises—both public and private.

Several years ago, the airlines in this country got themselves into deep trouble with their customers because they routinely broke their promises to people. The level of anger and frustration grew to the point where dramatic actions and schedule revisions took place. On the surface, the breaking of a promise may seem to be insignificant, but it undermines the moral fabric of relationships. Leaders become powerful people by keeping their promises.

- *Fairness.* Fairness is an underlying issue in relationships. This dimension is more complicated because each individual seems to have a unique personal definition and perception of what "fairness" really means. Because of this subjectivity, it may not always be possible to appear fair, but it is usually possible to avoid obvious unfairness. Here again, leaders become more powerful by getting this fairness dimension right more often than not. Leaders lose power when they are perceived to be acting unfairly or unjustly.

• *Respect for the Individual.* This fourth dimension builds on the first three dimensions. If people "truth tell," "promise keep," and "act fairly" (justly), they will be perceived as demonstrating respect for the individual. If each of these dimensions is viewed as a continuum having end points, respect for the individual would reflect the Kantian notion of treating people as "ends of worth and dignity" or treating people as "mere means."

When we fail to tell the truth, keep our promises, act fairly towards other people or indeed do them harm, we have treated them as "mere means." Sexual harassment, race discrimination, and age discrimination are vivid examples of people being treated as mere means as opposed to ends of worth and dignity. Leaders become more powerful by effectively treating people as ends of worth and dignity. When people treat others as worthwhile, they tend to reciprocate. This might be thought of as the basis for interactive empowerment.

BACK TO THE ROCK

The four dimensions discussed above exist in most if not all relationships. When people center their relationships on the rock, their quality is considered excellent. When they move off the rock, the quality tends to deteriorate. These are rather simple straightforward issues and yet, upon reflection, often not done well by most people.

Leaders become powerful people by getting these moral dimensions right (on the rock) more often than wrong (off the rock). The choice to be on or off the rock exists for each of us each day.

CHAPTER 49

Military Leadership

by Patrick L. Townsend and Joan E. Gebhardt, Partners in Townsend and Gebhardt

WHILE MILITARY LEADERS are often lampooned as power-mad autocrats, they tend to be more people-centered than their business counterparts.

United States business needs leadership. The distinction between leadership and management is becoming ever clearer as more books and articles are published on this topic.

Yet the journalistic-academic complex, which plays the lead role in defining what information is presented to American executives and executives-in-training, stubbornly refuses to draw from the experiences of the only segment of society that has debated and studied leadership for 2,500 years: the military.

What can the military teach business executives about leadership? Many lessons about adapting style, applying values and ethics, training subordinates and successors, and loving the people you lead.

STYLES OF LEADERSHIP

First, the military codifies the issues in a simple, realistic way. The U.S. Army Leadership Manual (FM 22-100) defines three styles of leadership—*authoritarian*, *participative*, and *delegative*.

1. Authoritarian. The first is described in pragmatic terms: "A leader is using the authoritarian leadership style when he tells his subordinates what we wants done, and how he wants it done, without getting their advice or ideas. Under the following conditions, the authoritarian approach is normally appropriate:

- *You have all of the information to solve the problem.*
- *You are short on time.*
- *Your subordinates are motivated.*

"Sometimes people think that a leader is using the authoritarian style. It is simply an abusive, unprofessional style of leadership."

The manual then explains that the way a leader insures that he has all possible time and information and his people are well-motivated is by practicing participative and delegative leadership most of the time.

2. Participative. This style involves "one or more subordinates in determining what to do and how to do it." In the case of participative leadership, "the leader maintains final decision-making authority."

3. Delegative. Using this style, "the leader delegates decision-making authority to a subordinate or group of subordinates." The leader "is still responsible for the results of his subordinates' decisions." It is an oft-repeated rule in military leadership that, "You can delegate authority but not responsibility."

APPLYING VALUES AND ETHICS

Second, the military emphasizes the character ethic over the personality ethic of leadership. For example, chapter headings in FM 22-100 include the following:

- "Professional Beliefs, Values, and Ethics"
- "The Character of a Leader"
- "Leadership That Provides Direction"
- "Principles of Leadership"
- "Know Yourself and Seek Self-Improvement"
- "Set the Example"
- "Keep Your People Informed"

Focus on accomplishing the mission and caring for, and about, the people assigned to a leader are the common threads that run throughout the military handbook. This focus becomes a springboard for discussions of the difference between management and leadership in other military sources, a debate which is concurrently taking place in the civilian community. In the *Marine Corps Gazette*, the difference is defined as, "A manager cares that the job gets done; a leader cares that the job gets done, and he or she cares about the people who do the job."

PRINCIPLES OF LOVE

In an article which received a commendation from the Marine Corps Combat Correspondents Association, a Marine officer discussed leadership as being a subset of love, adding that if a person wasn't capable of love, he or she would most likely not be much good at leadership.

There are many varieties of love, and one of the greatest is good leadership. Since leadership is a form of love, our knowledge and experience of the root concept can provide us with useful insights into leadership. Perhaps the most obvious is the act of caring for the welfare—the well-being, physical and mental—of others.

A person who would call himself or herself a leader of Marines must be capable of loving and being loved. To love someone is to make a commitment to him or her, a promise to work hard to improve conditions for them and to improve yourself. It is not a pledge to nag them until they finally shape up, but rather a promise to work with them toward mutual goals, a higher state.

A platoon commander, while laying the groundwork for the reputation that will follow him throughout his career, must truly love his men if he wishes to be known as a good leader. If he brings technical expertise and ambition but no warmth to his position, his troops will return his investment in like currency. They will do precisely what he says, but will not give the extra effort that is the mark of the well led. Neither will they overlook his faults nor compensate for his mistakes.

ONGOING TRAINING

What of all the stories that everyone has heard about sadistic drill instructors, power-mad officers, and devious, cruel sergeants? Stereotypical beliefs about how the military gets from here to there abound. For many, the words "autocratic" and "military" are interchangeable as adjectives in front of the word "management."

The stereotype was not manufactured out of thin air. There have been—and continue to be—enough incompetents in the uniforms of every country to sustain the unflattering, albeit generally inaccurate, image. The word "martinet," for example, is derived from the name of a particularly harsh 17th-century French general.

But the fact remains that the stereotype does not reflect reality. The military has been compelled to trust its people. In combat any person can become a casualty at any time; replacements must always be ready to step up, and in. Subordinates have to be told what is going on, and they have to be prepared to assume responsibility.

"Succession planning" is automatic—and very open. The military is made up of people, all busily training in some way to do something that they pray quietly at night never happens.

The peacetime version of this same phenomena is encouraged by the constant transfer of military personnel. It is rare to be in one geographical location for more than three years, rarer still to be in the same job that long. The training of one's subordinates—not just to do their jobs, but to assume the responsibility of the trainer—is a never-ending task.

The penalty for failure to involve, and insure the growth of, sub-ordinates is severe in the military. If a business manager chooses to be autocratic, to not enlist or use the input of any of the people who work with or for him or her, the worst thing that can happen is the inclusion of a pink slip in the next paycheck—devastating, but not fatal.

On the other hand, if a military leader in combat fails to draw on the knowledge, experience and intuition of subordinates, he could die as a result. Most unfair, he could take others with him. This potential for disaster makes choosing to build teams that maximize everyone's strengths, and to be participative and caring, a logical imperative.

William F. Ward was a man with one foot in each "world." At the time that he was the commanding general of the 77th Army Reserve Command, he was also president of Gestam, Inc., a real estate management firm. He was quoted in *Success* as saying:

> *The military is more people-oriented than business. My experience with business schools is that they teach a hell of a lot about the skills of management but very little about the qualities of leadership. And it shows. I've seen hundreds of companies where the CEO didn't care about people. He drove out all the good people. They wanted to go someplace where they were appreciated, where once in a while someone said, "Good job" or "Come in and let's talk about this problem." It's kind of strange because the military is perceived as being this great faceless group that shouts and screams. That only happens in Boot Camp. The military does that to take a personality and all of a sudden make him or her a member of a different society. But at the managerial levels in the military, the noncommissioned officer levels on up, employees have more to say about how they do their jobs than in most businesses. In its treatment of people, business has an opportunity to assume a great moral leadership role, but it has not done so yet.*

Business leaders can learn from military experience, and there may be an increasing willingness to do so. There are indications that the popular perception of the military is improving. The "military" as an organization is now held in high regard in public surveys (considerably ahead of "big business" and even further ahead of Congress). Couple this with the wide availability of written materials on military leadership—any military publication in the world, in any language, is sure to contain at least one article on leadership—and a valuable source of information is waiting to be discovered.

CHAPTER 50

Images of Cowboys and Leaders

by David M. Noer, Vice President of Training and Education at the Center for Creative Leadership

WE LIKE OUR heroes and villains strong and simple; we distrust ambiguity, equivocation, systems, and complexity.

In mellifluous tones, Willie Nelson tells us that his "heroes have always been cowboys." Many of us view top managers the same way.

Cowboys are macho and self-reliant—clearly differentiated good guys in a world where the divisions are easy; larger-than-life characters who, when we really think about it, seem shallow and contrived, somehow unreal, without the requisite frailties that make us human. I see the classic Clint Eastwood spaghetti-western where the hero rides into town and, amid interspersions of weird music and endless camera panning, wipes out dozens of bad guys while hardly breaking a sweat himself, and, in the end, rides away into the mist. Interesting guy, but would I want him for a neighbor? For sure, not a boss!

We tend to put our leaders on pedestals, to make them bigger than life. This "deification" plays out on both positive and negative sides. We believe that deeply rooted cultural and social problems can be solved if only we pick the right president. If he (or someday she) does well, we praise him; if not, we blame him, and woe betide him if he has the personal problems we accept—even defend—in us lesser humans.

Deep down we know that we can't cure underlying problems simply by shuffling "leaders." Our own quality programs teach us that problems are rooted in processes and systems. Why, then, do we persist in worshipping our leaders when they succeed and beating on them when they fail?

We want a *person* to praise or blame. Problems can be "fixed," and that's why we have leaders: They represent us. And if they can't do the job, we will get someone else. The media stir the broth. Top leaders are granted either godlike or goatlike status as they are paraded across our pages and screens.

We render our top leaders ineffective by deifying them. To the extent that we engender godlike qualities, we dehumanize them, push them away, and incapacitate them to deal with the human qualities of our organizations. Consequently, many leaders are figureheads and actors. This is not all their fault; nor is it all ours. It takes two to tango. On the one side, it's difficult to resist being treated like a god. On the other side, we scripted the roles they are acting out. And many other forces, including cultural expectations, cause our leaders to persist in this destructive relationship.

HOW TO HELP YOUR LEADERS

I offer four suggestions to help leaders break the cycle and help us avoid colluding with our leaders in ways that limit their effectiveness.

1. Resist the efforts—sincere though they may be—of people to turn you into a savior. You are not Clint Eastwood and will not get all the bad guys without lots of help. Find ways to show your humanity. If you don't have an answer, say so. If you are confused, let others know. If you are sad and emotional because your friends and colleagues are being laid off, act that way. To the extent you exhibit your human vulnerability, you enable others to take responsibility and display leadership behaviors.

2. Manage by "being" around, not "walking" around. An entire generation of managers has grown up perpetuating the myth of the charismatic leader "walking around," acting confident, and being a cheerleader. When Clint walks around assuring the townfolks that he, and he alone, will clean out the bad guys, it sets up a dependency relationship. I know of no evidence that charisma, which is what is being dispensed in the walks, has much to do with real leadership; in fact, I think it often gets in the way.

Of course, visiting with no charisma is also a problem. I have seen highly introverted and analytical leaders, because they have read a book or are responding to coaching, go out and attempt to fake it. It's like "Revenge of the Nerds" meets "Robocop:" Often they come off as badly cast actors in a very artificial role.

"Being around" means behaving authentically, being who you are and acting in accord with your true nature. Mingling is a good idea, but walking around with a script written by lawyers or PR agents comes off as contrived.

Another part of "being around" involves eschewing false, and therefore distance-inducing, status symbols. It is difficult to convince others that you are interested in empowering them and being part of their world when you wall them off with separate dining areas, reserved parking spaces, and secluded, often elaborately guarded, office suites.

3. Seek feedback. Being a cowboy is seductive. I'm sure the foothills of the Old West are filled with gunfighters who believed in their own invulnerability. Top leaders need to find objective information about themselves. Even in the best organizations, people are going to pull their punches when dealing with the top people. Feedback from multiple sources—from peers and subordinates as well as from bosses—can be a powerful tool. Leaders who are trying to share leadership need to be congruent, empower others, and find ways to get valid data on themselves.

4. Learn how to learn. Learning to learn isn't easy. For sure, cowboy leaders—colluding with those who would grant them omniscient, godlike qualities—do not easily open themselves to learning. The creation of a learning culture requires a dual application of courage: Formal leaders need the bravery to stop playing cowboy and to express their human vulnerability, and the rest of us need the fortitude to exercise leadership and not delegate upward.

CHAPTER 51

Caring Leaders

by H. Ross Perot, Chairman of Perot Systems, Inc.

TEACH THE PRINCIPLES of leadership because the principles never change, since human nature never changes.

A leader is a person that the rest of the team trusts and respects. As a leader, you have to earn that trust every minute of every day. It's very fragile. You can't take it for granted.

You will earn trust and respect if you have a mission and motivate people to come together and work toward that mission, recognizing that every person is different. There's something inside every one of us, no matter how obscure we might be, that says, "I'm unique. I'm special. There's only one person in the world like me. Treat me with dignity and respect." Now, if you talk about trusting people, you had better do it constantly. Shoot straight with people; treat them with dignity and respect.

One basic rule in my companies is you do not abuse people, especially people who report to you, because if you are abusive, they become intimidated. They're not going to be creative when they're intimidated. We make it very clear in employment interviews and training programs that we don't want anybody to look up or down at anybody else. Everybody is a full partner in our business; we are all equal, and we have one goal—to build the greatest company of its kind in the world, and to have fun doing it.

If you're looking to hire leaders, first look for people who are honest. People will not follow a person who is dishonest. Second, they've got to be highly self-motivated. Third, they've got to believe in what they're doing. Fourth, they've got to love other people and be excited about working with other people.

The leader's challenge is to work with people as individuals. You can't just categorize them like you can a box of bolts. Each person is unique, each one is different, and you play to their strengths and build on their strengths. And you don't try to jam square pegs into round holes.

BUILD A TALENTED TEAM

Surround yourself with people more talented than you are. That's the story of EDS. My idea for EDS was considered so unorthodox and so bad that nobody would put any capital into it. All we had was an idea, and a burning desire to make it materialize. We had to bootstrap everything. We had to compete all day, every day, with the greatest company in the computer industry, IBM. We had no chance, but we consistently beat them because of the brains, wits, and creative ability of the team. I was the least talented guy on the payroll, but I had some wonderful people around me. And we had dynamic leaders who galvanized the team.

The greatest thing you can do as a leader is build a united team. I've been around companies where the people at the top hated the people who did the work. That's a team that's going to fail.

To build a united team, treat everybody the same. Have one retirement plan. One health care plan. One dining room. One day, an executive of a big company visited me and said, "I can't believe you eat in the cafeteria." I said, "It's the only place to eat." As we went through the line, he said, "Ross, I can't believe you stand in line." And I said, "Well, these guys are bigger than I am. I have to." Then he was just amazed by how good the food was. He said, "What do you do to make the food so good in your cafeteria?" And I said, "I eat here."

Everyday I would go there and eat by myself, and the table would be filled with people from computer operators to systems engineers just covering me with their good ideas. Every great idea that made my company successful came from them, not from me.

When great things occur, thank people for what they've done, while they're still sweating from the effort.

Any time any member of your team or a member of your team's family has a serious health problem or a serious personal problem, have a standing order that you're to be notified 24 hours a day, seven days a week, and then make sure they get the same care your son or your daughter would get.

SPEAK, LISTEN, LEARN, ACT

Treat e-mail like you would a snake. Don't let anybody communicate with you with e-mail. Have people come in and talk to you face to face, eyeball to eyeball. It's important to have people communicate directly with you because they've got to learn how to talk. Teach them to speak by putting them in a situation where they have to speak. I've seen great individual performers become performers who manage divisions because they learned how to communicate.

Corporate America is finally listening to front-line workers, because that's where the best ideas are. In many of our companies, you have young people with MBAs telling management what the polls and the data show, but they never talk to the customers, never talk to the workers, and so they build, with the best of intentions, a product that nobody wants. As the companies deteriorate, they have to get their act back together and start listening to the customers.

Listening is fine, but if you don't hear people, you've wasted your time listening. Because hearing the message—absorbing it, analyzing it, and tapping the full potential of that idea—will spell the difference between success and failure.

DEAL DIRECTLY WITH PEOPLE

When we interview people for positions in the company we make it clear that if anybody lies, cheats, steals, or takes advantage of another person—and we define taking advantage of another person as being a corporate politician who wants to move ahead at the expense of others—first we make sure that it is true, and then no matter where they are in the world, they come to my office, and I personally terminate them as a signal to everybody that we don't do that.

When someone is not working up to expectations, talk candidly with them. Not everyone who wants to be on an Olympic team can perform at the Olympic level. But they can be a roaring success somewhere else. So be graceful, and help them get relocated and make a smooth transition. Let them find a job, and let them announce they're leaving. Turn a problem into a victory for that person.

If your department, division, team, or organization is not working the way it needs to, bring the key players together, drop the cards on the table, and say, "We have a problem that is going to result in failure for this company. Let's brainstorm what we need to do to correct it."

One challenge will be to get them to stop being defensive. Often the team that creates the problem is unable to unhook from it. You may need to bring in a new team, and say, "All right, we have this problem. Everybody knows we have this problem. What do you think we should do about it?" And since they didn't create it, incredibly creative ideas will flow. You've got to tap the potential. Reach down to all those fighters who are restless and say, "Okay, how do we do it?" They'll tell you.

CHALLENGE YOUR GOALS

Everything changes. Today's products will be obsolete soon. And that's part of the challenge. Change is a constant. So look forward to it and lead it. If you dread it, you're dead. If your company is successful, you're probably becoming complacent. Success breeds arrogance and complacency; adversity breeds strength.

To get everyone to focus on the same goal, you live it in everything you do. For example, the building in which they work should be spotlessly clean. If everything they see is world-class, then everything they do will tend to be world-class. Everybody thrives on competing with other teams in the company—and so you build this positive spirit.

Goals excite people. On a yellow sheet of paper, I wrote out what our goals would be before we started. And that became our road map. All of our goals were dynamic, all subject to review. But we always said, "There are some we won't touch, like honesty and integrity. That's always going to be a goal."

Your goals should be direct, simple, succinct. Give every person in your company a copy of those goals. Stick it in your wallet. They define who you are, what you are, and what you're going to be.

LOVE IT OR LEAVE IT

I love business. Business is fun. The people whom I associate with are the best part of it. I love being with the customer. When you're out in the field in the middle of the action, that is pure fun.

If you don't love what you're doing and you're not excited every day, you're probably on the wrong track. You ought to try something else. Now if it's just tough but you still love it, great. Going through difficult times is like hammering an iron on an anvil. The more you hit it, the harder it gets. The tough times you go through will make you tough; they will make your team tough.

If you're a genius, you have a tremendous disadvantage (growing a company). Your only chance to build a great company is to surround yourself with talented people, set them free, and not intimidate them with your genius, but motivate them with your genius, stand back, and let them be the stars.

Successful people learn from failure. They get stronger and better as a result of their mistakes. Their huge successes are built squarely on the rubble of their failure.

Many people don't see themselves as leaders, and not everyone will be a leader. If everybody had to be a leader, we wouldn't have some of the genius individual performers. There is a very important place for the superstar genius creator, but to get the multiplier, you've got to have the leader.

Most people can develop leadership skills. To lead a group of people, you have to talk, listen, hear, and then take action. Before you put anybody in a leadership role, teach them these fundamentals. To train people as technicians and not train them how to lead and inspire the people is to fail in the leaders' mission.

CHAPTER 52

Leadership Means Telling the Truth

by James C. Shaffer, Principal of Towers Perrin

A NEW DEAL needs to be defined—and with it a new relationship based on shared interests and partnership.

When new Amtrak chairman Tom Downs first met with his leadership team, he implored them to follow one rule—tell the truth. This simple, three-word maxim is becoming the filter Amtrak people use to drive decisions and behavior as they seek to reinvent America's passenger railroad.

Telling the truth doesn't always come easy. As Downs says, "A lot of executives find it easier not to tell the truth by avoiding reality, facts, and things that seem to get in the way of success. But, we can't solve problems unless we tell each other the truth."

Stimulating the movement to increased openness is a confluence of two forces—changing values and economic necessity. There's a growing recognition that leaders need to establish a different relationship with their people than they've maintained in the past. And, more leaders are realizing that success comes from people who are held accountable for results they control.

The shift is from patriarchy to partnership. Patriarchy is grounded in an adult-child relationship of dependency. In the patriarchal relationship, the deal between the organization and its people is: "If you're loyal, work hard and do as you are told, we'll provide pay increases and security. We'll take care of you." In recent years, that deal was broken as many companies laid off thousands of people. Loyalty and hard work no longer translate into pay and security.

THE NEW DEAL

Today's leaders know that empowerment and high performance come from a partnership built on sharing information—something akin to full disclosure. "Full disclosure is a critical dividing line between parenting and partnership," writes Peter Block in his book, *Stewardship.* "The things a parent would never tell a child have to be told to a partner. Truth untold to a partner is betrayal."

Jack Stack, president and CEO of the SRC Corporation, a rebuilder of engines and engine components says, "The more people know about a company, the better that company will perform. This is an iron-clad rule. You will always be more successful in business by sharing information with the people you work with than by keeping them in the dark."

What does the new partnership of full disclosure look like?

• *Communicating the new deal.* Full disclosure starts with communicating the new deal. An organization creating a partnership with its people believes in a deal based on a mutually beneficial relationship. One west coast organization's stated deal is that if employees develop skills the organization needs, apply them in ways that help the organization succeed, and behave in a way that's consistent with the desired values, the organization will provide a challenging work environment, support for the employees' development, and a reward linked to their contribution. And, the employees will be part of a revitalized industry leader. The new deal must be driven by the business strategy. And, it must be clearly communicated through what is both said and done to be credible to employees.

• *Explaining the business context.* Full disclosure means communicating the business context—carefully explaining what the business is, and how it works. That includes the forces shaping the markets, what makes the business improve and suffer, competitive information, customer data, supplier information, and so on. It must be an honest and accurate portrayal of the operating environment. Part of this is building business literacy. SRC teaches its people about business and how it runs. "We try to take the ignorance out of the workplace and force people to get involved, not with threats and intimidation but with education," Stack says.

Building business literacy means sharing financial information, so people can understand their options and the results of their choices. Stack calls it open book management, "the best way I know to keep people focused on the important issues facing a company."

• *Sharing the vision.* Full disclosure means communicating a clear picture of what the organization is attempting to become. This vision shouldn't be a simple-minded statement, wallet card, or wall chart. It represents the future condition toward which the entire organization must be directed.

- *Building values.* Full disclosure means clarifying the organization's values in everything that's said and done. Values shape the culture; culture drives behavior. The culture acts as a tiebreaker when people consider "how-to-act" options. For instance, when employees in a customer-focused organization are faced with the choice of returning a customer's phone call or returning the boss's phone call, they will always return the customer's call first. Values must be consistent with business strategy.
- *Sharing rewards.* Full disclosure means sharing success and failure, gains and shortfalls, honestly. Mechanisms take the form of various stock ownership and profit-sharing plans.
- *Clarifying roles.* Full disclosure means clarifying roles. Where people are asked to perform multiple roles in a given day—from project leader in the morning to subject matter or functional expert in the afternoon—rigid job descriptions are anachronisms. But, people still need to understand their roles and where they fit. Full disclosure takes down walls, says Jack Stack. "When you communicate with people through the financial statements, knowledge gets to them quickly without being distorted by internal rivalries. If everyone is looking at the whole business, it's harder for departments to make excuses at one another's expense."
- *Sharing performance results.* Performance results must be widely communicated. Full disclosure means that the entire team understands the team's performance as well as that of its members. Organizations that create partnerships work hard to make sure that all resources are available to help each team member create high performance.

ALIGNING THE "SAY" AND THE "DO"

Many managers believe that communication is principally generated through media such as memos, newsletters, and audio-visual presentations. And so they use these media and consider the job done. Actually, the communication that influences behavior most is generated from leadership style and behavior and through the structure and systems. Only a small portion of behavior-changing communication comes from the media.

Fully informed employees are more likely to create competitive advantage than uninformed employees, especially if they believe they're the direct beneficiaries of improvement. One international food products company is well known for its external secrecy, yet it shares financial information widely with its people. "Our people know that it's in their best interests to protect their interests. Why would they try to damage themselves and all they work for?"

GETTING STARTED

To build a new partnership based on openness and trust, take the following seven steps.

1. Create leadership understanding of the new deal. Base the new deal on a solid human resource strategy that's tied to your business strategy.

2. Develop a communication philosophy that will guide organizational openness. Is it full disclosure or something short of it? Whatever your philosophy, understand its implications to the business.

3. Develop a communication strategy that focuses on moving information up, down, and laterally in a way that is consistent with the new communication philosophy.

4. Educate people about the business. Help them understand the new rules, what it takes to win, what causes losses.

5. Teach people how to use the information—how to manage it to achieve results.

6. Align the infrastructure so it sends consistent messages and helps people who are trying to improve the business.

7. Tie rewards to results, either through ownership plans or through profit-sharing arrangements.

Moving toward partnership means eliminating the fear many managers feel about giving up the power associated with information. But, failing to share only means perpetuating the patriarchal relationship of the past. And that relationship will put an organization at a major competitive disadvantage.

CHAPTER 53

Leading by Covenant, Not by Contract

 by Delmar L. Landen, Chairman of Landen, Wells & Associates, Inc.

THE ORGANIZATION of the past decades was one of glitz and glamour. The successful organization of the 21st century will be one of symbols and substance.

Symbols are representations of what is valued. They convey both our dreams and our deeds. They embody our history and signify our future. They connote our accomplishments and challenge our performance. The *substance* underlying our symbols must be achievement, measured not only in terms of meeting certain goals and objectives, but also in affirming the constant striving for fulfillment, actualization, and satisfaction.

Substance must be what we are all about. We must accept our responsibility for creating and nurturing organizations of character and integrity. We do this by exhibiting these qualities and by recognizing that organizations derive their character and integrity from the character and integrity manifested by their members.

The consuming public has expressed its desire for quality, value, and excellence and made known its desire for leaders to show greater statesmanship and craftsmanship. Leaders must now respond to this challenge, working to define and attain new and loftier standards of performance. Sadly, our leaders are seemingly ill-equipped to meet and grasp this challenge.

As a human creation, the organization is the only instrument through which future goals are defined, pursued, and accomplished. It is the means by which quality is determined, value is produced, and excellence is pursued. Its character and integrity define and determine the character and integrity of its products and services. The organization has no meaning, no substance, no direction, no future other than that which individuals give to it.

The quality of the enterprise must be equal to the goals it seeks. All too many organizations extol the merits of quality but lack the commitment to take the difficult steps that make quality the transcending standard and symbol of their existence.

LEADING BY COVENANTS

Creating and sustaining organizations of symbols and substance can't be achieved through contracts, procedural manuals, and edicts. Nor can they be mandated. They can only be fashioned out of the values, beliefs, and convictions that define and compel the human spirit. Thus, we need to create human relationships which are bound together by covenants, not contracts. We need to fashion organizations out of shared values, shared ideals, shared ideas, shared goals, shared beliefs, and shared visions. Covenants are bonds. They are shaped from our values, molded by our deeds, and nurtured by our convictions. They are living testimonials to our heritage. They are standards of our conduct and performance. They are symbols of our future.

The creation of covenants occurs in the natural events of history. Their early formation emerges from the values, convictions, deeds, and decisions of the founders. They are perpetuated by others because they validate the character of the institution, are valued by its members, provide for its continuity, and instill in its members the essence of the enterprise and its reasons for existing.

In recent years, conscious efforts have been made to create new organizational forms. The need to do this is driven mainly by the inability of existing organizations to fulfill their many obligations. In rare instances, the impetus has resulted from the convictions of leaders whose visions of the future compel the molding of covenantal relationships. These covenants provide energizing and enabling conditions that elevate organizations to higher levels of aspiration and achievement.

Transformational leaders, while fashioning covenantal relationships and elevating the status of organizations, also seek to uplift the human spirit to ever higher levels of ethics, integrity, and morality.

Aligning people with future visions occurs through the combined influence of the behavior of leaders and the cultures of enterprises. For leaders to communicate a vision with the force of persuasion, the words they employ, the symbols they use, and the deeds they perform must have the capacity to shape the character of individuals and mold the cultures of organizations.

Leaders are people who fashion visions of distant futures and capture the imagination of others. Leaders inspire commitment and align the desires and deeds of others with future organizational goals. The role of management is to provide stability, consistency, and control—to guide complex systems. The role of leadership is to produce change, to create movement, to empower and transform.

Transformation has become an economic necessity. As instrumentalities of production, the classical organization, with its emphasis on hierarchical control, served well during periods of stability and predictability. Management systems based on contracts, consistency, and control were in keeping with those forms and with the needs and demands of the marketplace. However, the marketplace has changed; many organizations have not.

SHIFTING PARADIGMS

In his book, *Rebirth of the Corporation*, D. Quinn Mills describes the cluster organization: "Clusters involve a philosophy of work and human behavior that requires a new way of thinking," he notes, adding that one of the strengths of cluster organizations is that people who have the knowledge to do something also have the obligation to do it. This, of course, presupposes that people are empowered to act. Since there is no hierarchy to dictate performance, the commitment to act is derived from the prevailing norms of the culture. These in turn are the product of experiences, past victories and failures, the assumptions and values on which the organization was founded and by which it is nurtured, and those myriad occurrences which define and shape each enterprise's unique qualities.

The fluid nature of the cluster organization is characterized by the fluidity in working relationships among cluster members, and with the clusters and their internal and external environments.

Cluster relationships can't be achieved contractually. Contracts, by their very nature, provide specification, definition, and detail. In clusters, the desire is for generalization, direction, and abstraction. The boundaries within which clusters flourish are shaped by covenants, not by contracts.

The rebirth of the corporation can be created only when it is based upon a different set of assumptions about human nature and the nature of work. General Motors, General Electric, Xerox, and Motorola are among those organizations in the throes of reinventing themselves. Each has approached its transformation differently. Regardless of where they started, ultimately they, as do all organizations who are committed to change, must deal creatively with these organizational properties which bind people together in the pursuit of common objectives. The shaping and nurturing of covenantal relationships emerging out of the collective experiences and deliberations of the organization's members is the best, if not the only, way to accomplish this.

CUSTOMER-DRIVEN ORGANIZATIONS

As more organizations begin to shift their emphasis from production to quality, they realize that to achieve sustained improvements in quality they must achieve sustained improvements in all dimensions. Early efforts to achieve continuous improvements in quality, based upon the techniques of statistical process control and Japanese quality circles, failed because the management systems and prerequisite cultural conditions to their success simply did not exist in most corporations.

A similar fate now faces many efforts in Total Quality Management. A study done by the U.S. General Accounting Office identified six improvement efforts common to the 20 companies that were among the highest-scoring applicants for the Malcolm Baldrige National Award. These six features involved the following practices:

- *Corporate attention was focused on meeting customer quality requirements.*
- *Management led the way in disseminating TQM values throughout the organization.*
- *Employees were asked and empowered to continuously improve all key business processes.*
- *Management nurtured a flexible and responsive corporate culture.*
- *Management systems supported fact-based decision making.*
- *Partnerships with suppliers improved product or service quality.*

Transcending these features is the overriding realization that successful organizations must be customer-driven, not product-driven. Achieving customer-driven organizations requires top-level leadership that manifests its commitment to quality by its daily actions, continuously building quality values in the organization.

COVENANTAL VALUES

The importance of overarching values was manifestly apparent in an incident with Tylenol. When the incident occurred, the senior management of Johnson & Johnson, with the leadership of James Burke, focused its attention on the company's credo. Based upon the beliefs, values and commitments inherent in the credo, the decision to recall all Tylenol products throughout the nation was the natural decision to make. As it happened, it was also a very wise business decision.

This incident serves to reinforce the importance of preserving the integrity of organizations. Enunciating certain beliefs requires a commitment to action equal to their proclamations. Johnson & Johnson met this test with great honor. Exxon, however, in the Valdez incident, did not. The business and public relations reverberations from these two examples are testimonials to the obligation for leaders to uphold their own integrity and that of their institutions.

The creation of bonds of commitment and excellence grows out of the uninhibited sharing of those values which define our humanity and symbolize our democratic institutions.

Since work is so central to our lives and so fundamental in defining who and what we are, the nature of our work and the context within which we work are vital to our well-being. If, as the Eastern philosophers believe, the function of work is to uplift the human spirit and to develop the human character, both the content and context of work are nutrients which nourish human and organization growth and development.

The infinite potential for improvement residing within ourselves and our institutions will be unleashed when the rights and obligations we enjoy as citizens are the same standards by which we define work and our working lives. Achievement of integrity in workmanship that parallels integrity in citizenship can be advanced immeasurably by defining our relationships to our work and our institutions of work based on covenantal values and ideals. The pursuit for self-actualization is born within the human spirit and nourished by its experiences. Covenants can become the source through which the pursuit of excellence and the search for self-actualization are spawned, guided, and nurtured.

To people in authority, this means they must be social architects, creating organizations that embody those values and ideals that bind people together in pursuit of common destinies.

Today's managers must be leaders. They must fashion shared visions. They must provide direction. As Max DePree suggests, "The first responsibility of a leader is to define reality." Beyond this, managers must create, through their decisions and deeds, covenantal relationships that motivate, inspire, and align the goals of individuals, groups, and organizations toward a common future.

Today's organizational symbol is excellence. Like a vision of the future, excellence is a direction, not a destination. It is always within our view, but never within our grasp. As such, those values which define our institutions must provide the bonds which bridge human and organizational character.

Tomorrow's organization must manifest a sense of wholeness, achieving a harmony within itself, among its members, and with the larger society. It must have the capacity to learn, to grow and develop. It must be able to recreate its own future. Organizations of this character, capacity, and competence can only derive their strength from their members, who in turn derive theirs from the organization. This spirit of unity, this covenant and purposefulness, will create the spiritual foundation for excellence to become commonplace and self-actualization a living reality.

CHAPTER 54

Leaders Care for the Spirit

 by Bill Westfall, Vice President of Galliger Westfall, Inc.

MANAGERS CARE for the body of the organization; leaders care for the spirit; and great leadership does both!

Captain Donald D. Brooks exited the Marine helicopter that had ferried him from headquarters, Chu Lai, to a sun-soaked hill just east of a group of villages in Vietnam known as Tan Hy. As he did so, he looked into the faces of nearly 150 Marines grouped to welcome him as their new commander. They were not happy faces. They were the faces of a group that had been subjected for the past six months to the petty tirades of a company commander who was more concerned about his barrack's reputation than he was the safety, welfare, and morale of his charges.

Brooks was inheriting a well-trained but dispirited company. As the helicopter faded from sight, he relaxed, moving easily among the men who at first parted and then surrounded him. He slowly turned, saying in a supportive tone so all could hear, "Men, why don't you remove those utility jackets and let the sun get to those body sores?"

The previous commander forbade the removal of utility jackets when in the company perimeter, even though they were miles from the prying eyes of command personnel. He feared an unmilitary appearance should some unexpected visitor suddenly arrive.

Before his arrival, Brooks had properly assessed the fading spirit of his new command. He recognized the over-supervision of the past commander as the cause and, in one sentence, won the hearts of those he would so successfully lead. Brooks had done the right thing by failing to do the thing right. He allowed the removal of the utility jackets.

This was the first of many such reversals in procedure from his predecessor's rigid and petty style. In days, this dispirited group of Marines turned back two separate groups of Viet Cong in a daring midnight raid. Incoming mortars and the grenades of two infiltrators began a night-long battle that required vigilance until sunlight. The sun found a vanquished enemy while Brooks' company escaped with just two superficially wounded who refused evacuation. It was the same group of men in the same area with the same non-commissioned officers (NCOs) and junior officers who shared the same mission. Only one variable had changed: the leadership. Within days, it was a different company because of the wisdom of one man, their new leader.

As a young Marine NCO detached to that company, I never forgot the experience. It stunned me. How can one person in a leadership role reverse a whole pattern of performance of so many? Since that time, I have watched the same phenomena in police departments all over the United States.

INACTION: A LEARNED RESPONSE

In his work on human performance, Charles Garfield has argued, "People are not born to inaction, they learn it (in organizations)." He further states, "Peak performers are not average people with something added, but average people with nothing taken away." That translates to "the less those around me take from me, the more productive I will be, the more I will realize my potential, the more I can give back." Brooks' predecessor, by his petty concerns, robbed his subordinates of their potential and eventually their spirit. Brooks restored both in days.

Peter Drucker completed a study of the Los Angeles Police Department more than twenty years ago that was never published. After talking with officers for six weeks, he made several observations. One of the most salient and insightful was, "You police are so concerned with doing things right that you fail to do the right things." Although initially the statement may sound like a riddle, it is amazingly accurate in the wake of Warren Bennis's determinations about superleaders. Bennis concluded that, "Managers do things right while leaders do the right thing." It would appear that what Drucker was saying is that police management is so concerned with managing that they fail to lead.

I, too, have worked with police forces around the nation, and I have conducted research in many aspects of their management and leadership. In an article dealing with community-oriented policing, Kelling and Wilson stated, "Police management is driven more by the constraints of the job than by the goals of the job." We are so concerned with avoiding wrong that we often fail to do what's right. It's a defensive posture like a coach trying to protect a lead rather than marshalling team resources to win. Ray Meyer, famed basketball coach at

DePaul, once commented after a losing game which ended one of the nation's longest winning streaks, "Good, now we can start playing to win rather than playing not to lose." This posture of trying not to lose seems to rob the participants and their organizations of their potential and then eventually their spirit.

Here is a summary of observations related to the difference between management and leadership.

MANAGEMENT	LEADERSHIP
Does the thing right	Does the right thing
Tangible	Intangible
Referee	Cheerleader
Directs	Coaches
What you do	How you do it
Pronounces	Facilitates
Responsible	Responsive
Has a view on the mission	Has a vision of the mission
Views world from inside	Views world from outside
Chateau leadership	Front-line leadership
What you say	How you say it
No gut stake in enterprise	Gut stake in enterprise
Preserving life	Passion for life
Driven by constraints	Driven by goals
Looks for things done wrong	Looks for things done right
Runs a cost center	Runs an effort center
Quantitative	Qualitative
Initiates programs	Initiates an ongoing process
Develops programs	Develops people
Concerned with programs	Concerned with people
Concerned with efficiency	Concerned with efficacy
Sometimes plays the hero	Plays the hero no more

From this list, we see a pattern of roles that leaders play. They seem to do the right thing at the right time. They are like great coaches who don't handle the ball, score the touchdown, or put the ball through the hoop. They prepare their people, develop them, challenge them, encourage them, and touch them with their vision and the passion for that vision. As Charles Garfield says, "They give their people a place to stand, so like Archimedes they can move the world." Leaders know that if they do these things many of the management concerns of programs, balanced budgets, and profits will result. Walt Disney said, "Do what you love, and the money will come." Wasn't he really saying, find your passion and follow it? Leaders help us identify, define, and fan our passions for life.

In his book *Leadership Is an Art*, Max DePree talks about organizations having both a body and a spirit. After reading his book, one concludes you can have an organization that from all appearances is working but whose spirit is dead. We've all worked in places like that before. The lights are on in the building, people come to work, are paid—there is movement and the appearance of a job being done. A closer look reveals that in reality there is nothing happening. The body is comatose.

Conversely, we find other organizations that are housed in substandard surroundings, who have woefully strained budgets and few resources, but the whole places just hum with activity and, to a person, they have a passion for life. The people have missions that are meaningful, they are challenged, have respect for one another and accomplish remarkable things, even under the worst of conditions. They are like the character in George Bernard Shaw's *Man and Superman,* who asserted, "Life's no brief candle to me. It is like a splendid torch which I have got hold of for just a moment, and I want to make it burn as brightly as possible before handing it on to the next generation." What makes the difference? In one the body is functioning, but the spirit is dead; the reverse is true of the second—the body is crippled, but the spirit is alive and healthy. And it is the intangible spirit of a group that causes a business or organization to grow and reach its potential.

The role of the manager is to care for the body of the organization, while the role of the leader is to care for the spirit of the organization. Great leadership does both!

Peter Drucker also observed, "Police are so concerned with doing things right, they promote for the absence of wrongdoing rather than for the presence of initiative, innovation, and leadership. As a result, bright, young police officers recognize that success can be found by occupying high-profile, low-risk positions."

If this is accurate, organizations tend to promote insecure, shallow, one-dimensional leadership that can turn on the lights in their buildings but turn the lights off in their people.

Organizations spend a great deal of time and effort to select and recruit potential peak performers. Why, after just two or three years, do we often find a dispirited, cynical employees instead of peak performers? Something has taken place in the process of their work to alter their beliefs, attitudes, and feelings. A French writer once observed, "When the police function is assumed by a person of intelligence and of heart, by someone of humanity and of integrity, then nothing is more useful, nothing is more vital, and nothing is more exciting." An officer, one of six accused of beating a known drug dealer to death who had anonymously threatened one of the group, defended himself by saying, "I'm not an animal, I'm not a supervisor's nightmare. I'm a professional, I'm a good cop." He then added, "Do you have any idea how tough our job is? You know, we can't win—we just can't win." What happened to him, one who once was so vital, so useful, and so exciting? His spirit dead, he and five more like him are accused of taking into their hands the very law that they swore to uphold. How sad for us all.

We see our officers involved in long, inconclusive, and often frustrated struggles with their criminal public, the criminal justice system, and all too often their own administrations. I have observed that many suffer a death of the spirit which is the result of the contradiction of their courage on the one hand and the obvious futility of their effort on the other.

This changing nation and this changing world will require even more of our future generation of police officers. We can no longer seek out and promote one-dimensional, high profile, low-risk leadership. They must prepare themselves, their careers paths reflecting the badly needed balance while, as Keegan says, "Playing the hero no more." And, as MacCoby points out, we cannot afford to educate this generation of leadership—they are going to have to learn on the job, taking responsibility for their own development.

We must have leaders who understand that the most important contribution they make is the care of the spirit of their people and their organization. Peter Drucker has said: "Doing the right thing is what makes knowledge work effective."

We might also add that it nourishes the spirit as well.

As leaders, we must remind ourselves that contained within every dilemma is a two-pronged question. One prong contains the managerial issues, and the second prong the leadership issues. The management prong is doing the thing right, while the leadership prong is doing the right thing. Leaders understand this, and when doing the thing right flies in the face of doing the right thing they know how to put the right spin on this contention and bring the situation to a successful conclusion. That is what sets them apart. Police are very adept at identifying the managerial issues. They must learn how to identify the leadership issues. To make a decision simply based on the managerial concerns robs an organization of spirit.

Once identified, the leadership issues often take moral courage to pursue. The human spirit, while intangible, is remarkable. History and sport have proven that time and again.

As I mentioned earlier, I have traveled to nearly every state in the United States and worked with thousands of police officers. They are a remarkable people. For all they see and experience, they are like Robert Service's ideal in his poem, "The Law of the Yukon:" "Not men and women who are weaklings, subtle, suave, and mild, but men and women with the hearts of vikings and the simple faith of a child."

They each have taught me something. However, their greatest legacy to me, to us all for that matter, is that the human spirit cannot be plundered. It cannot be taken away. You can only give it up.

I have often wondered what happened to Donald Brooks. What he did in his first introduction as the leader of that Marine infantry company was only the first of many subtle and intangible illustrations of "doing the right thing" that made a significant difference in the performance of those young Marines whose lives he touched. I have been even more curious about what would have happened had he not assumed command of that company. How many lives might have been lost had Brooks not taken command?

In this age of empowerment, we must develop leadership at the lowest levels. We will have to find immediate ways to teach leadership on the job, for time will not allow solely for traditional classroom instruction. Those who seek to be leaders must pursue mentors who are role models of successful traits. They must network with peers who, like themselves, thirst to give back so "the torch might burn brighter for future generations." They must care for both management and leadership issues, and thereby take care of the organizational spirit. Doing so is like fresh air and sun healing aggravating sores.

INDEX

EXECUTIVE
Excellence®

Since 1984, *Executive Excellence* has provided business leaders and managers with the best and latest thinking on leadership development, managerial effectiveness, and organizational productivity. Each issue is filled with insights and answers from top business executives, trainers, and consultants—information you won't find in any other publication.

"Excellent! This is one of the finest newsletters I've seen in the field."
—Tom Peters, co-author of *In Search of Excellence*

"Executive Excellence *is the* Harvard Business Review *in USA Today* format."
—Stephen R. Covey, author of *The 7 Habits of Highly Effective People*

"Executive Excellence is the best executive advisory newsletter anywhere in the world—it's just a matter of time before a lot more people find that out."
—Ken Blanchard, co-author of *The One-Minute Manager*

CONTRIBUTING EDITORS INCLUDE

Stephen R. Covey

Ken Blanchard

Marjorie Blanchard

Charles Garfield

Peter Senge

Gifford Pinchot

Elizabeth Pinchot

Warren Bennis

For more information about *Executive Excellence* or *Personal Excellence*, or for information regarding books, audio tapes, CD-ROMs, custom editions, reprints, and other products, please call

Executive Excellence Publishing at:

1-800-304-9782
or visit our web site: **http://www.eep.com**